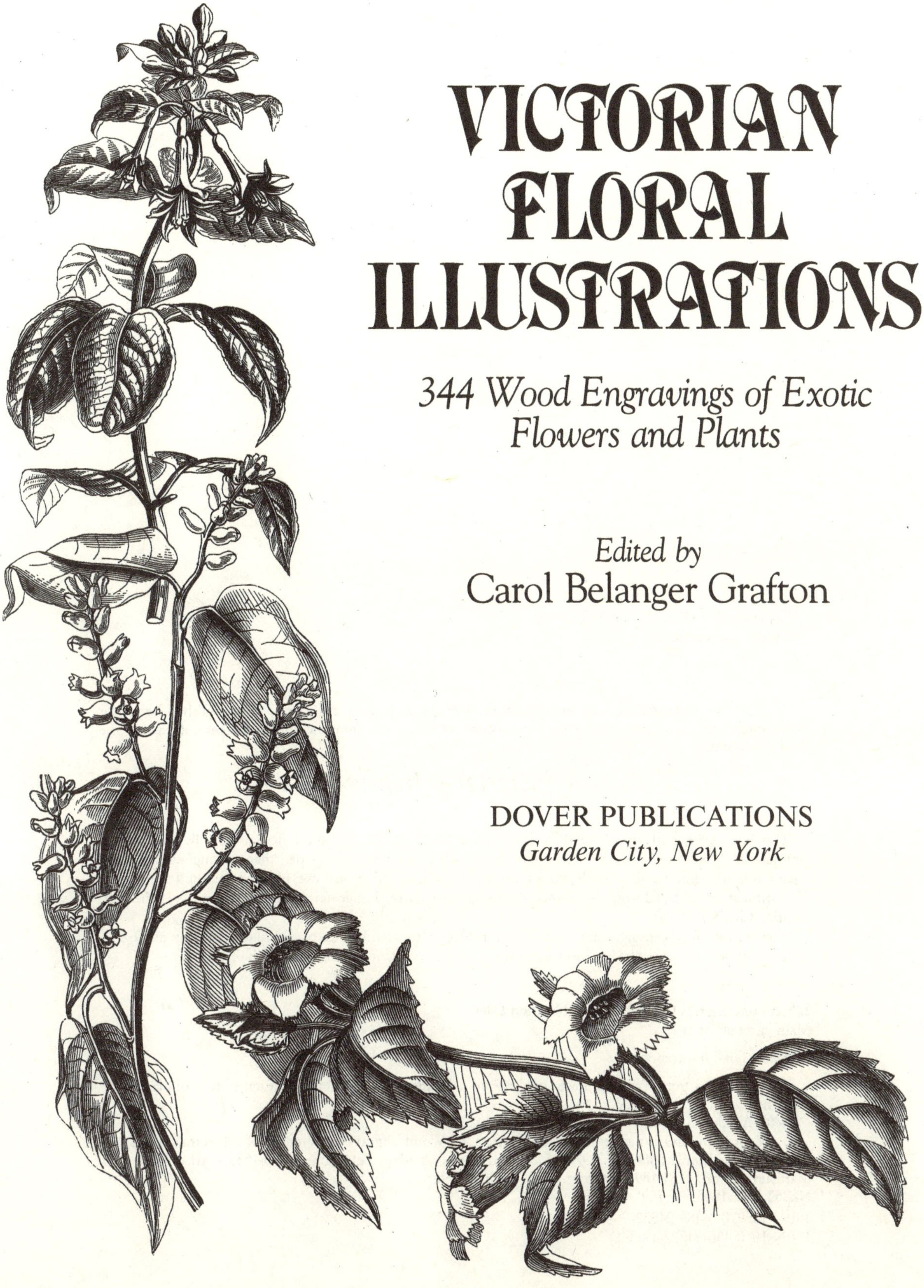

VICTORIAN FLORAL ILLUSTRATIONS

344 Wood Engravings of Exotic Flowers and Plants

Edited by
Carol Belanger Grafton

DOVER PUBLICATIONS
Garden City, New York

Victorian Floral Illustrations: 344 Wood Engravings of Exotic Flowers and Plants, first published by Dover Publications, Inc., is a new selection and arrangement of illustrations from the printed sources indicated in the Publisher's Note.

DOVER *Pictorial Archive* SERIES

Library of Congress Cataloging in Publication Data
Main entry under title:

Victorian floral illustrations.

Plates reprinted from: Paxton's flower garden / by J. Lindley, 1850-1853 and Natural history of plants / by A. Kerner von Marilaun, 1902.
Includes index.
1. Decoration and ornament—Plant forms. 2. Wood-engraving, Victorian. I. Grafton, Carol Belanger. II. Lindley, John, 1799-1865. Paxton's flower garden. Selections. 1850-1853. III. Kerner von Marilaun, Anton, 1831-1898. Pflanzenleben. English. Selections. 1902.
NE953.V5 1985 769′.434 84-21207

ISBN-13: 978-0-486-24822-6
ISBN-10: 0-486-24822-4 (pbk.)

Printed in Canada
24822424 2026
www.doverpublications.com

PUBLISHER'S NOTE

The 344 wood engravings that compose this collection of exotic flowers and plants are derived from two sources: *Paxton's Flower Garden* by Professor John Lindley and Sir Joseph Paxton, published by Bradbury and Evans, London, 1850–1 (Vol. I) and 1853 (Vols. II and III), and *The Natural History of Plants: Their Forms, Growth, Reproduction, and Distribution* from the German of Anton Kerner von Marilaun by F. W. Oliver, published by Blackie & Son, Limited, London, 1902 (Vols. I and II). These two botanical texts are classics in the field and furnish a wealth of technical commentary on the illustrations that have been selected for *Victorian Floral Illustrations*.

The captions in the present volume are not exhaustive citations, but are identifications gleaned from the original texts. The Latin binomial nomenclature—genus and species designation—is provided along with a brief description of the plant or flower, its native region (sometimes modernized) and, if it is a flower, the coloration of the blossoms. Latin plant names are periodically revised by botanists and, for some of the plants included here, may no longer be the same as they were 80 or 130 years ago, but for the purposes of this volume, which is not intended as a botanical text, updating has not been attempted.

These engravings are compelling by their clarity and novelty; the quality of detail invites careful scrutiny and enhances our perception of the marvelous variety of flora. Often the flowering, or inflorescence, is the focus of these renderings; however, there are also detailed studies and even dissected floral elements that are meant to illustrate the reproduction, growth and form of a particular plant and the diseases that prey upon it. Orchid lovers will be pleased to find that over one-tenth of this volume is devoted to orchids.

Of the 344 illustrations, 92 are from *The Natural History of Plants*: numbers 15, 18–24, 36, 64, 65, 67, 70, 71, 73, 84–87, 90, 93, 96–108, 122, 143–156, 159, 173, 196–206, 208, 215, 218, 222, 230–234, 244, 246–248, 254, 260, 262, 264–268, 278, 281, 285, 289, 290, 327, 338, 339, 344. The remainder are from *Paxton's Flower Garden*.

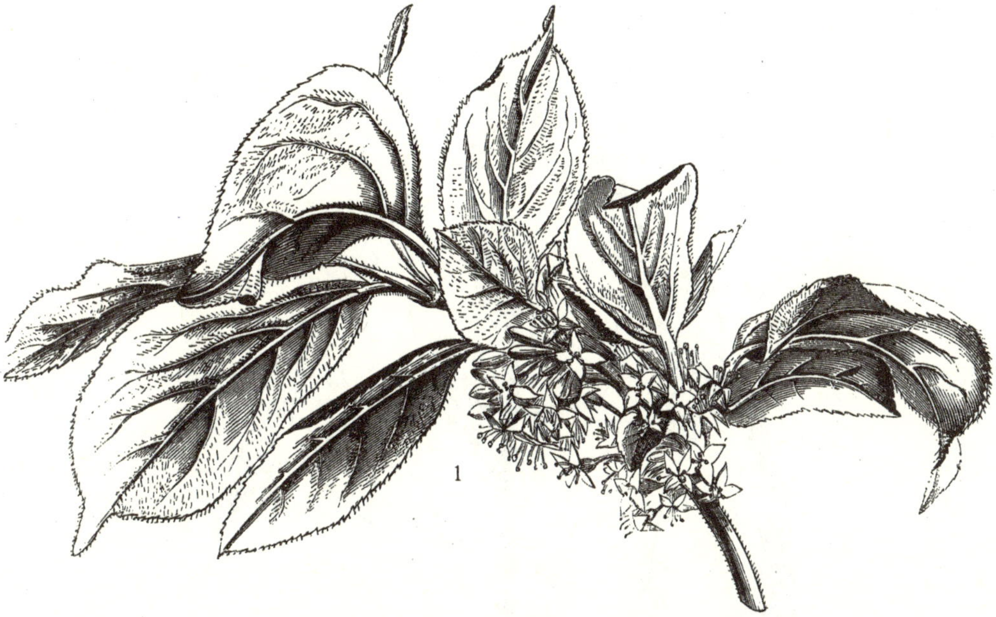

1

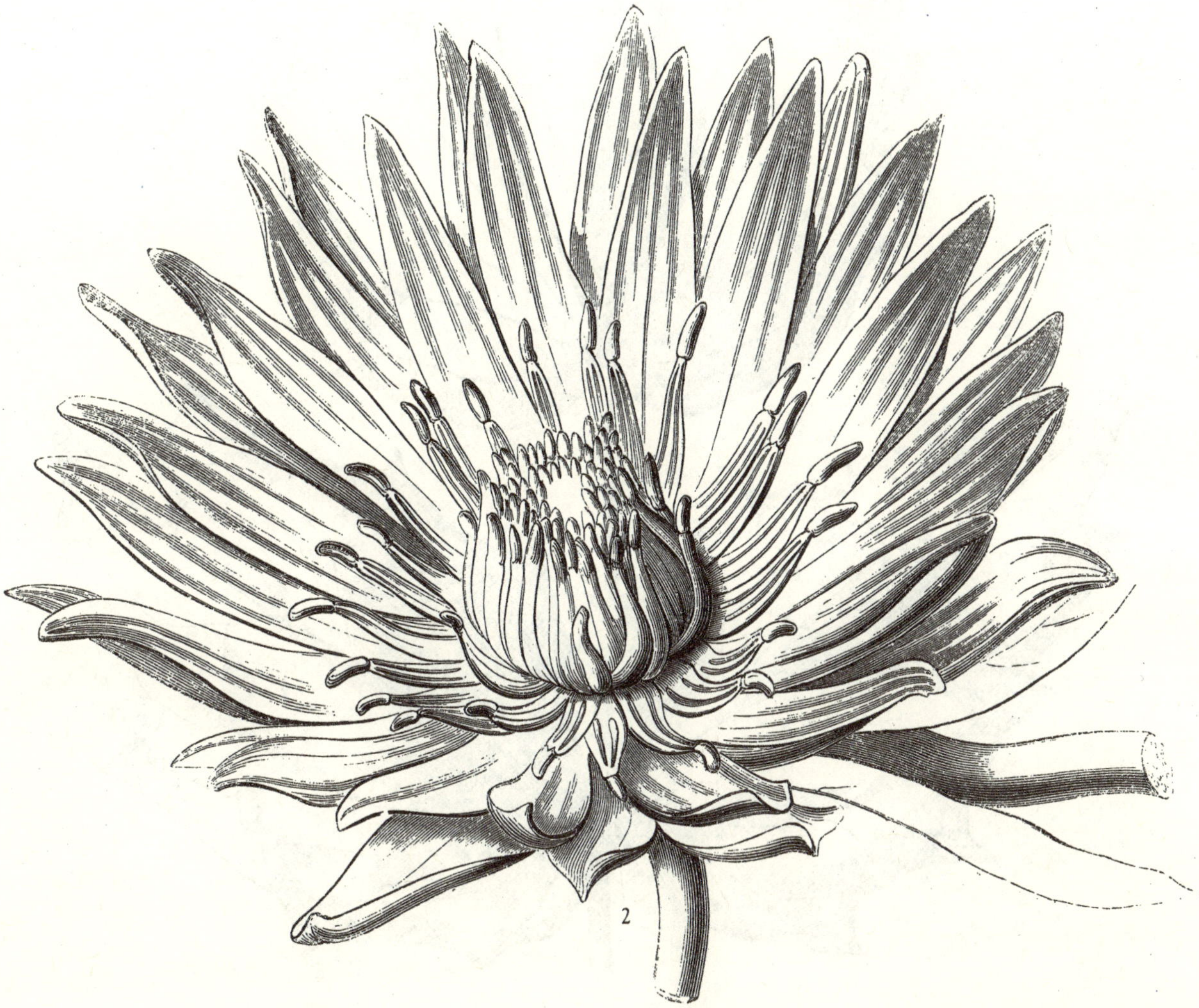

2

1. *Rhamnus hirsutus.* A buckthorn with green flowers; from the temperate regions of the Northern Hemisphere. 2. *Nymphaea scutifolia.* A water lily with large blue flowers; from the Republic of South Africa.

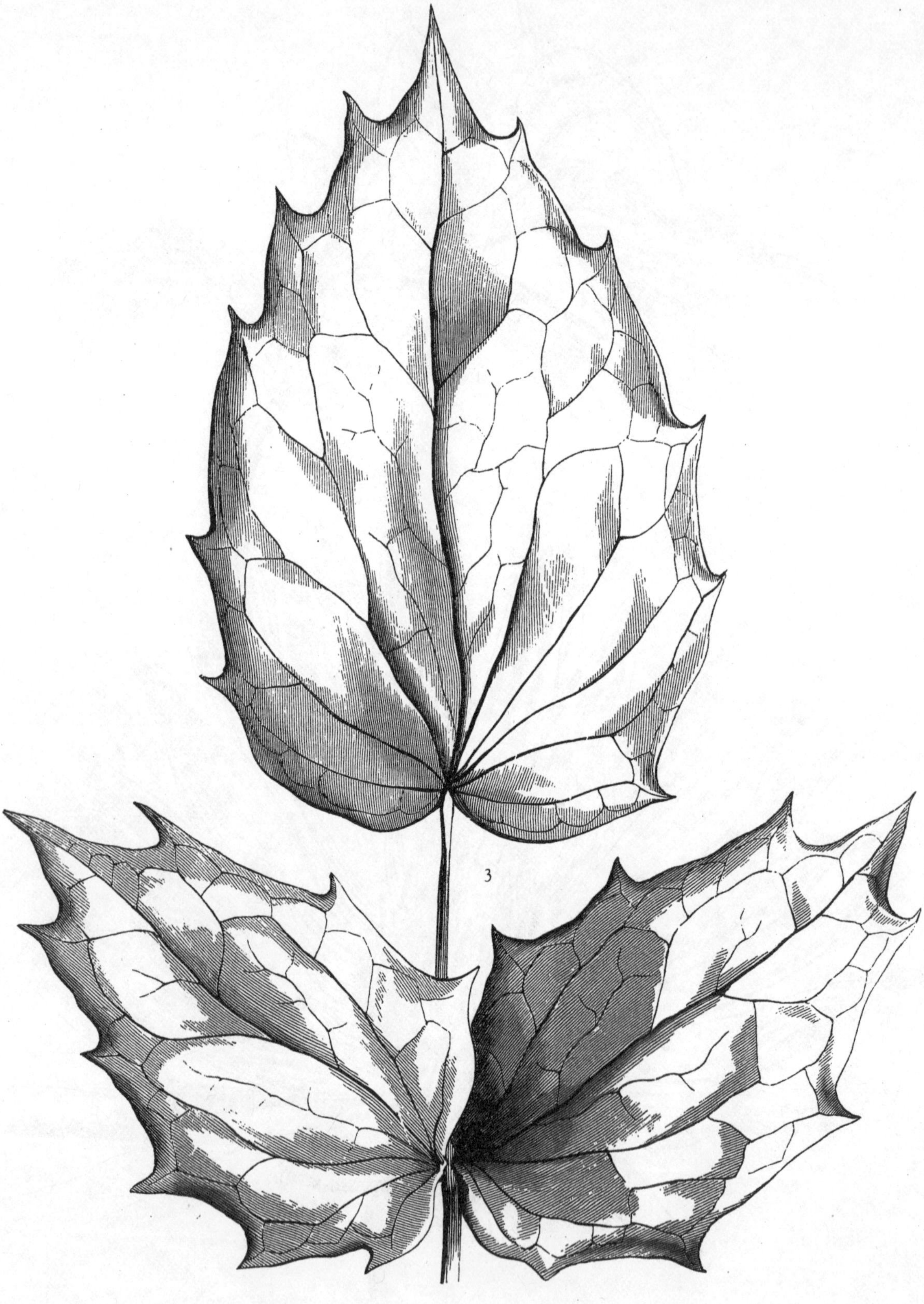

3. *Oncidium hastatum.* An orchid with large variegated flowers and a white lip sometimes tinged with green; from Mexico and Brazil.

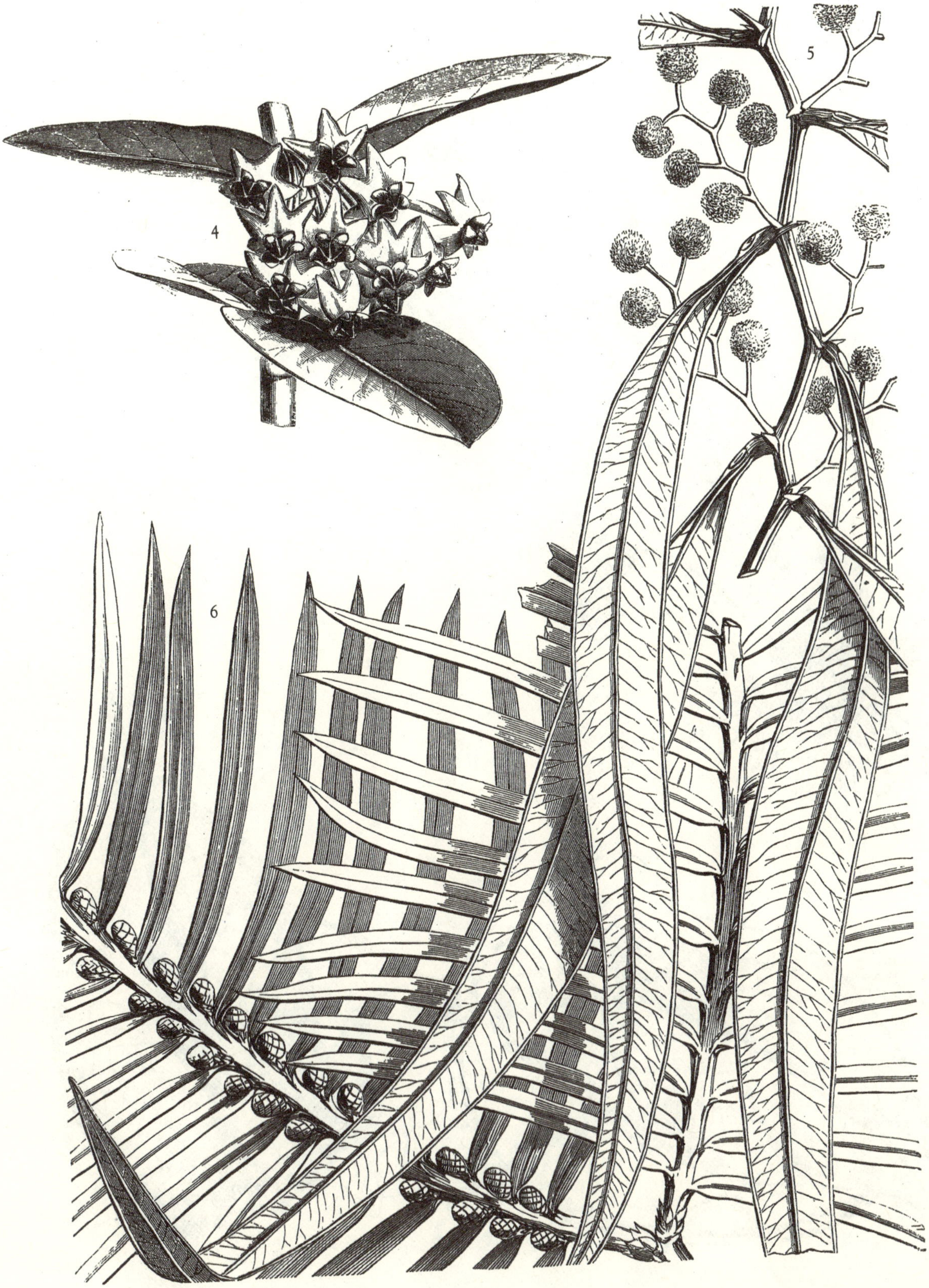

4. *Hoya cumingiana.* A climbing shrub with greenish-yellow flowers; from the Philippines. 5. *Acacia macradenia.* A bush with innumerable zigzag spikes of yellow heads; from Australia. 6. *Cephalotaxus fortuni.* A shrub with long, narrow, deep green leaves; from the north of China.

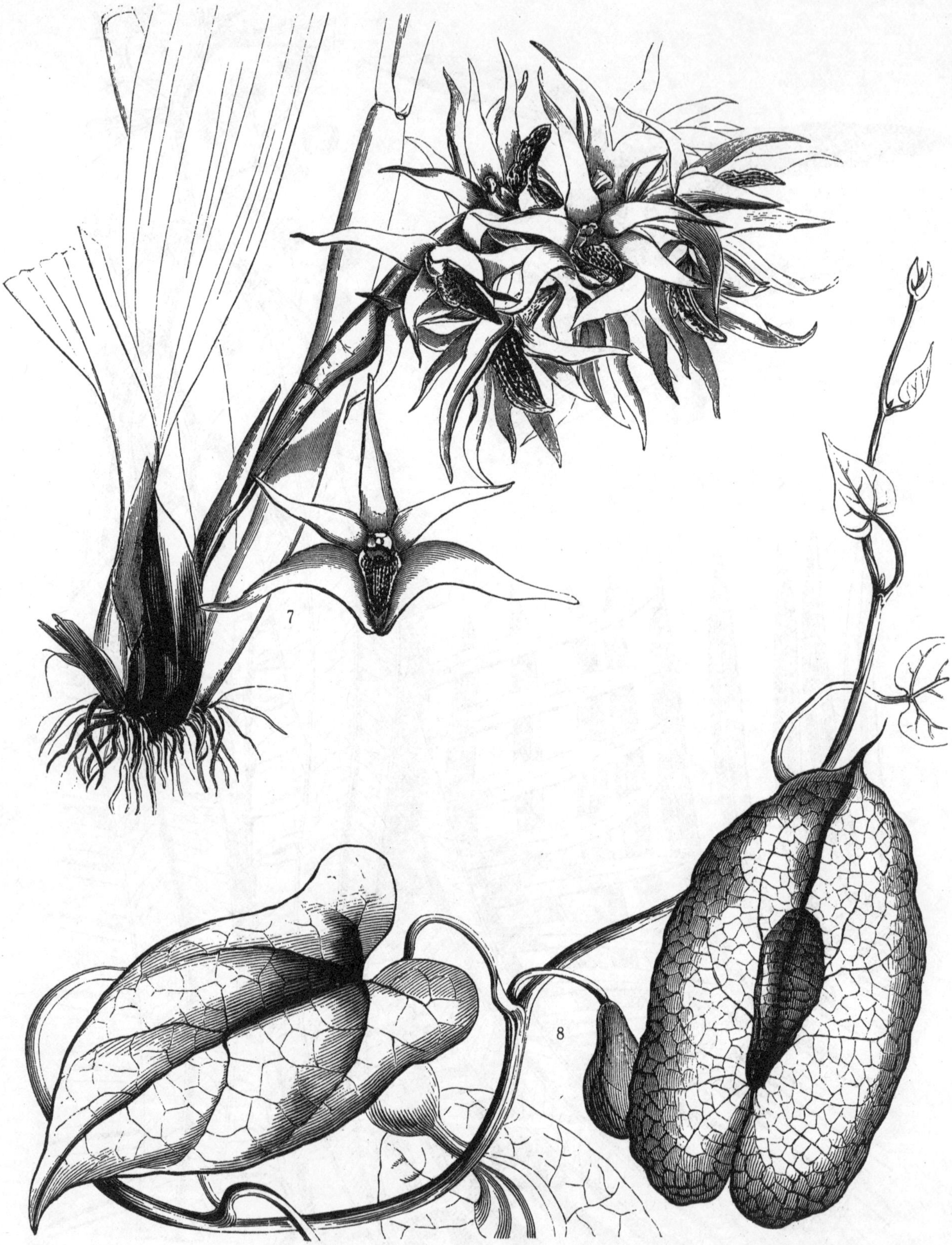

7. *Maxillaria elongata.* A terrestrial orchid with pale yellow and brown flowers; from Central America. 8. *Aristolochia picta.* A birthwort with purple flowers; from Venezuela.

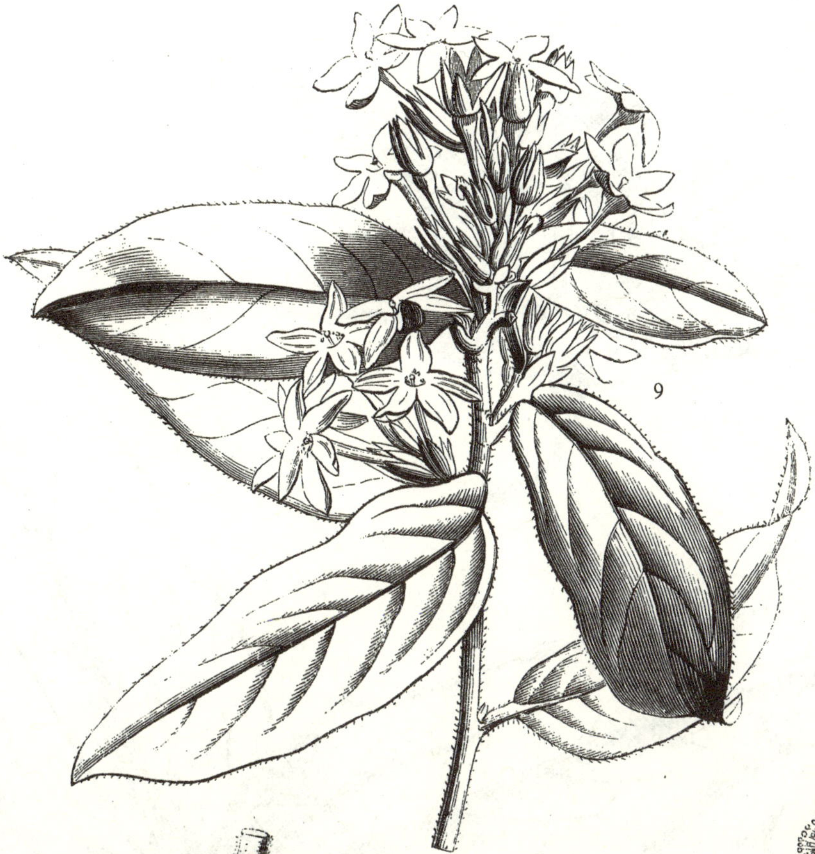

9

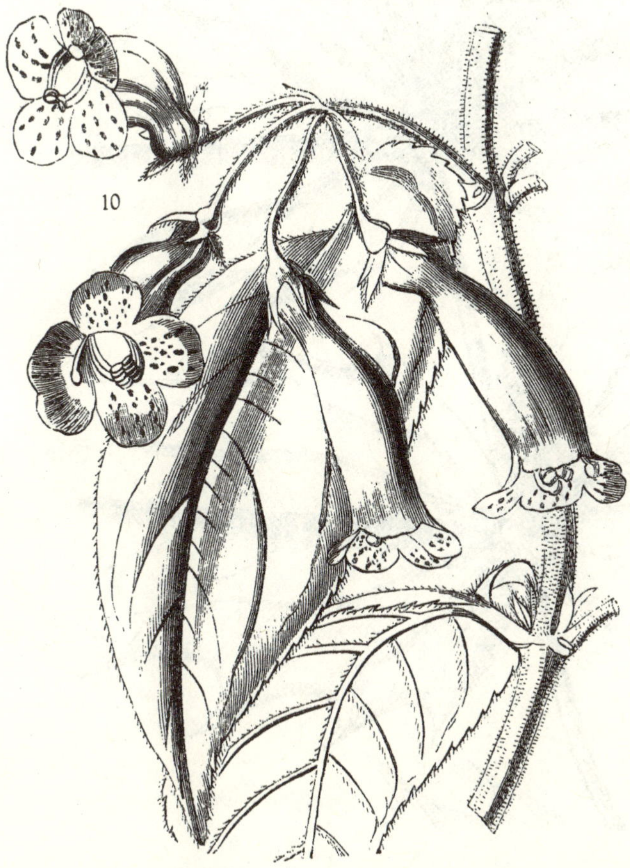

10

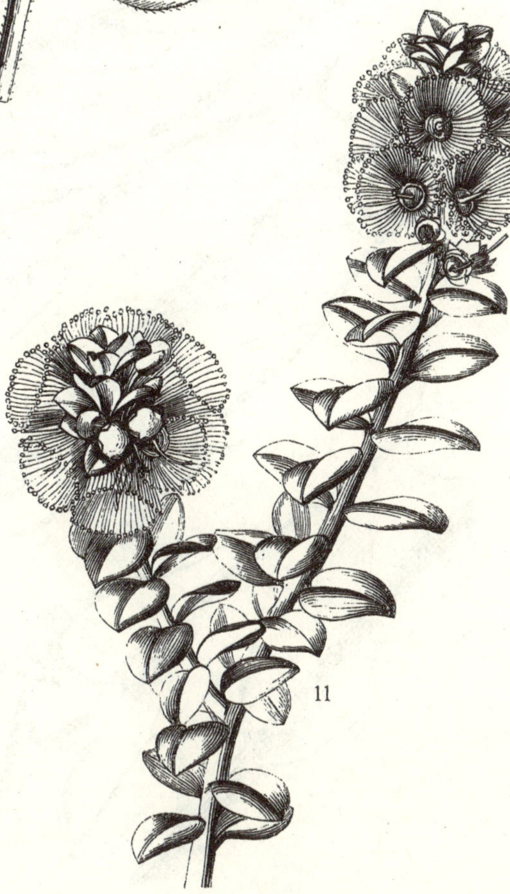

11

9. *Cestrum calycinum.* A shrub with green flowers; from Argentina. 10. *Moussonia elegans.* An herb with orange and yellow flowers; from Guatemala. 11. *Metrosideros buxifolia.* An evergreen bush with box-like leaves and heads of pale yellowish-white flowers; from New Zealand.

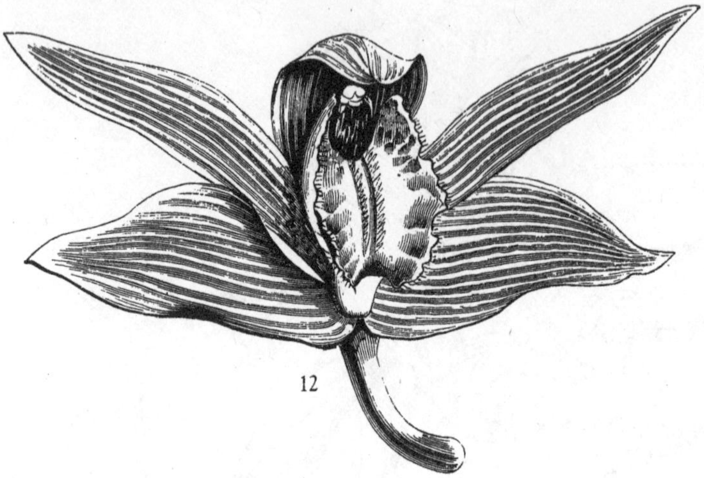

12

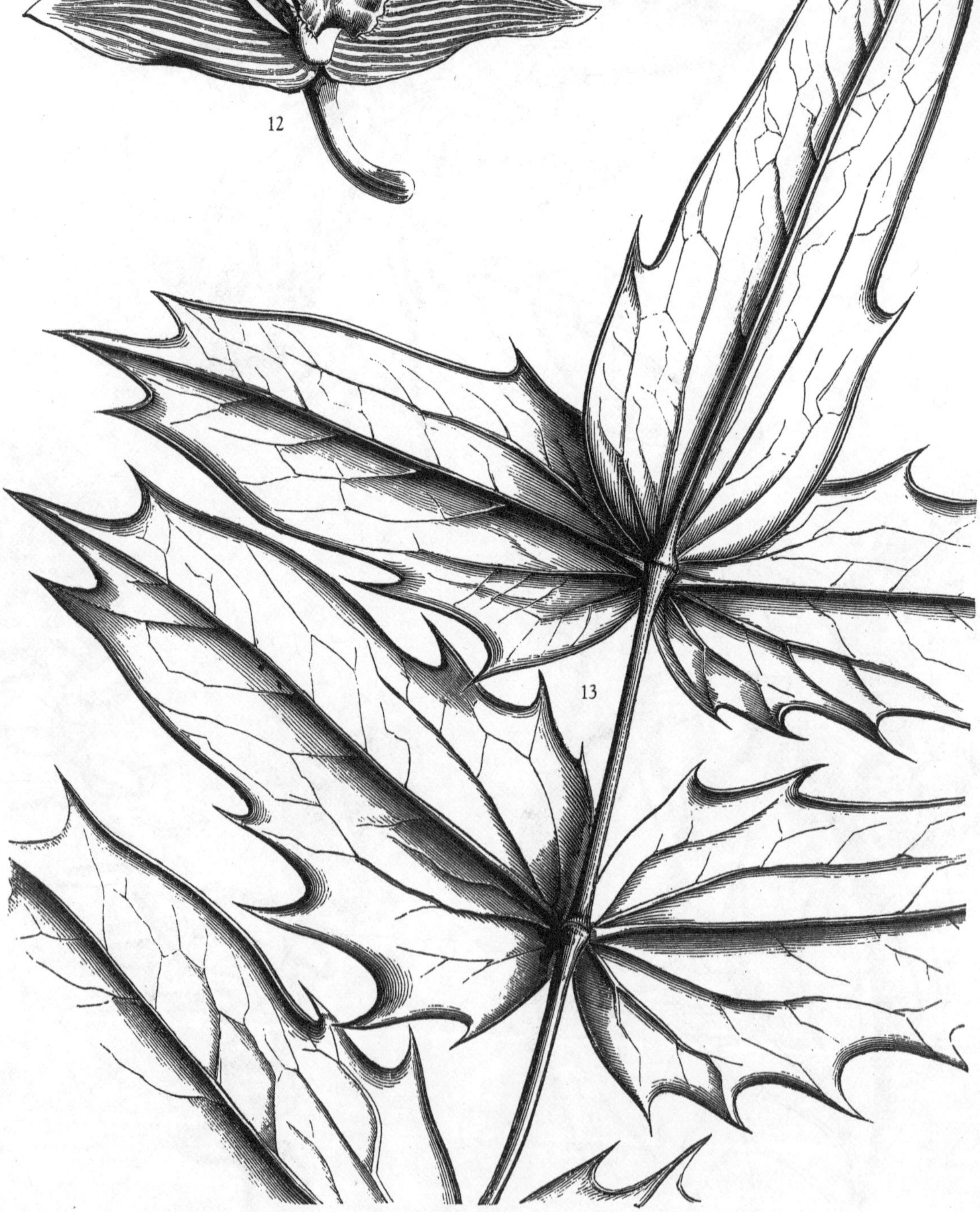

13

12. *Cymbidium giganteum.* A terrestrial orchid, flowers deep warm yellow with a richly spotted brown lip; from Nepal. 13. *Berberis trifurca.* A hardy evergreen shrub; from China.

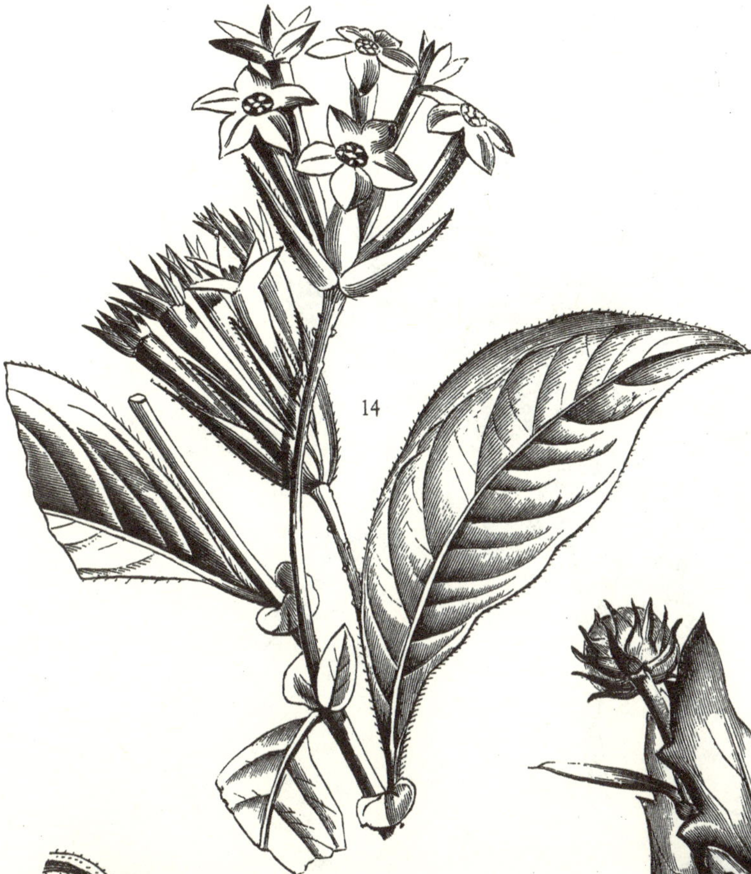

14

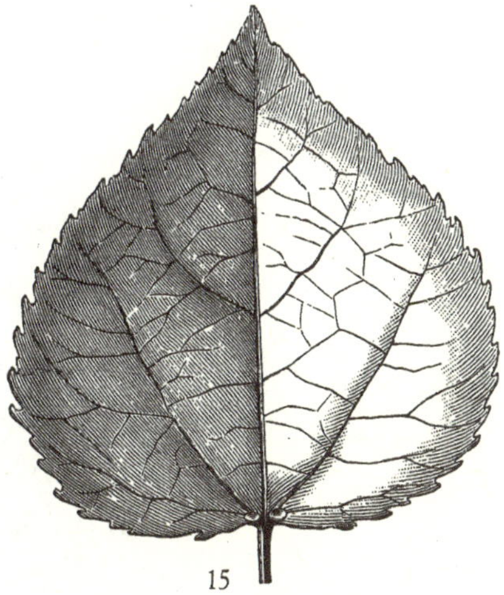

15

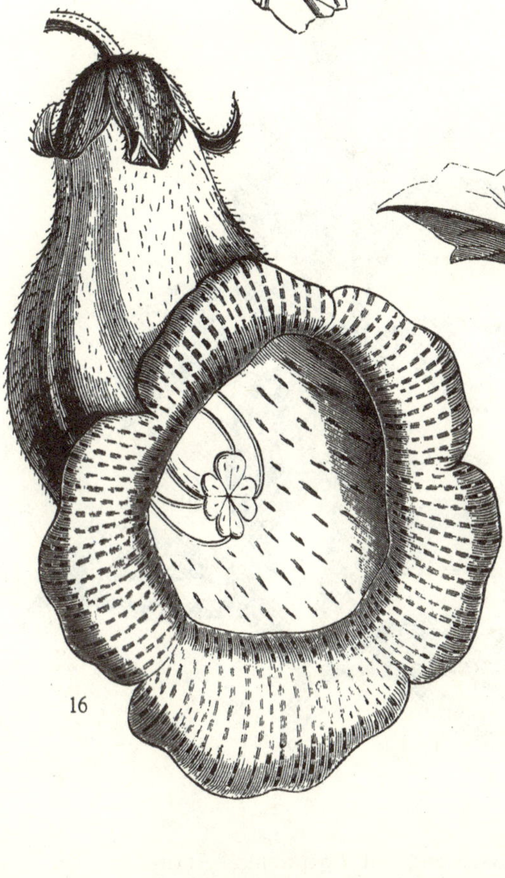

16

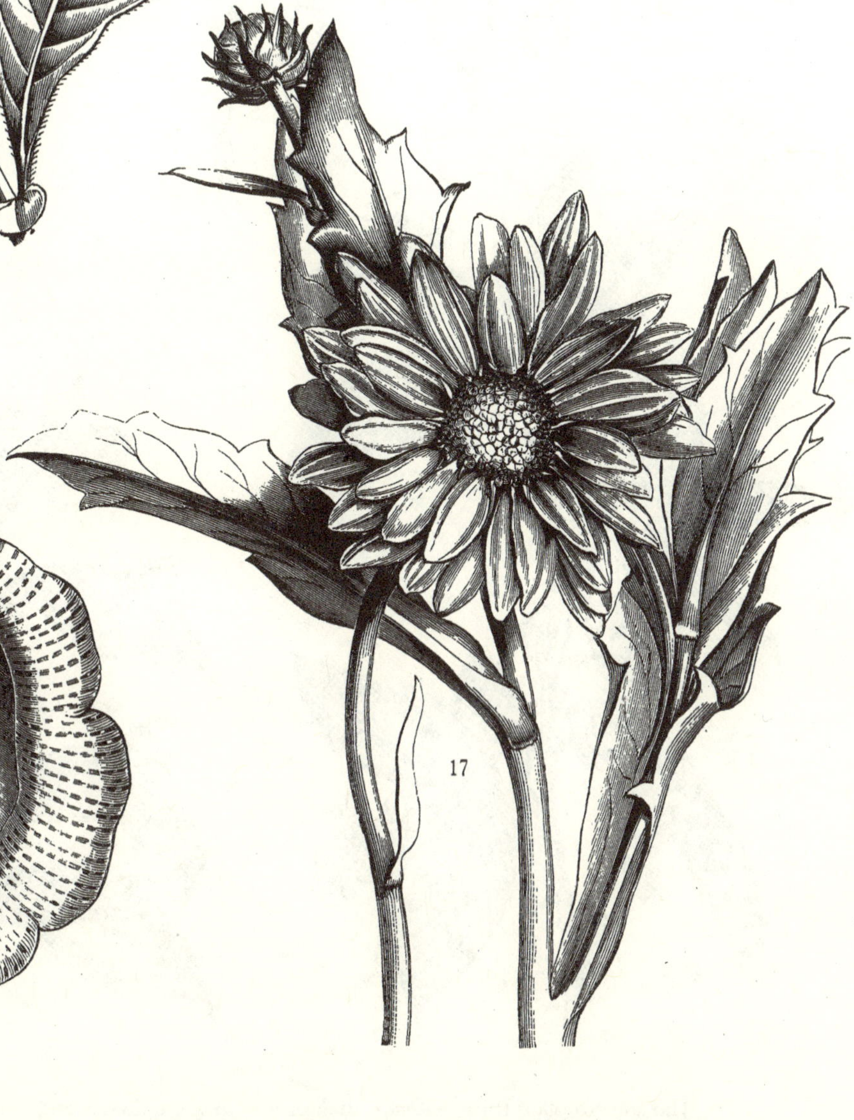

17

14. *Cestrum bracteatum.* A green-flowered shrub; from Brazil. 15. A leaf from a shoot of the aspen (*Populus tremula*); from Europe. 16. *Campanea grandiflora.* A large shrub, flowers white with crimson dots in lines; from Colombia and Panama. 17. *Grindelia speciosa.* A hardy undershrub with large yellow flower heads; from Argentina.

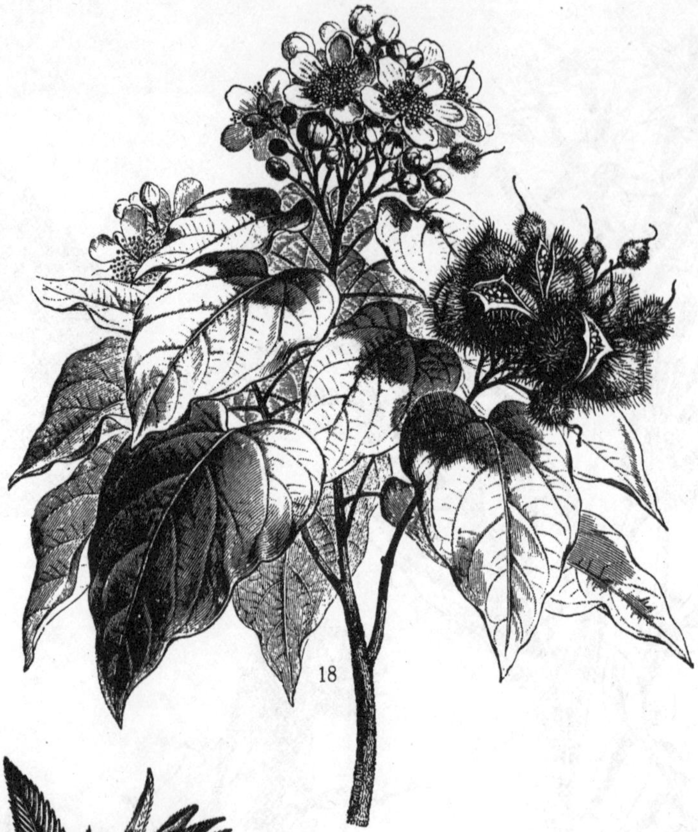

18

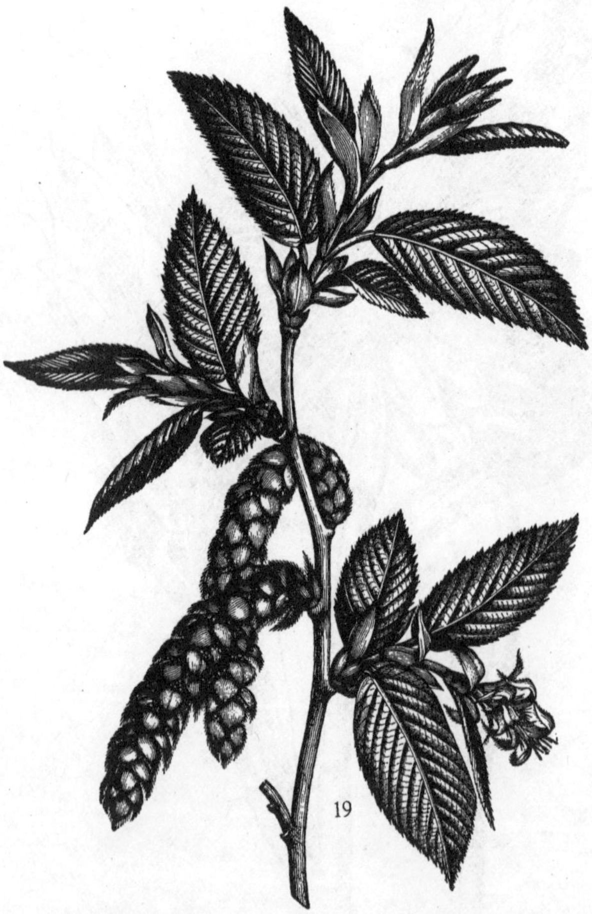

19

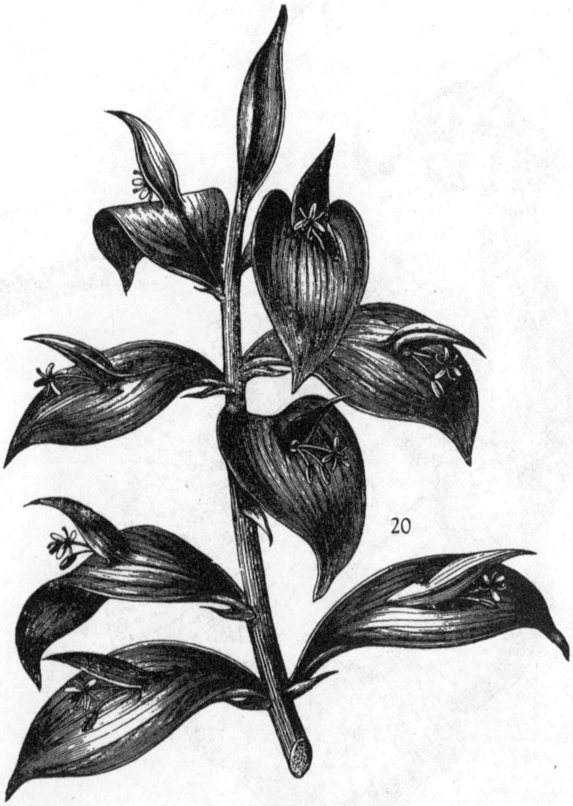

20

18. The annatto plant (*Bixa orellana*). Pink or rose to white flowers and fruit; from tropical America. 19. Birch (*Betula alba*). With fruit; from the Northern Hemisphere (see also Fig. 67). 20. A shoot of butcher's broom (*Ruscus hypoglossum*). An evergreen shrub; from southern Europe (see also Fig. 90).

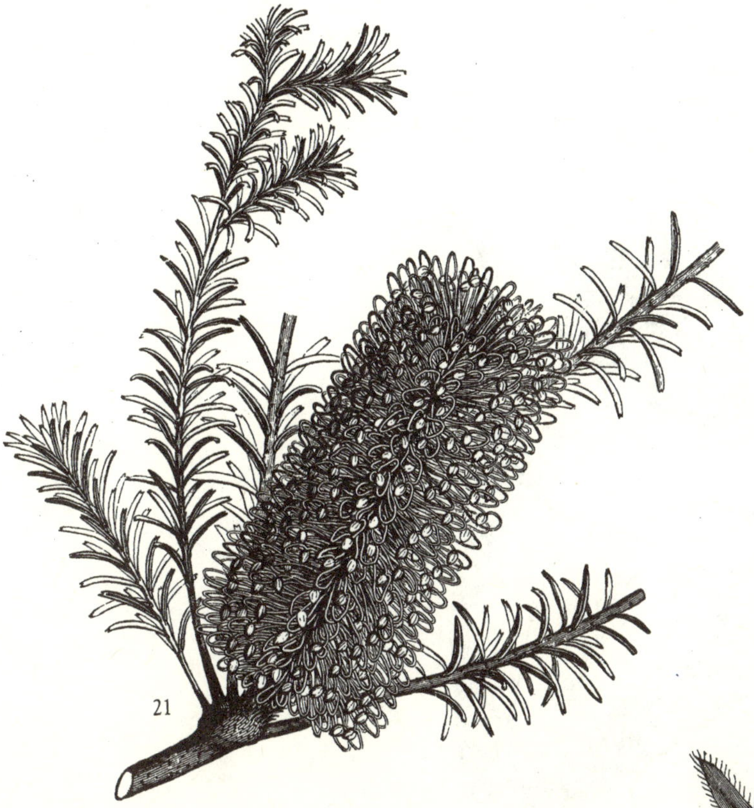

21

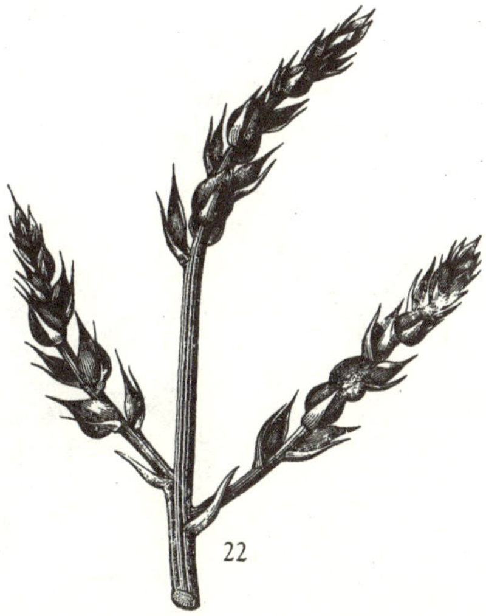

22

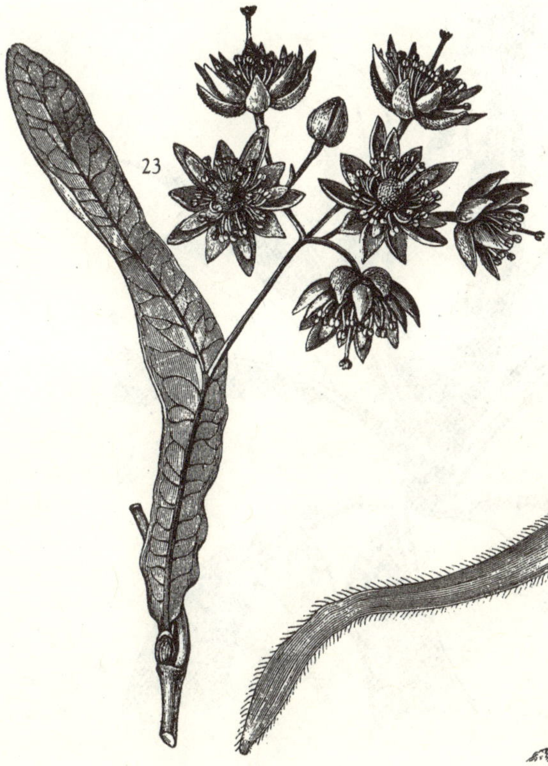

23

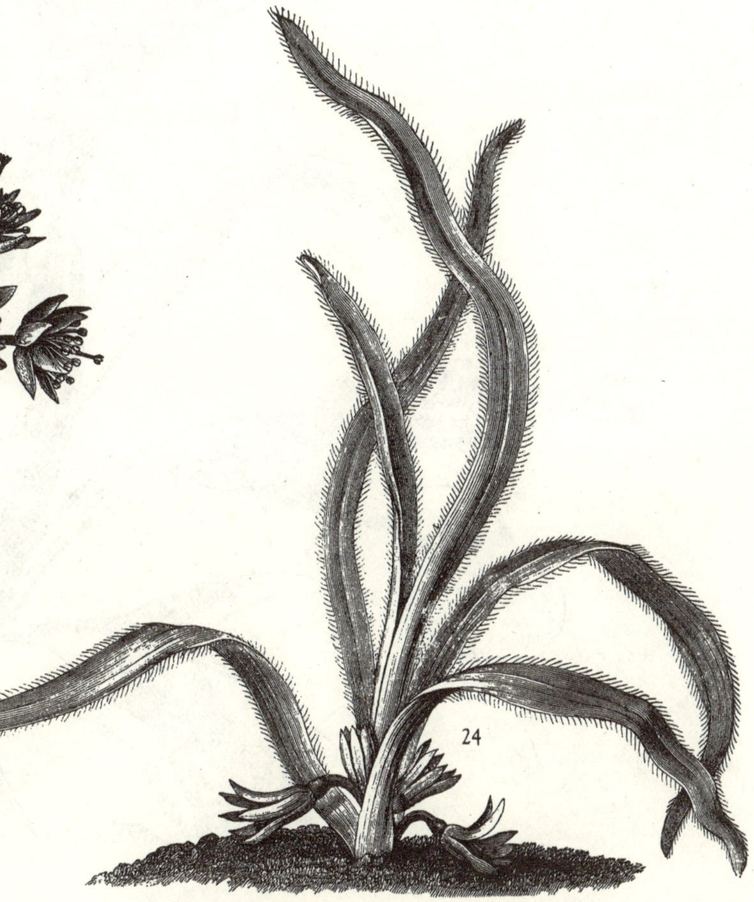

24

21. *Banksia ericifolia.* An evergreen shrub with golden-yellow flowers; from Australia (see also Fig. 153). 22. A young shoot of *Ruscus aculeatus* (butcher's broom). An evergreen shrub with small greenish flowers and red berries; from the Azores and western Europe (see also Fig. 233). 23. Flower of the linden tree *(Tilia argentea)*. From Europe and Asia. 24. *Allium chamaemoly.* An onion; from southern Europe and north Africa (see also Fig. 215).

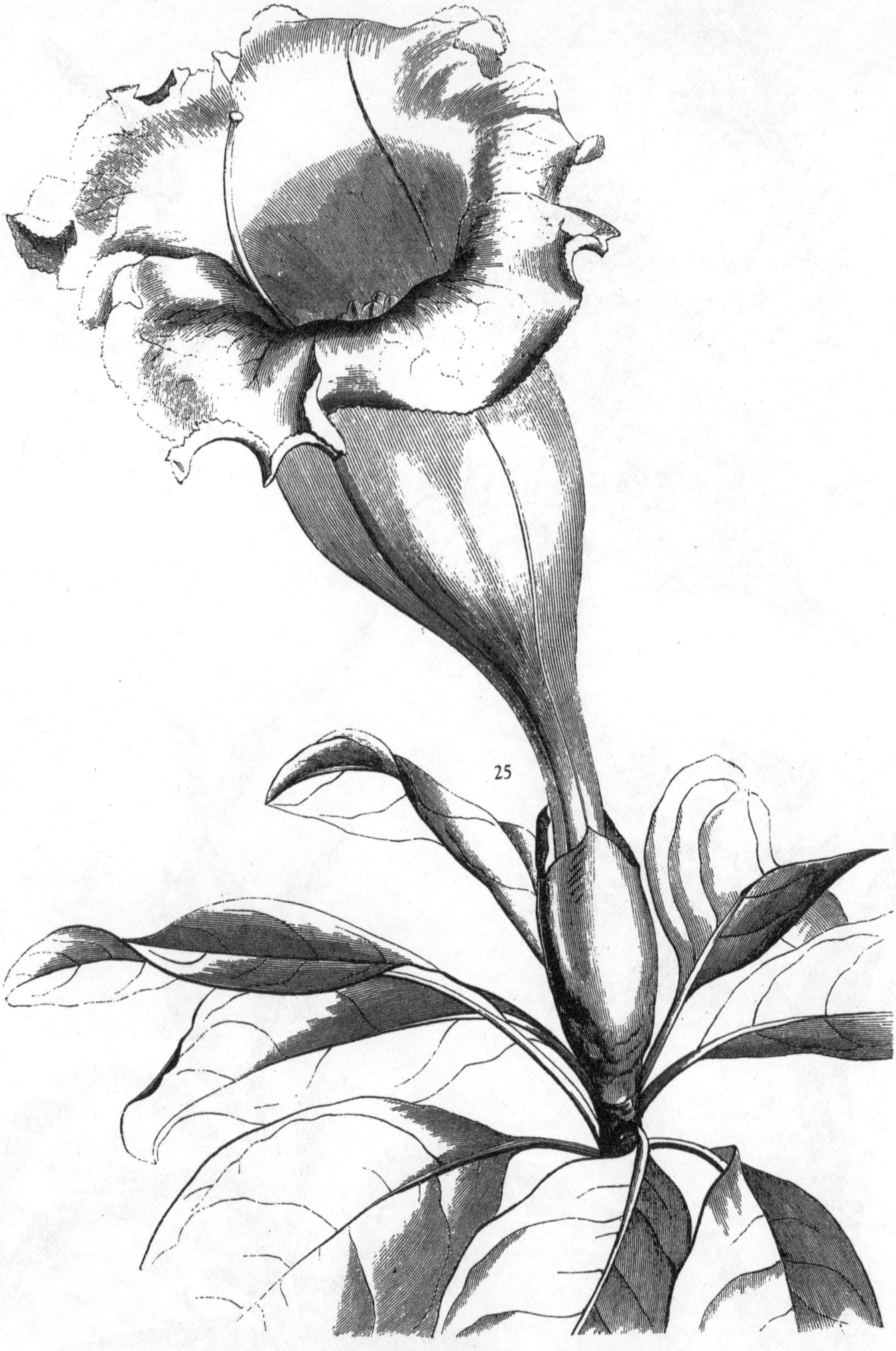

25. *Solandra laevis.* A nightshade; from Guatemala.

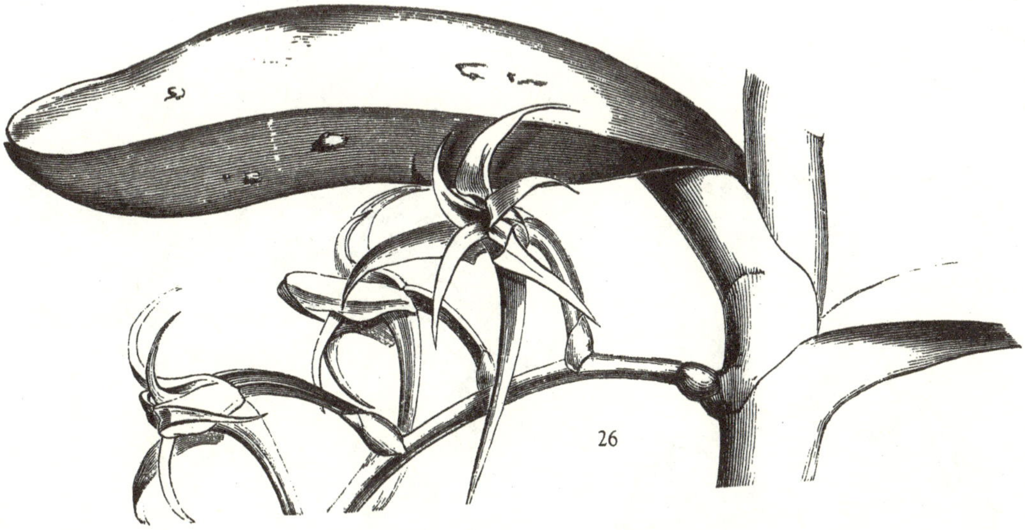

26

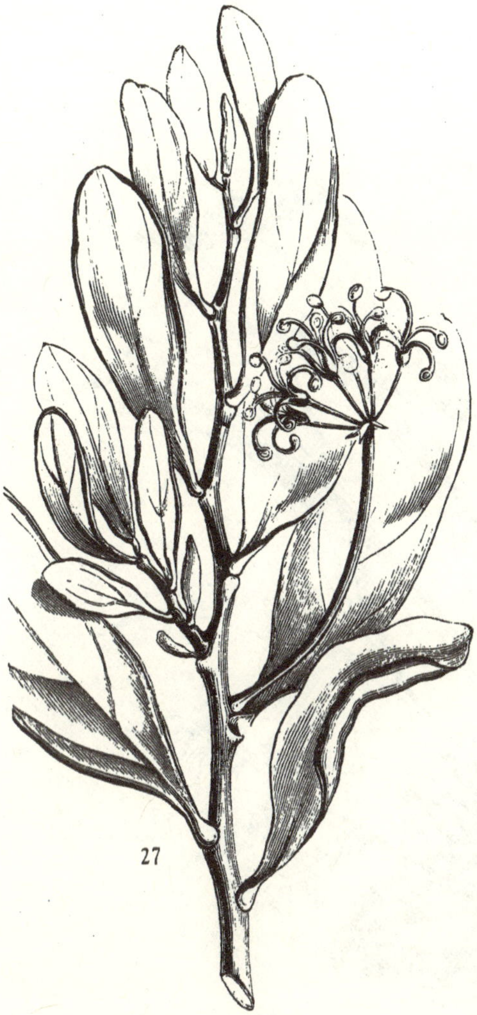

27

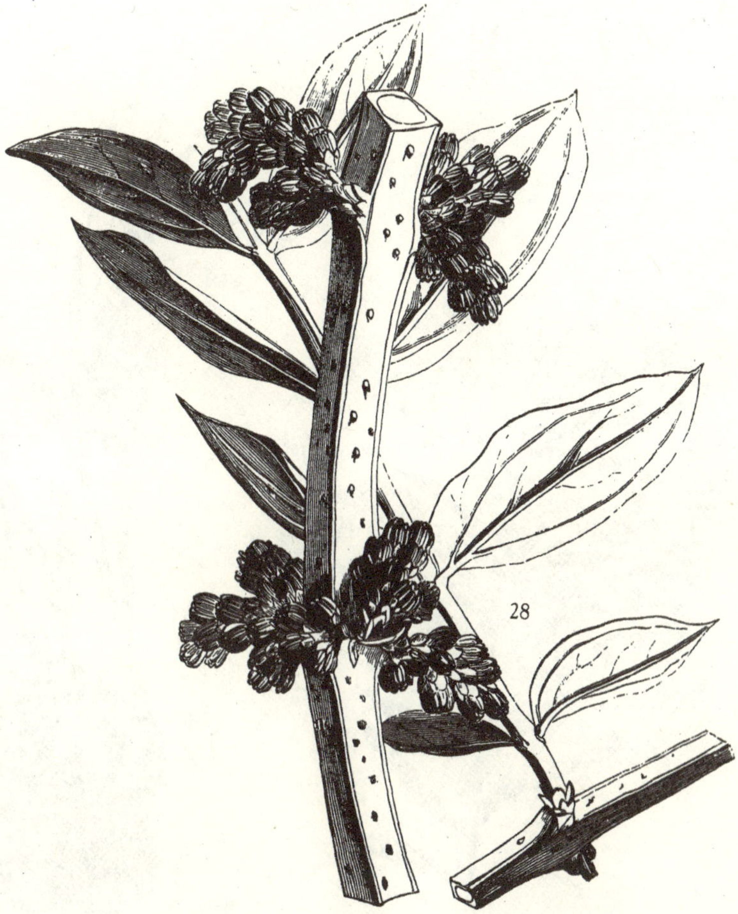

28

26. *Angraecum arcuatum.* A white-flowered orchid; from the Republic of South Africa. 27. *Stenocarpus forsteri.* An evergreen shrub; from New Caledonia. 28. *Coriaria nepalensis.* A large shrub with clusters of brownish-red flowers; from northern India.

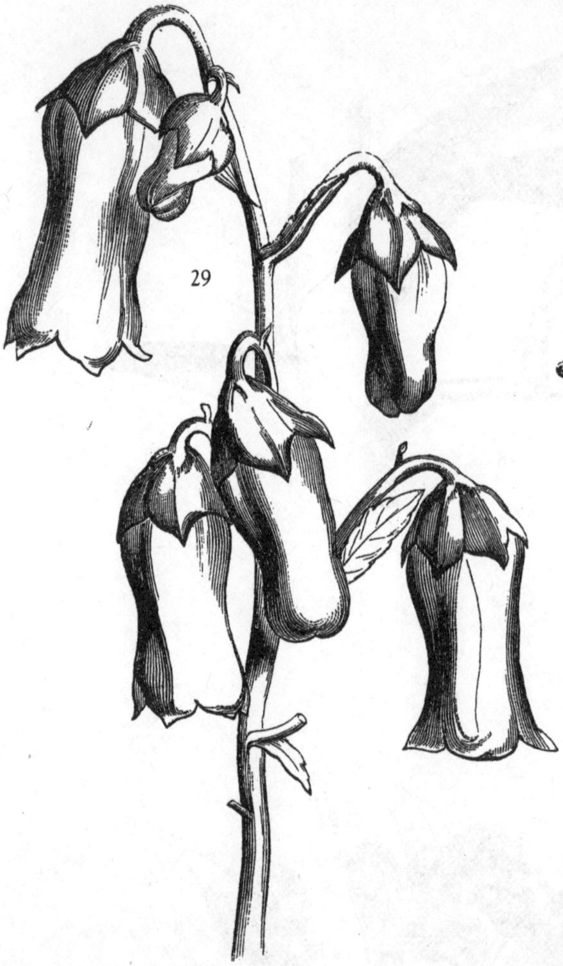

29

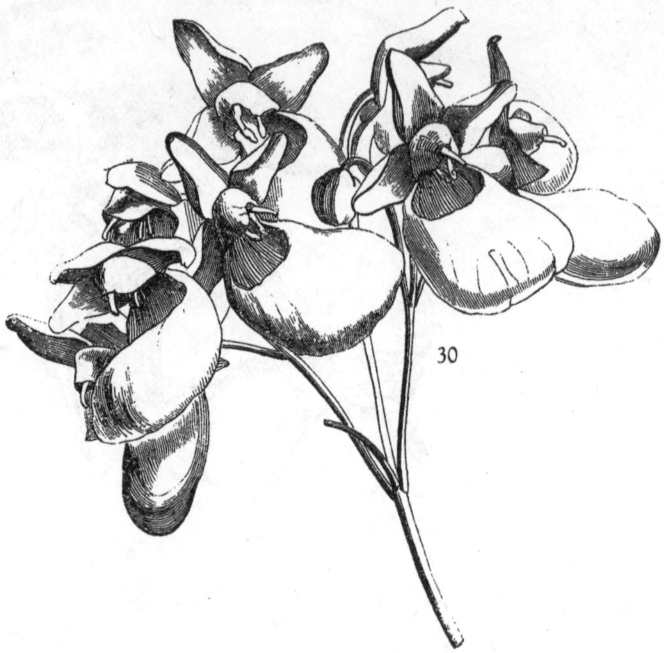

30

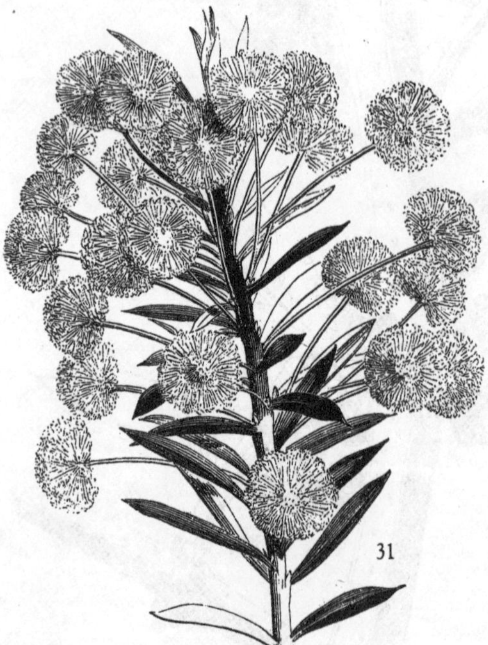

31

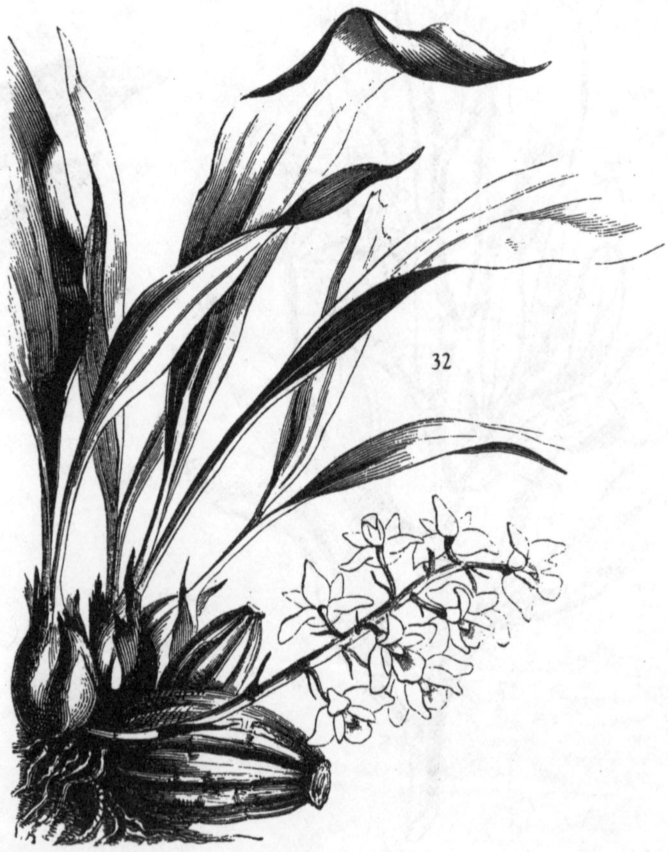

32

29. *Campanula vidalii.* A shrubby perennial with large dirty-white flowers; from the Azores. 30. *Calceolaria tetragona.* A broad-leaved shrubby plant with large pale yellow flowers; from Peru (see also Fig. 162). 31. *Acacia diffusa.* A leguminous bush with numerous balls of bright yellow flowers; from Tasmania. 32. *Maxillaria concava.* A pale yellow orchid; from tropical America.

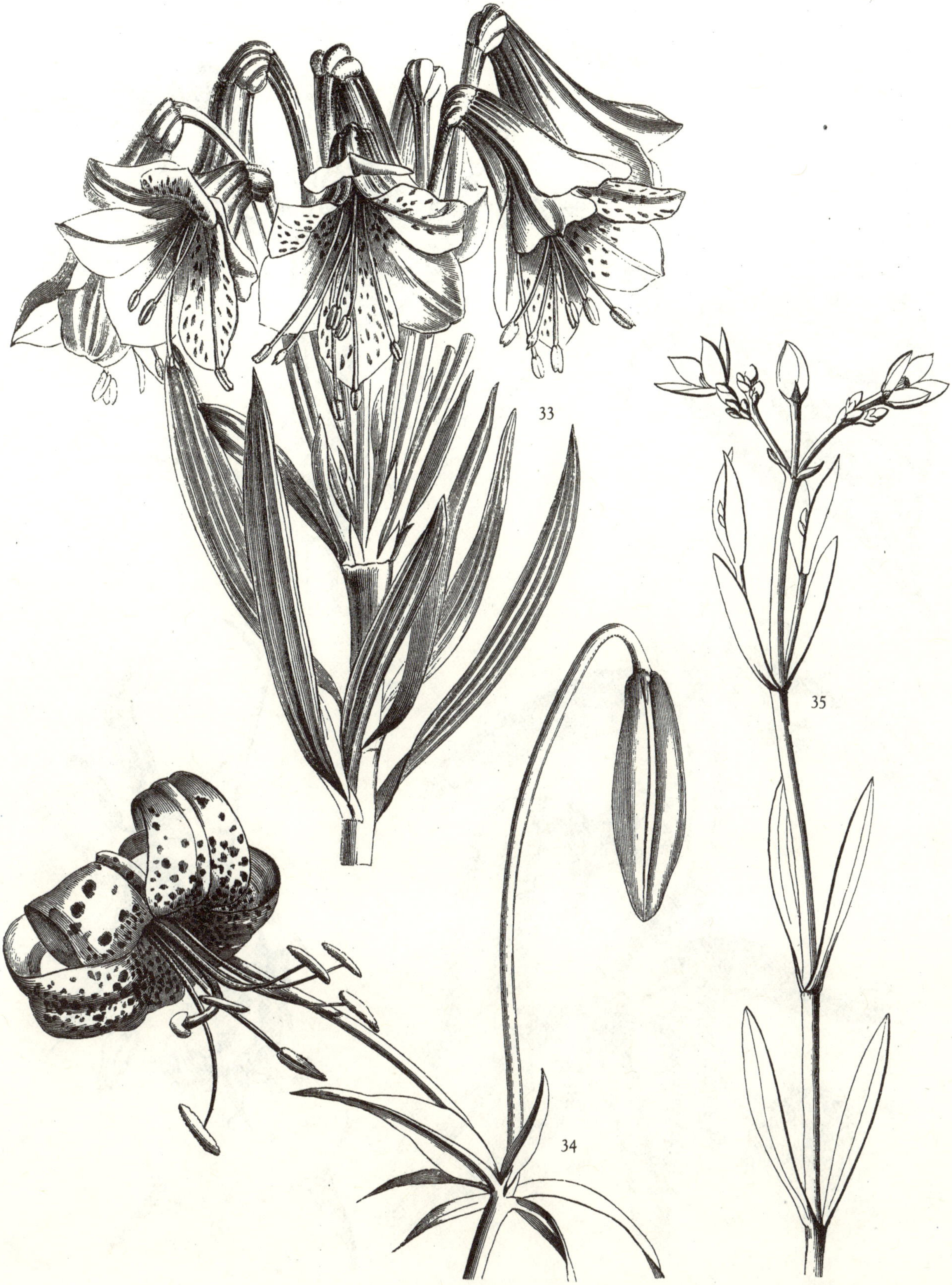

33. *Alstromeria plantaginea.* A herb with rich bell-shaped flowers of deep orange, lined with yellow, tipped with green and spotted with dark brown bars; from Brazil. 34. *Lilium canadense.* A lily with orange flowers spotted with crimson; from California. 35. *Boronia spathulata.* An evergreen with small pink flowers; from Australia.

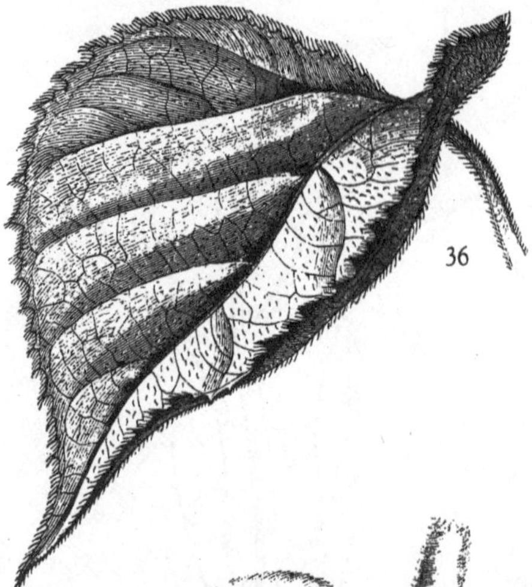

36

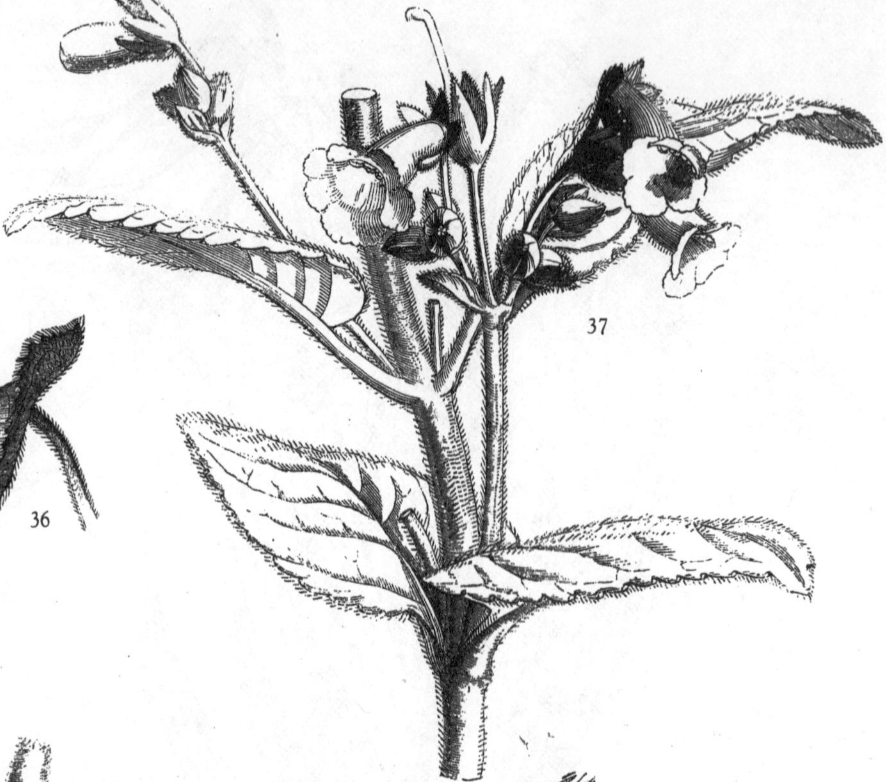

37

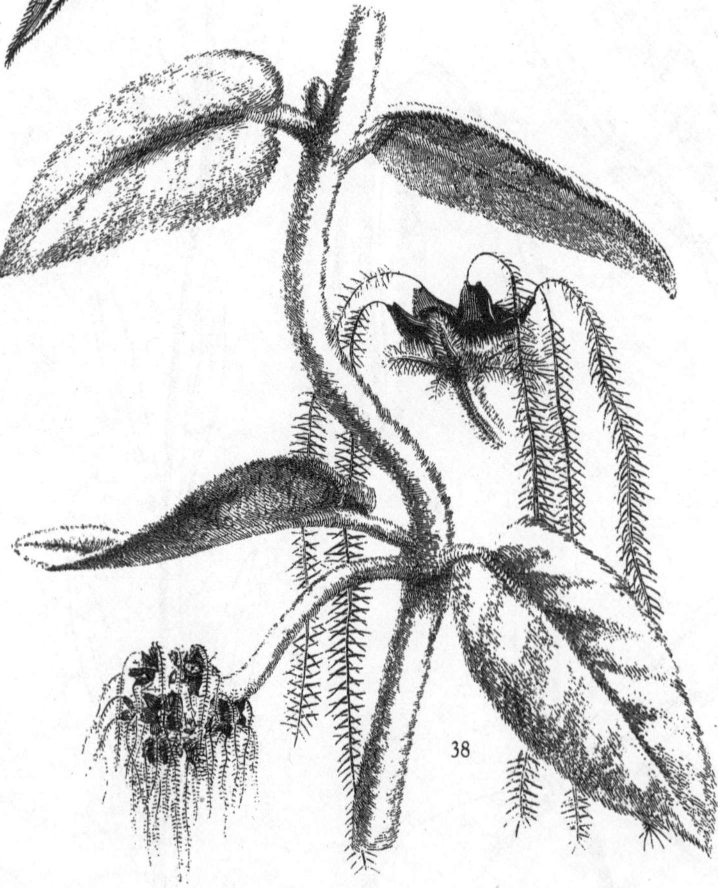

38

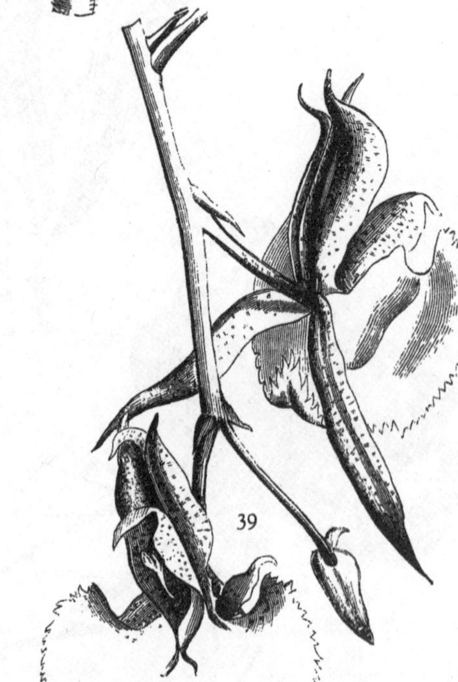

39

36. A leaf of the paper mulberry tree *(Broussonetia papyrifera)*. From east Asia and Polynesia. 37. *Achimenes viscida.* A herbaceous plant with woolly leaves and red and white flowers; from the Mexico-to-Panama area. 38. *Trichosacme lanata.* A woolly herb with small, dark purple flowers with long tails; from Mexico. 39. *Catasetum fimbriatum.* A terrestrial orchid with dirty-white and pink flowers; from Brazil, Uruguay and Paraguay.

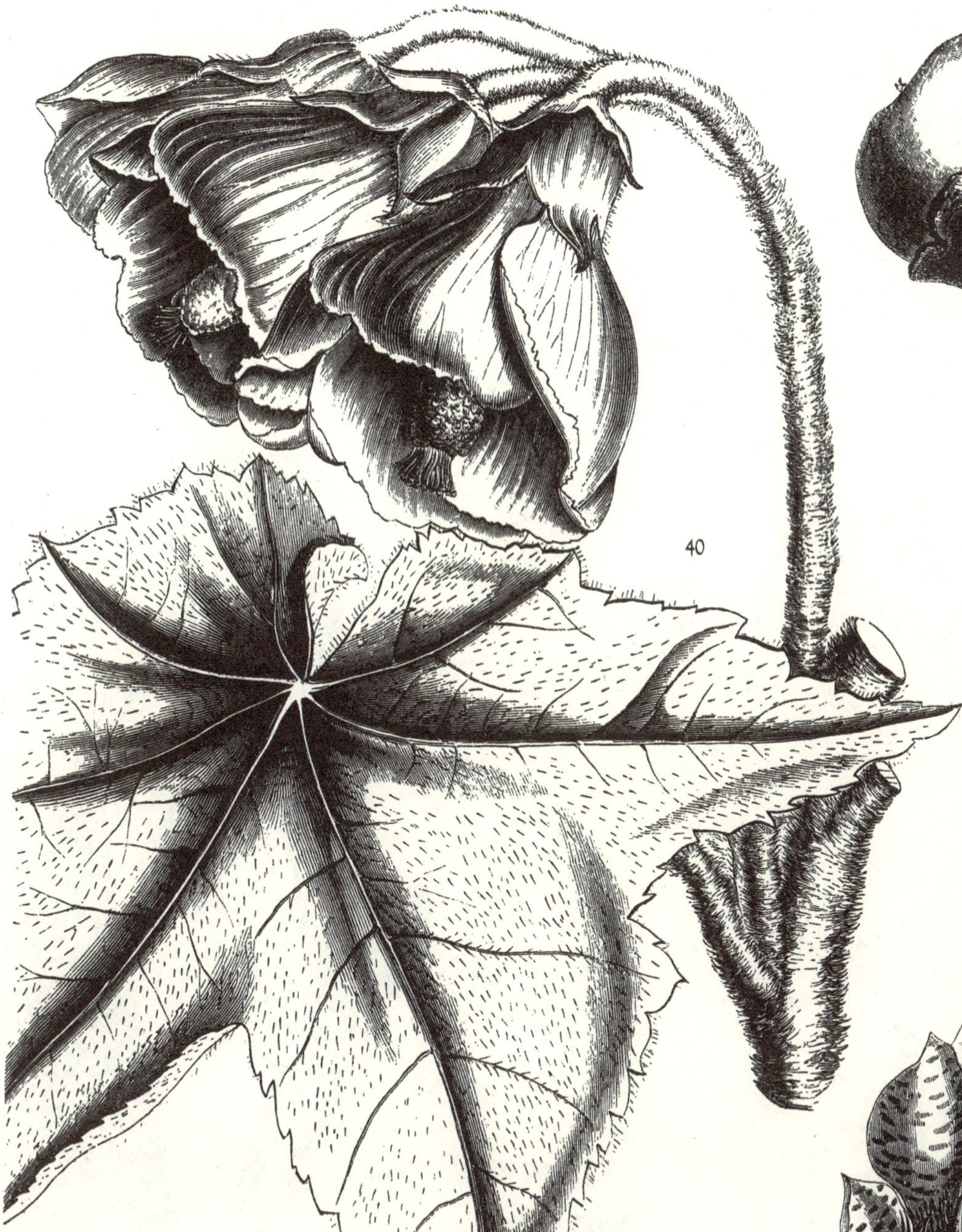

40

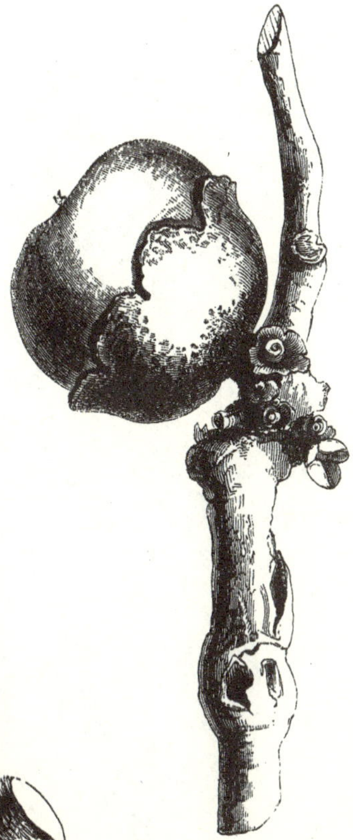

41

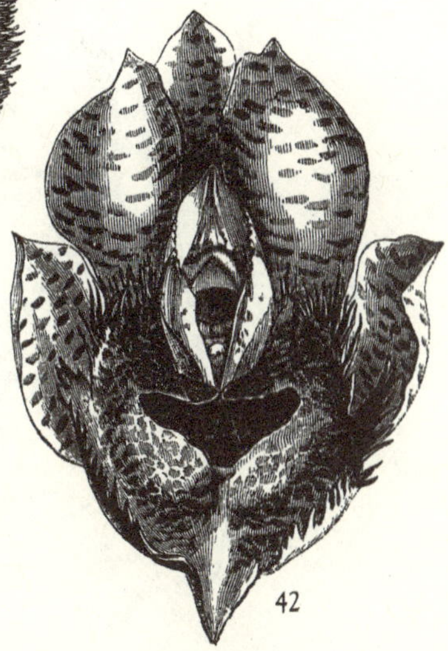

42

40. *Sphaeralcea nutans.* A coarse purple-flowered shrub; from Guatemala. 41. *Diospyros amplexicaulis.* A persimmon; from Mauritius. 42. *Catasetum sanguineum.* A terrestrial orchid with greenish flowers speckled with brown or dull red; from Central America.

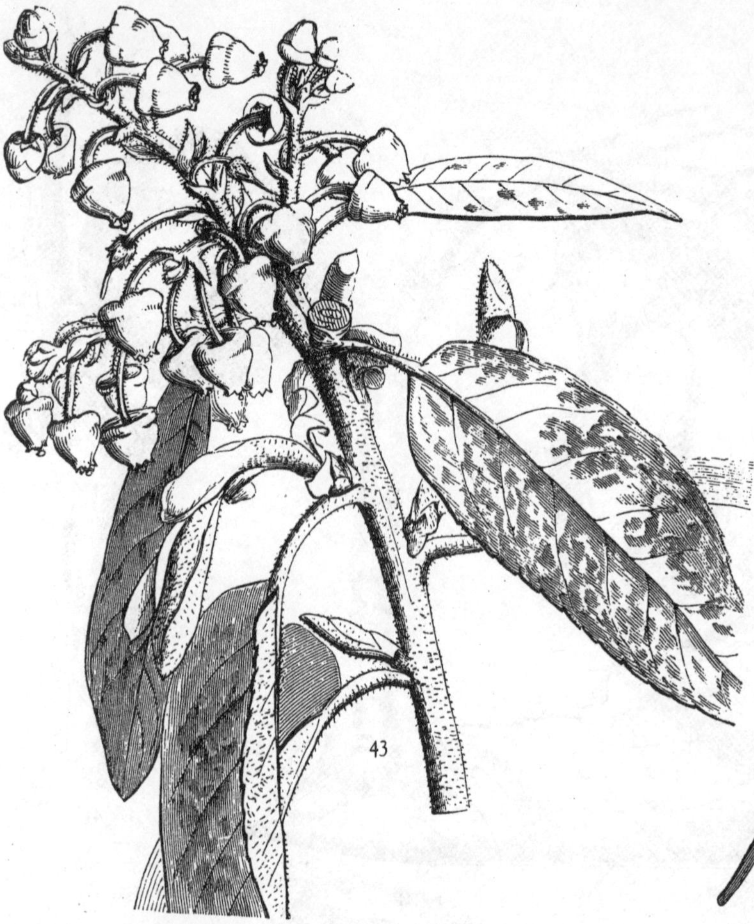
43

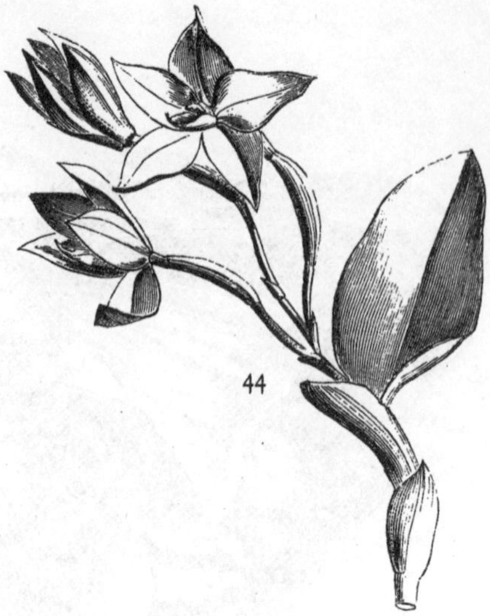
44

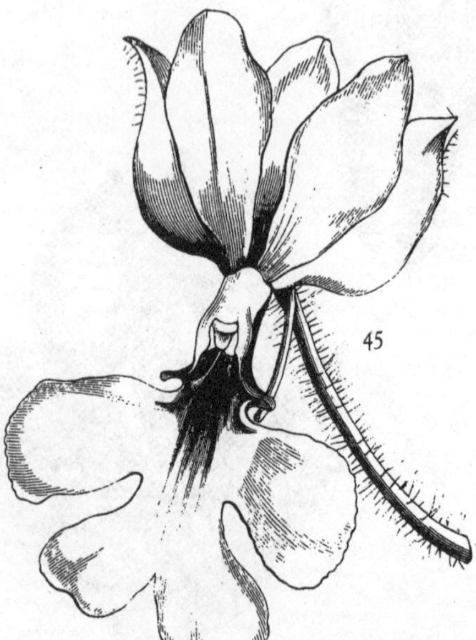
45

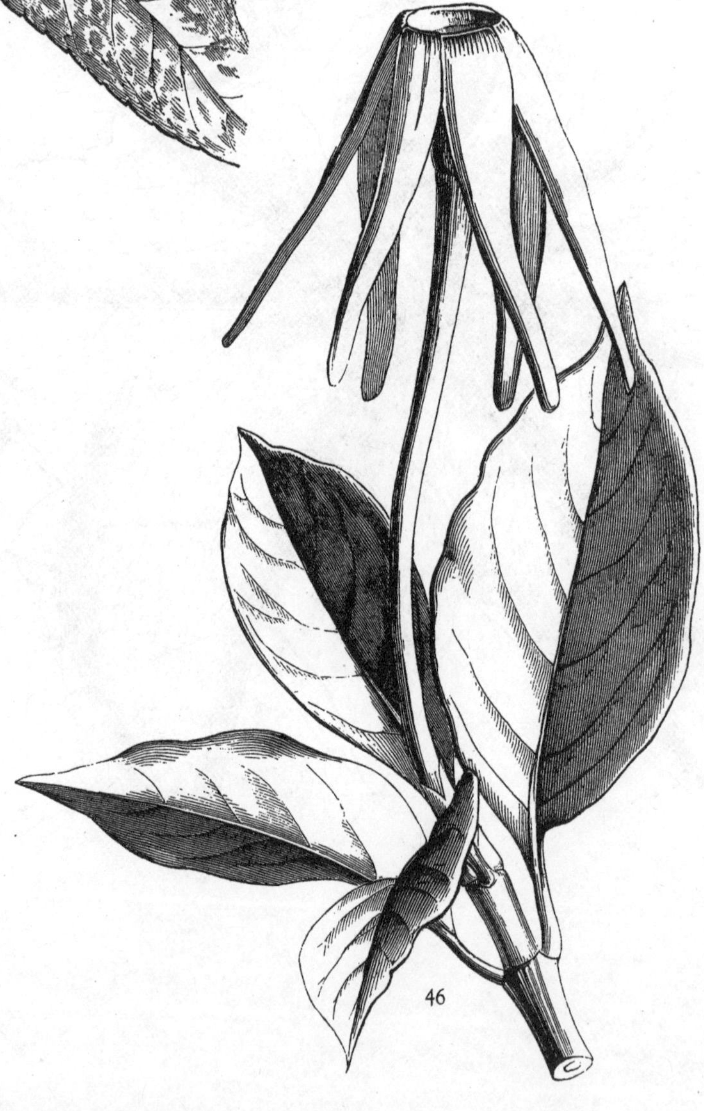
46

43. *Arbutus varians.* An evergreen shrub with white and pink flowers; from Mexico. 44. *Sophronitis ceruna.* An orchid with small brilliant scarlet flowers with a yellow lip; from Brazil. 45. *Calanthe vestita.* A terrestrial orchid with white flowers with a deep stain of bright crimson in the middle of the lip; from Burma (see also Fig. 193). 46. *Hillia parasitica.* A creeper with long trumpet-shaped, cream-colored flowers; from the West Indies.

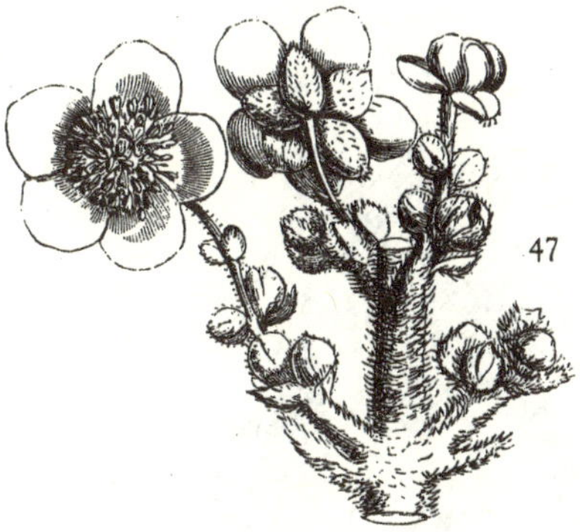

47

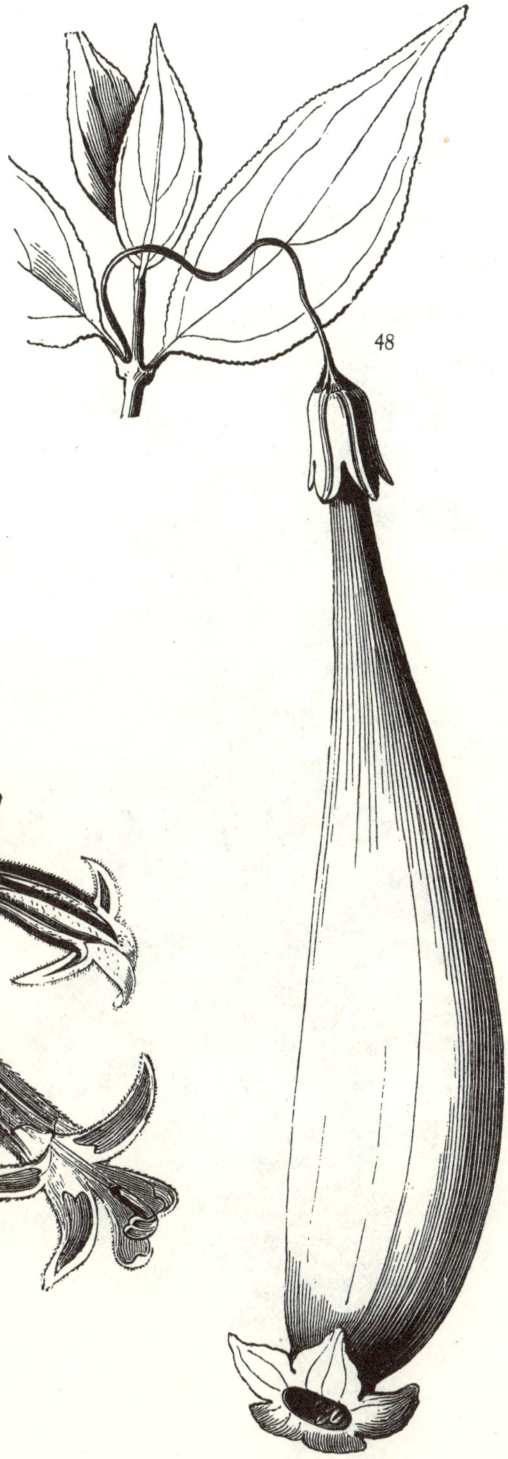

48

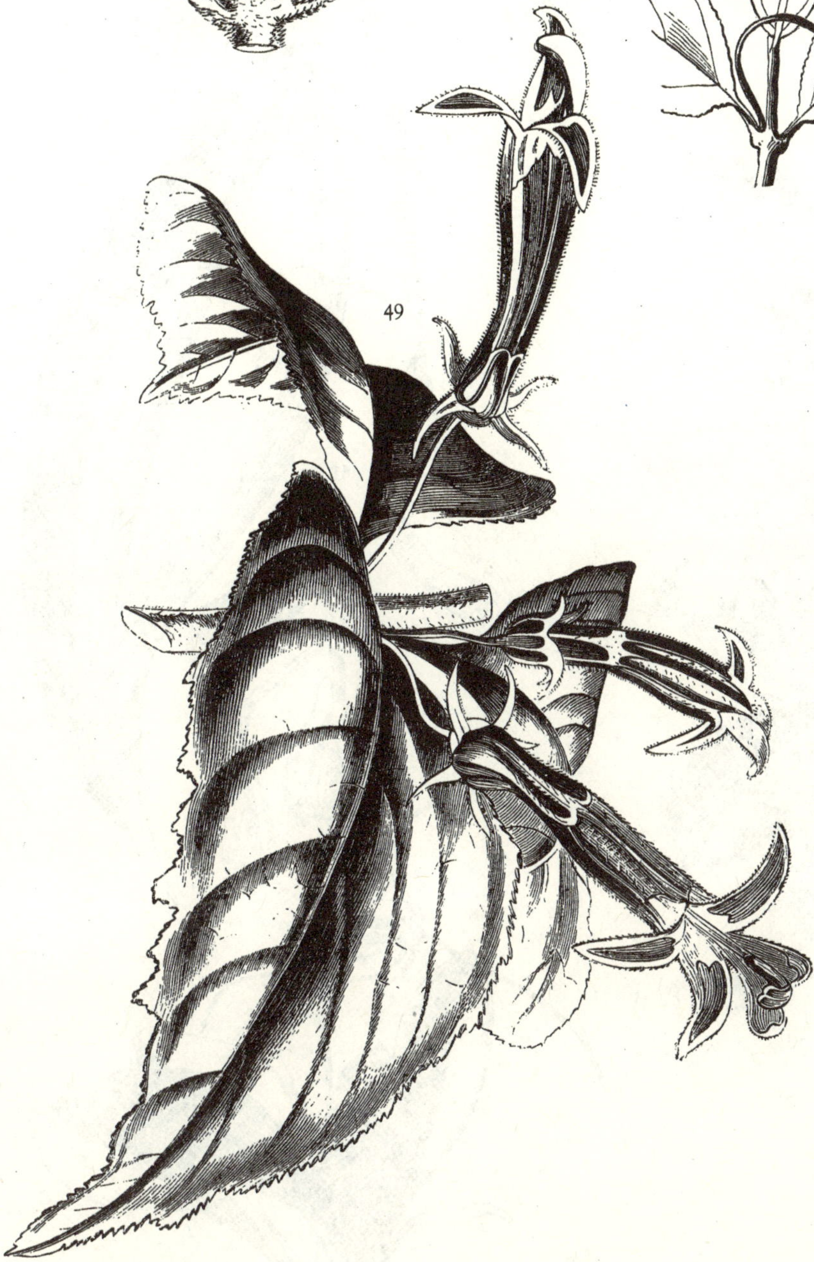

49

47. *Saurauja macrophylla.* A soft, shaggy white-flowered shrub; from Guatemala (see also Fig. 223). 48. *Lisianthus princeps.* A shrub with very long scarlet, yellow and green flowers; from Colombia and Panama. 49. *Siphocampylus orbignyanus.* A plant with dark-green leaves and crimson and green flowers; from Bolivia.

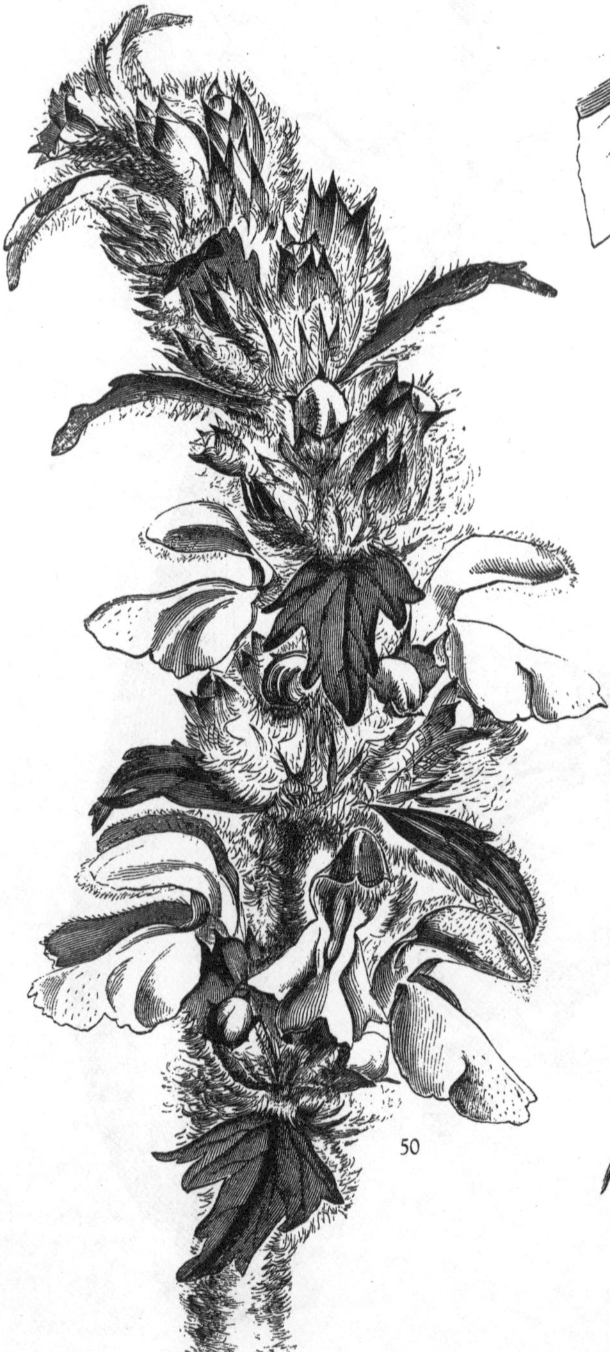

50

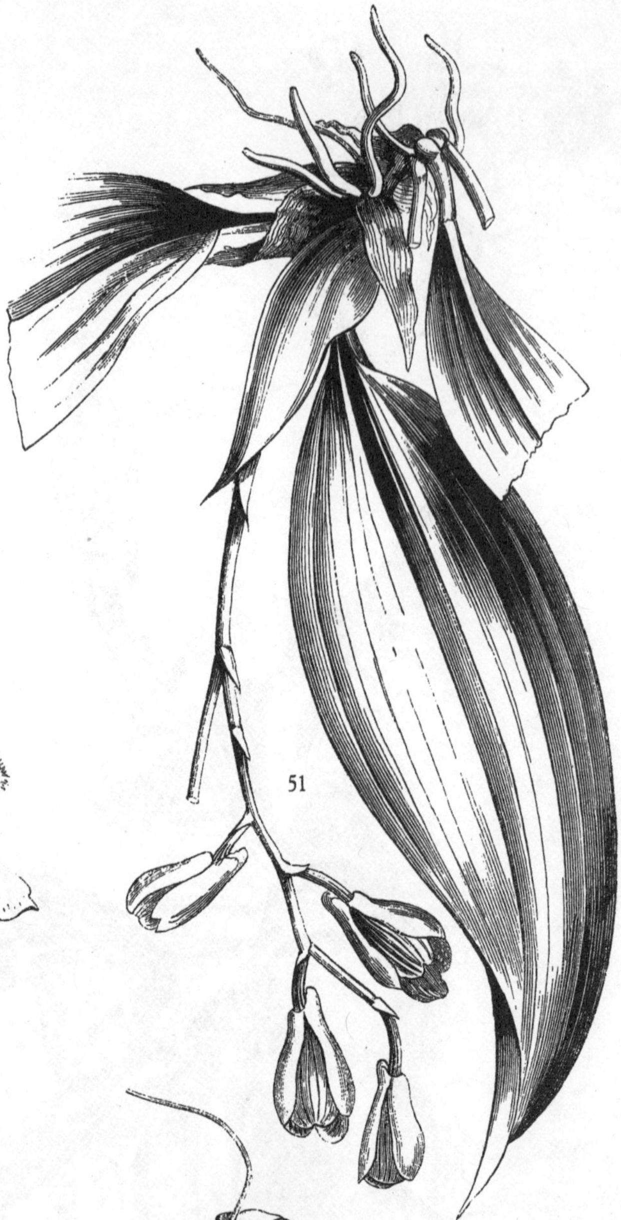

51

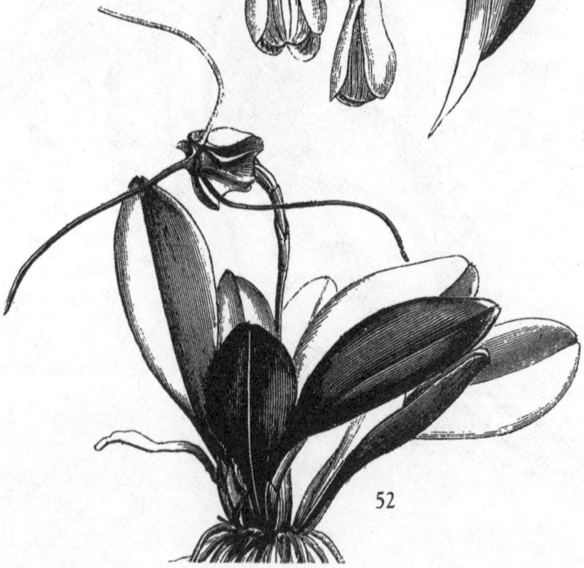

52

50. *Eremostachys laciniata.* A hardy perennial with large yellow flowers; from the Caucasus.
51. *Scelochilus ottonis.* An orchid with yellow flowers with a few red streaks; from Venezuela.
52. *Masdevallia wageneriana.* A small, dull pale red orchid; from Venezuela.

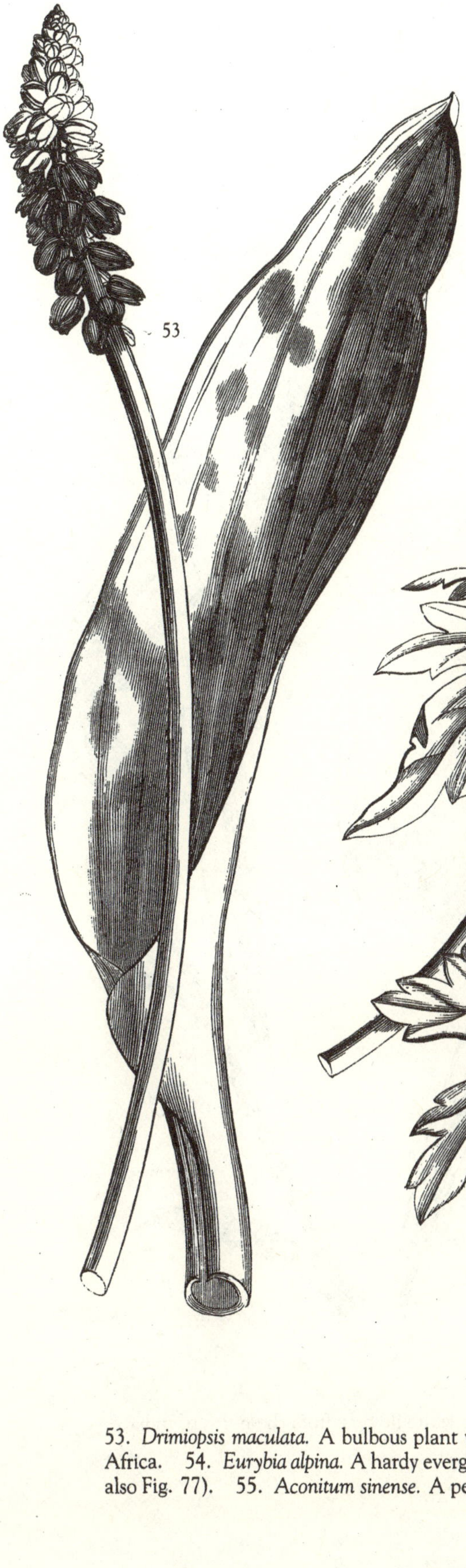

53

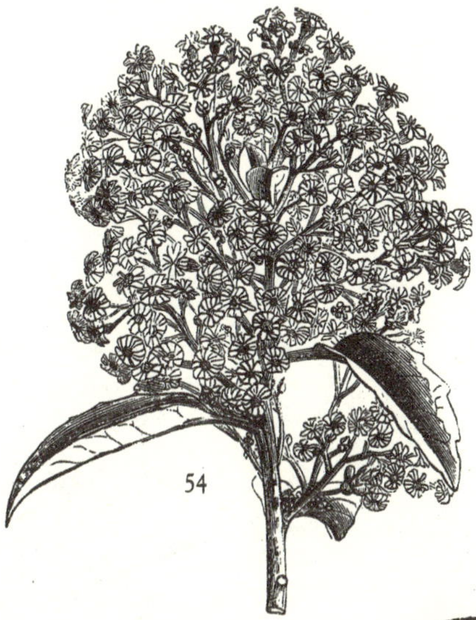

54

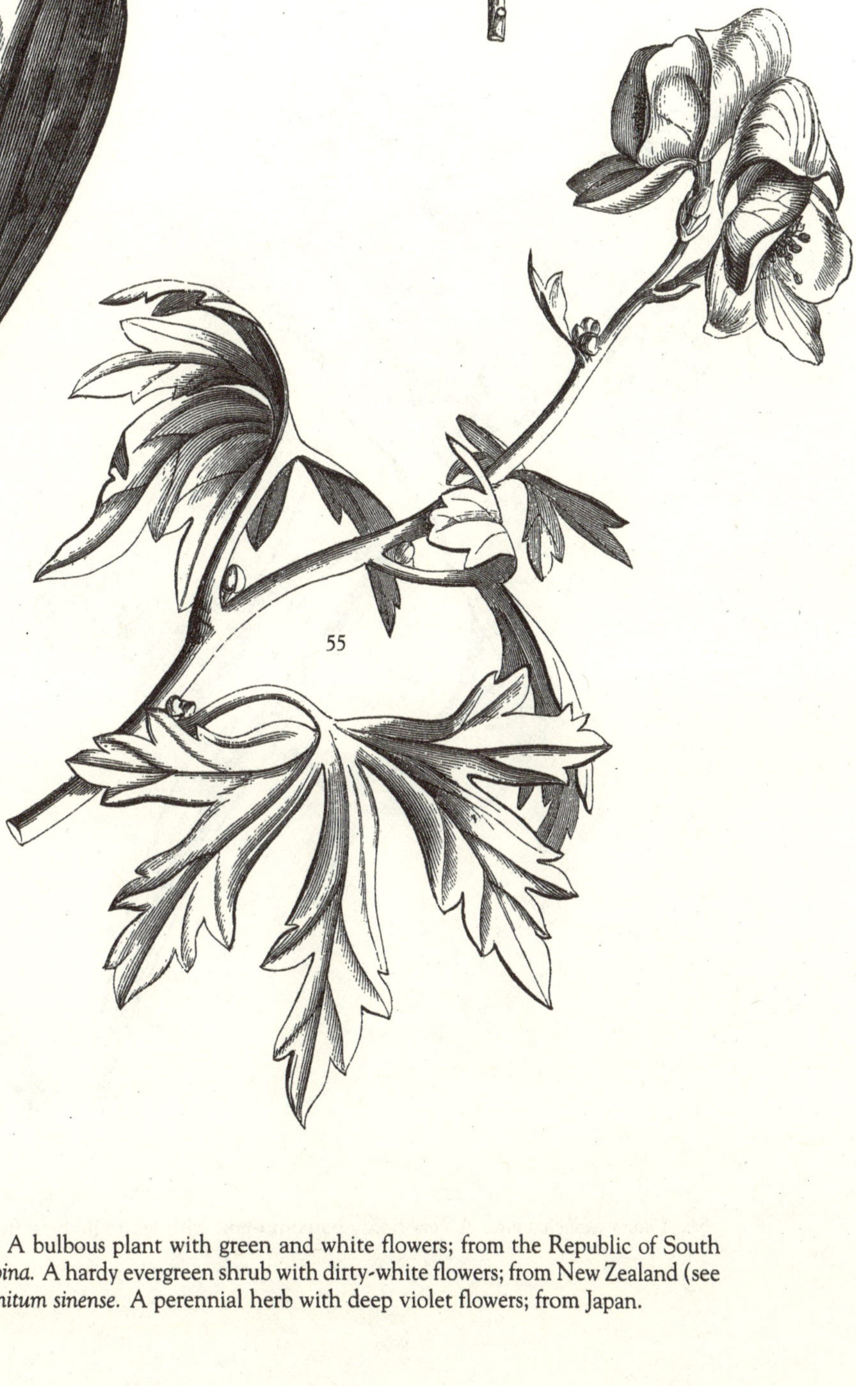

55

53. *Drimiopsis maculata.* A bulbous plant with green and white flowers; from the Republic of South Africa. 54. *Eurybia alpina.* A hardy evergreen shrub with dirty-white flowers; from New Zealand (see also Fig. 77). 55. *Aconitum sinense.* A perennial herb with deep violet flowers; from Japan.

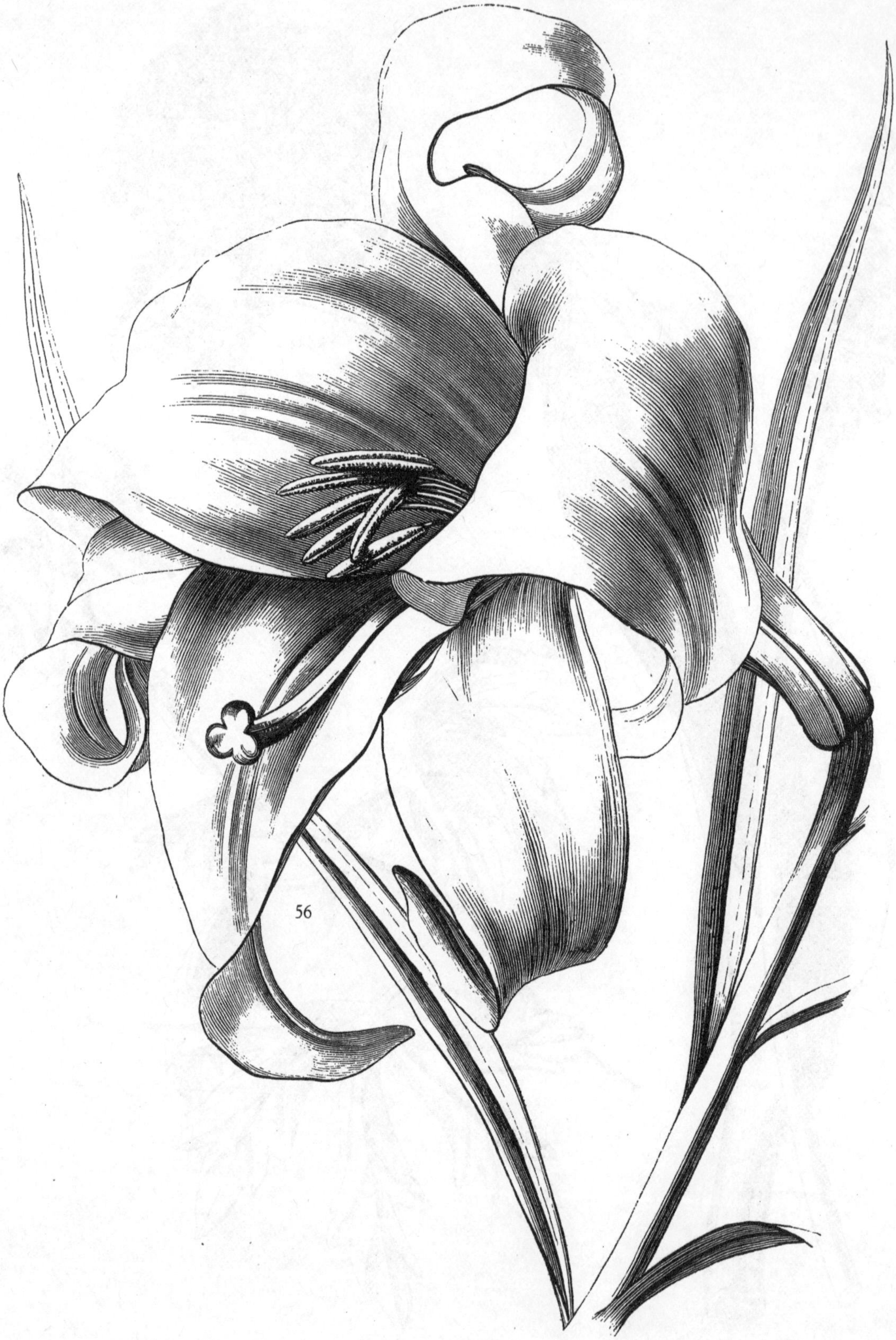

56. *Lilium wallichianum.* A very hardy bulbous plant with white flowers; from the north of India.

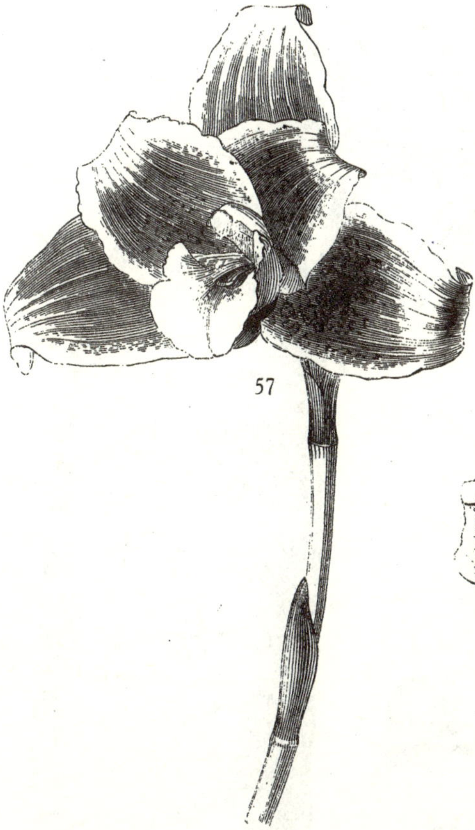

57

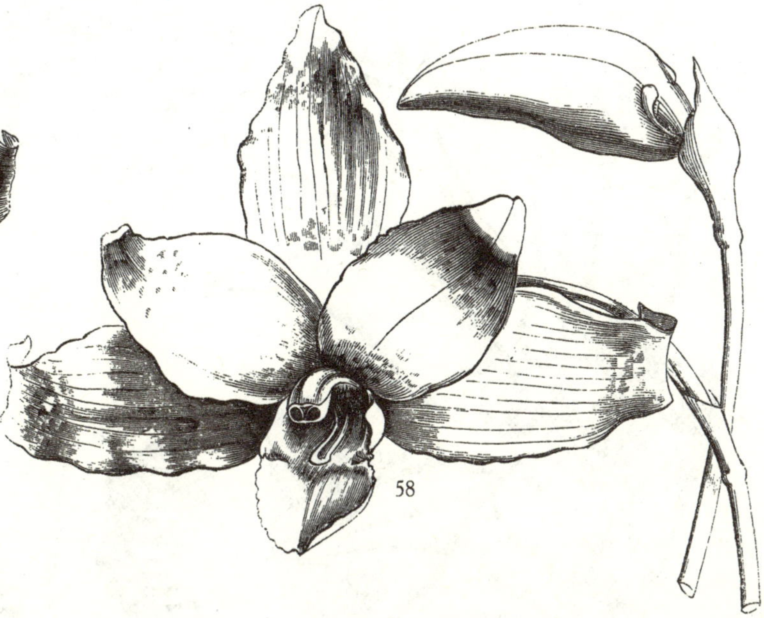

58

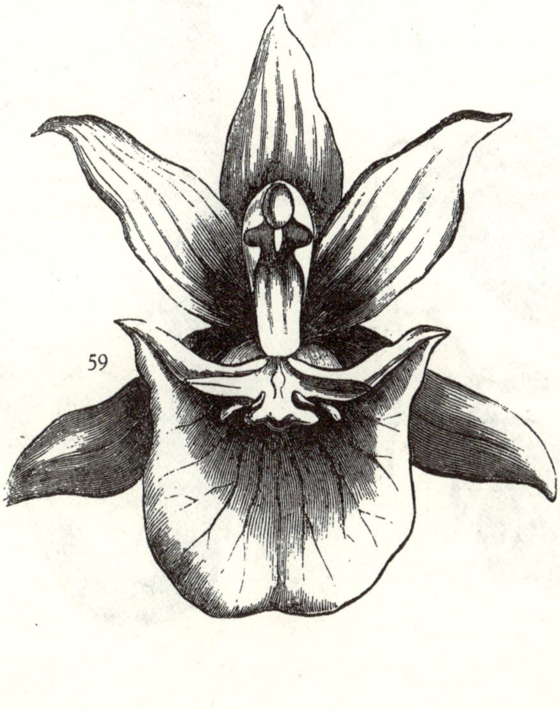

59

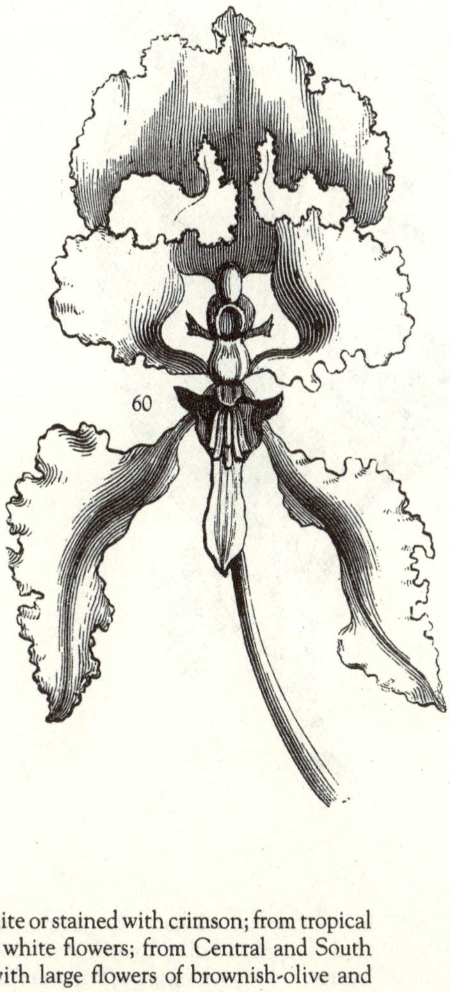

60

57 & 58. *Lycaste leucantha.* An orchid with flowers that are white or stained with crimson; from tropical America. 59. *Warrea candida.* An orchid with purple and white flowers; from Central and South America. 60. *Oncidium serratum.* A half-twining orchid with large flowers of brownish-olive and brilliant yellow; from Peru.

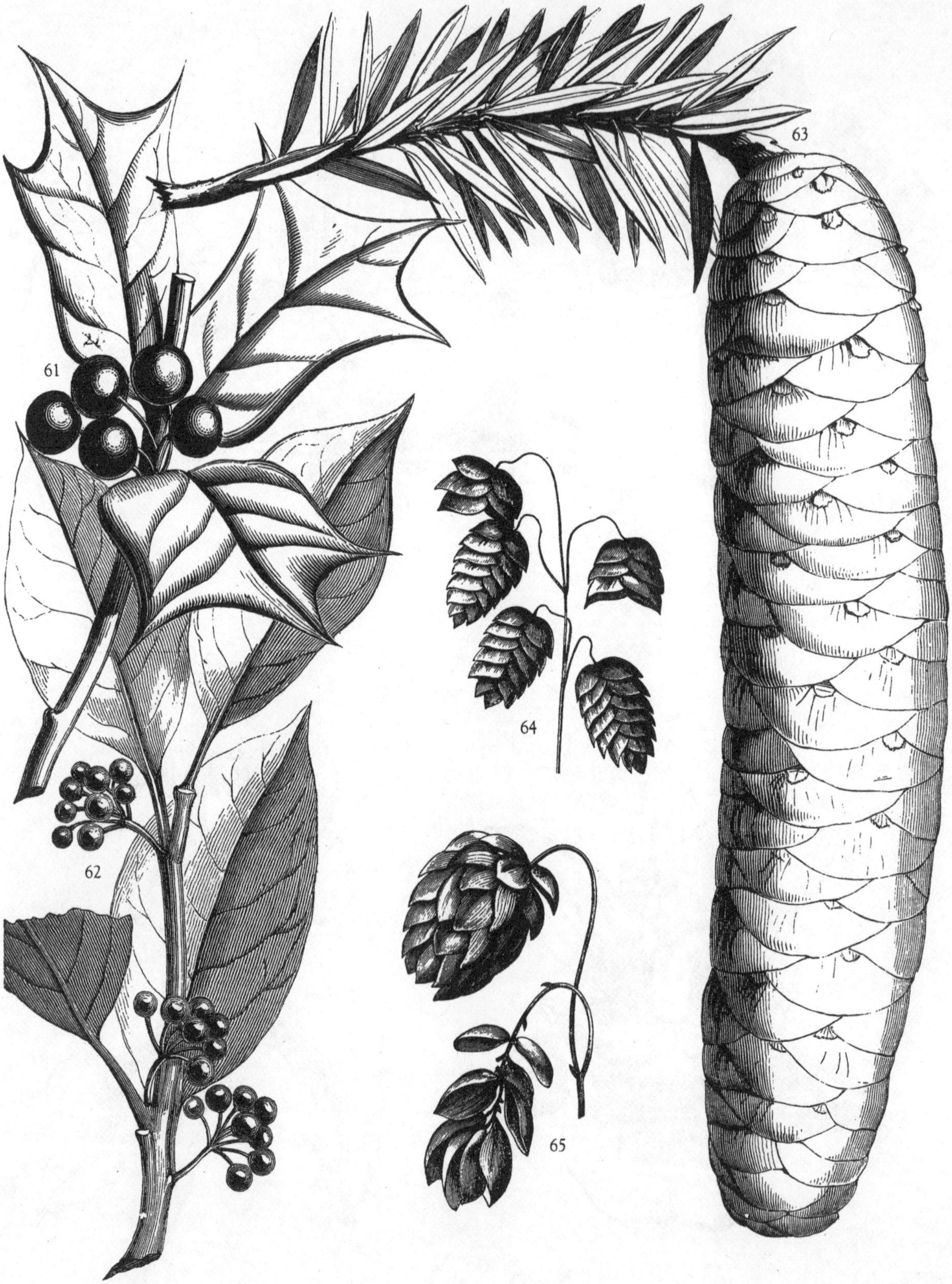

61. *Ilex cornuta.* A hardy evergreen holly; from the north of China. 62. *Ilex microcarpa.* Another hardy evergreen holly; from China. 63. *Abies jezoënsis.* A spruce with leaves of brilliant green; from Japan. 64. Quaking grass *(Briza maxima)*. From California and Texas. 65. Common hop *(Humulus lupulus)*. From the temperate Northern Hemisphere.

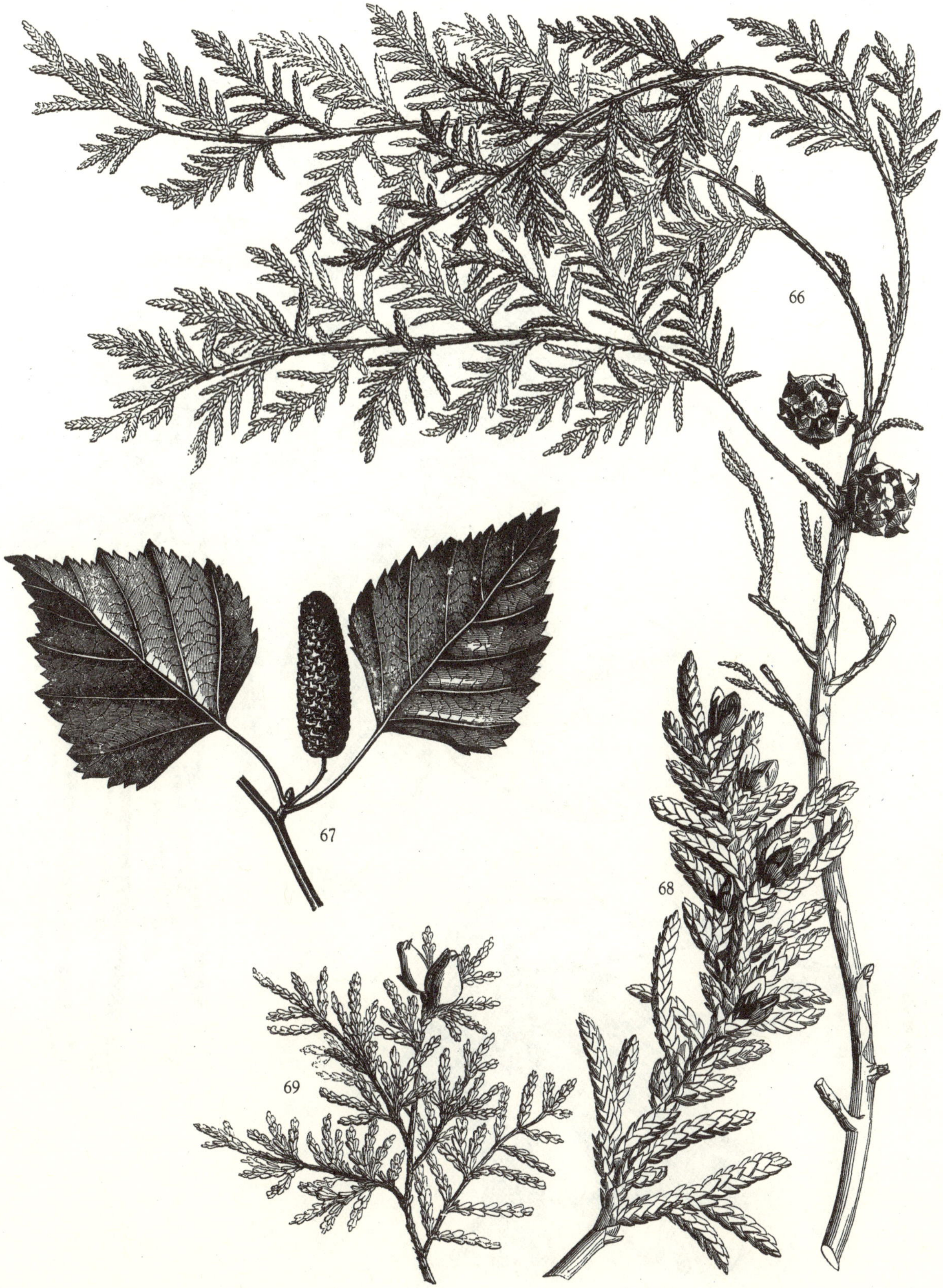

66. Mourning cypress (*Cupressus funebris*). From China. 67. A ripe female catkin of birch (*Betula alba*). See Fig. 19. 68. *Libocedrus tetragona.* An evergreen coniferous tree; from the cold southern regions of South America. 69. Chilean incense cedar (*Libocedrus chilensis*).

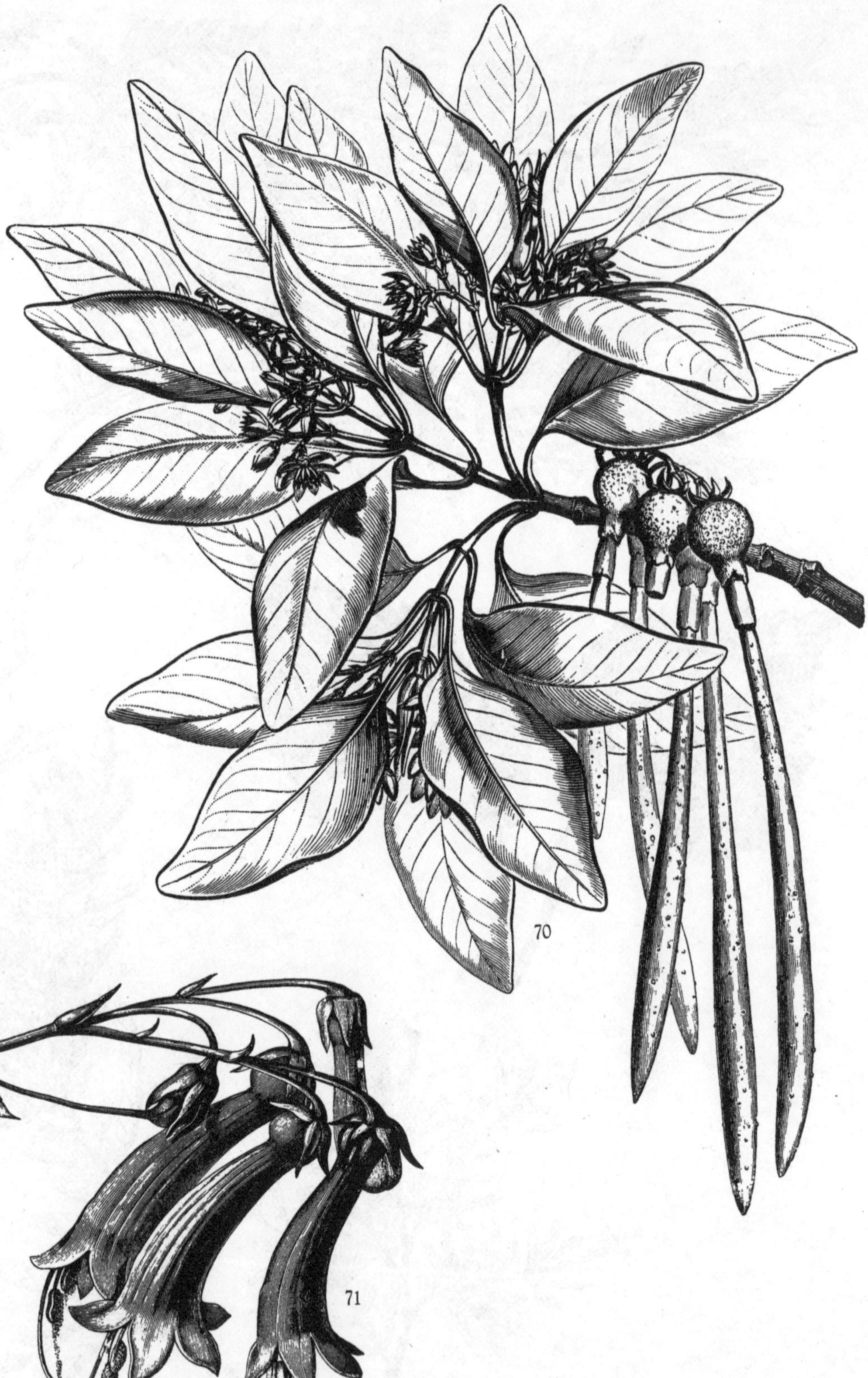

70

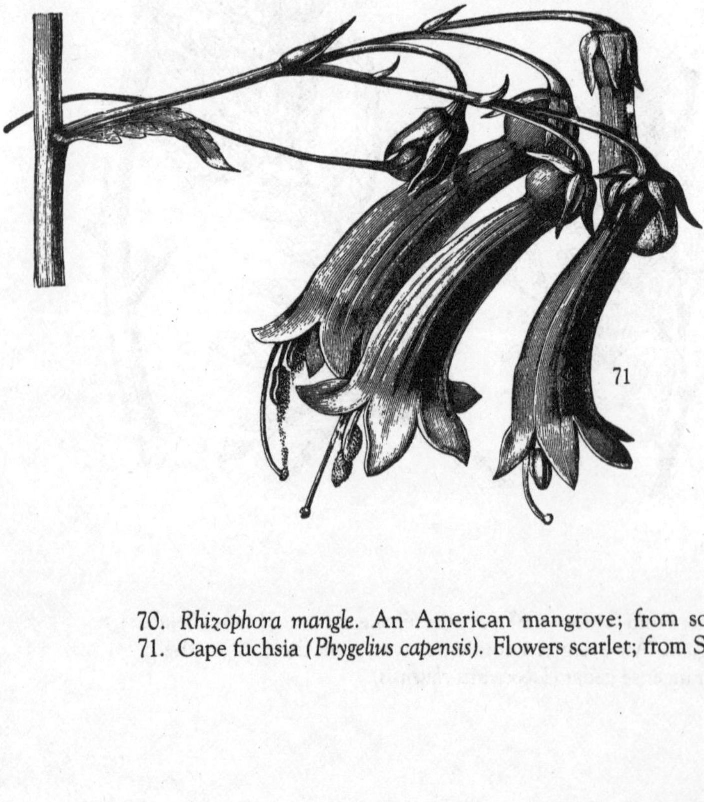

71

70. *Rhizophora mangle.* An American mangrove; from southern Florida and tropical America.
71. Cape fuchsia *(Phygelius capensis).* Flowers scarlet; from South Africa.

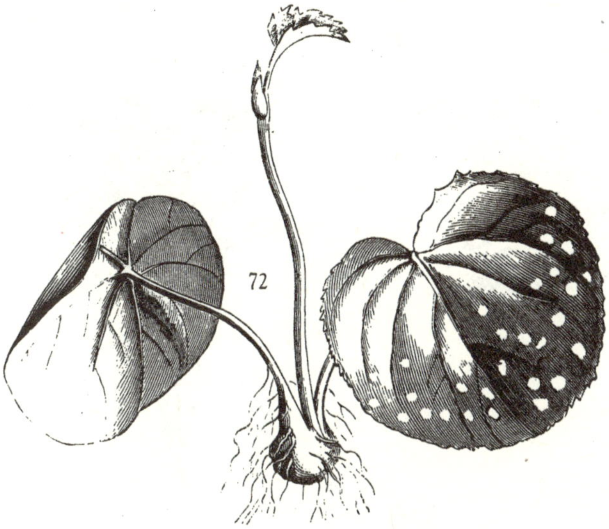

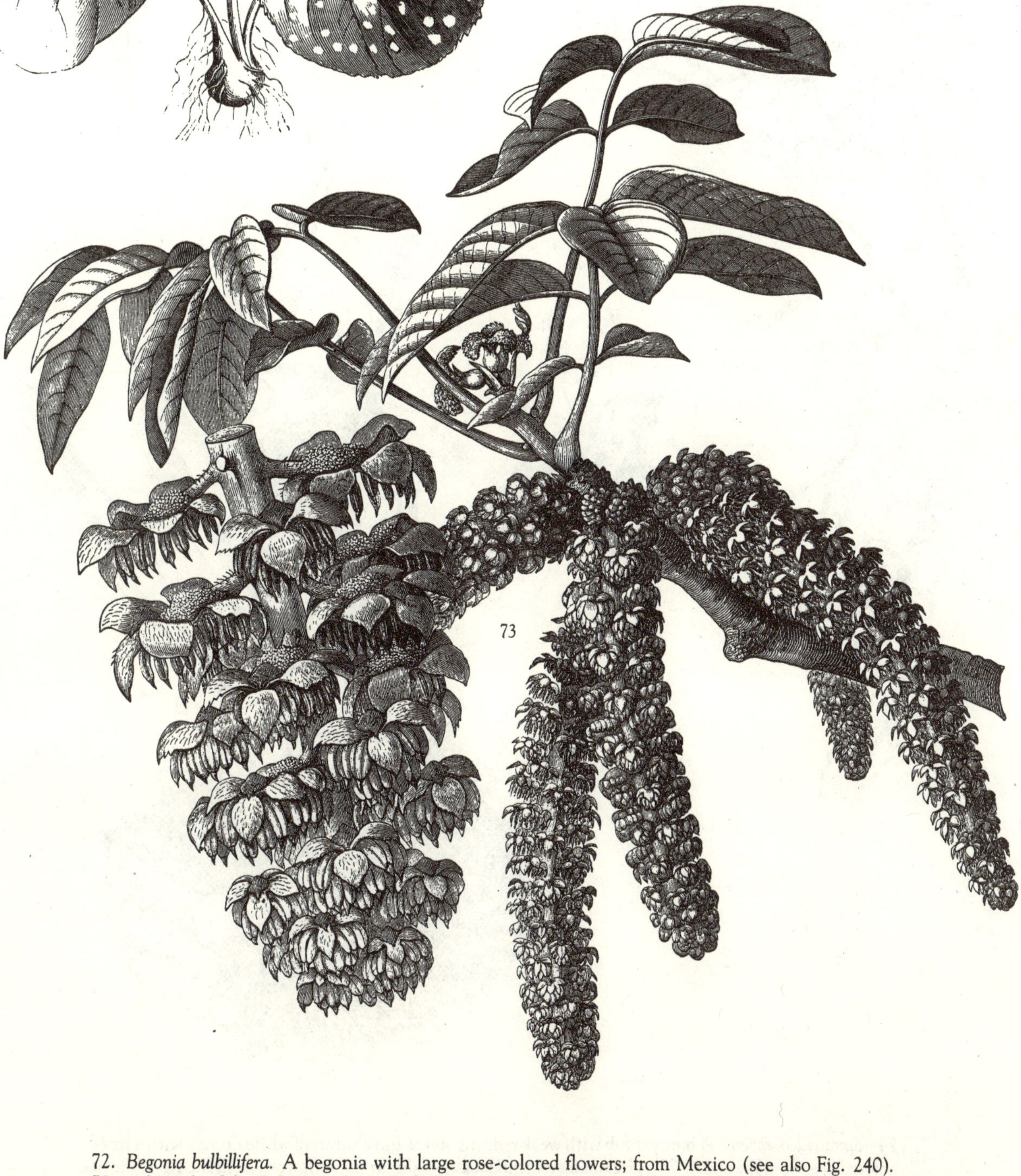

72. *Begonia bulbillifera.* A begonia with large rose-colored flowers; from Mexico (see also Fig. 240).
73. A branch of the Persian walnut *(Juglans regia)*. Shows hanging male catkins and a small cluster of female flowers; to the left is an enlarged drawing of the male catkin; from southeastern Europe and western Asia (see also Figs. 155 & 248).

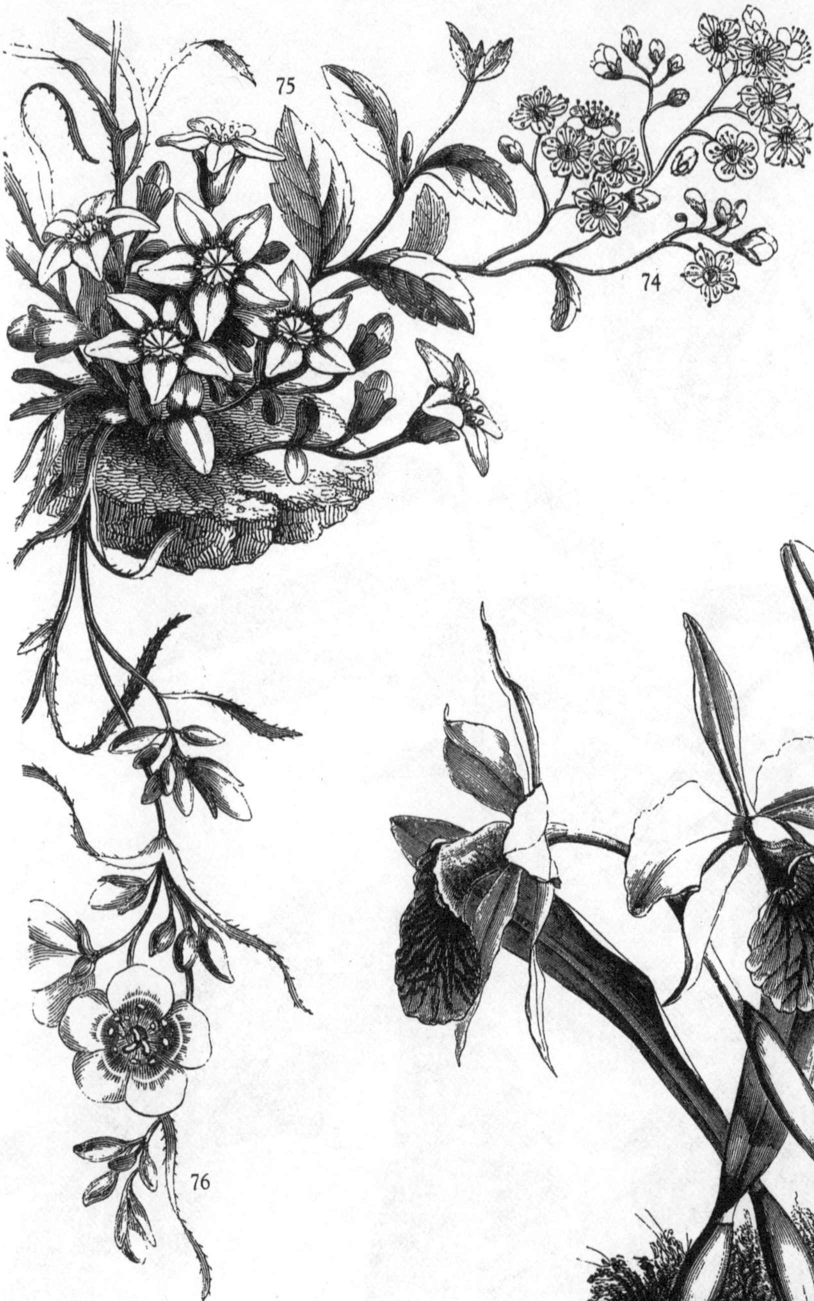

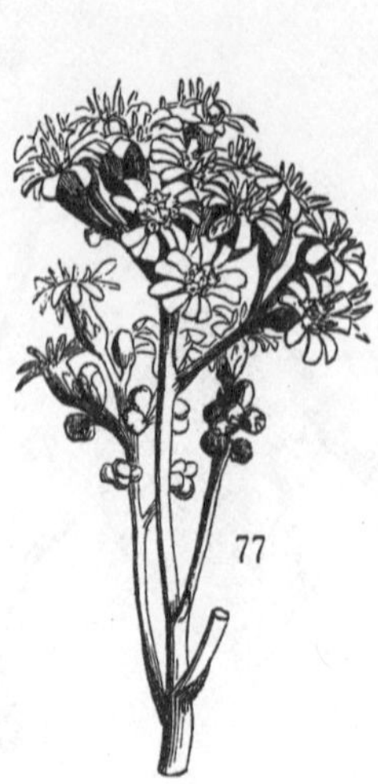

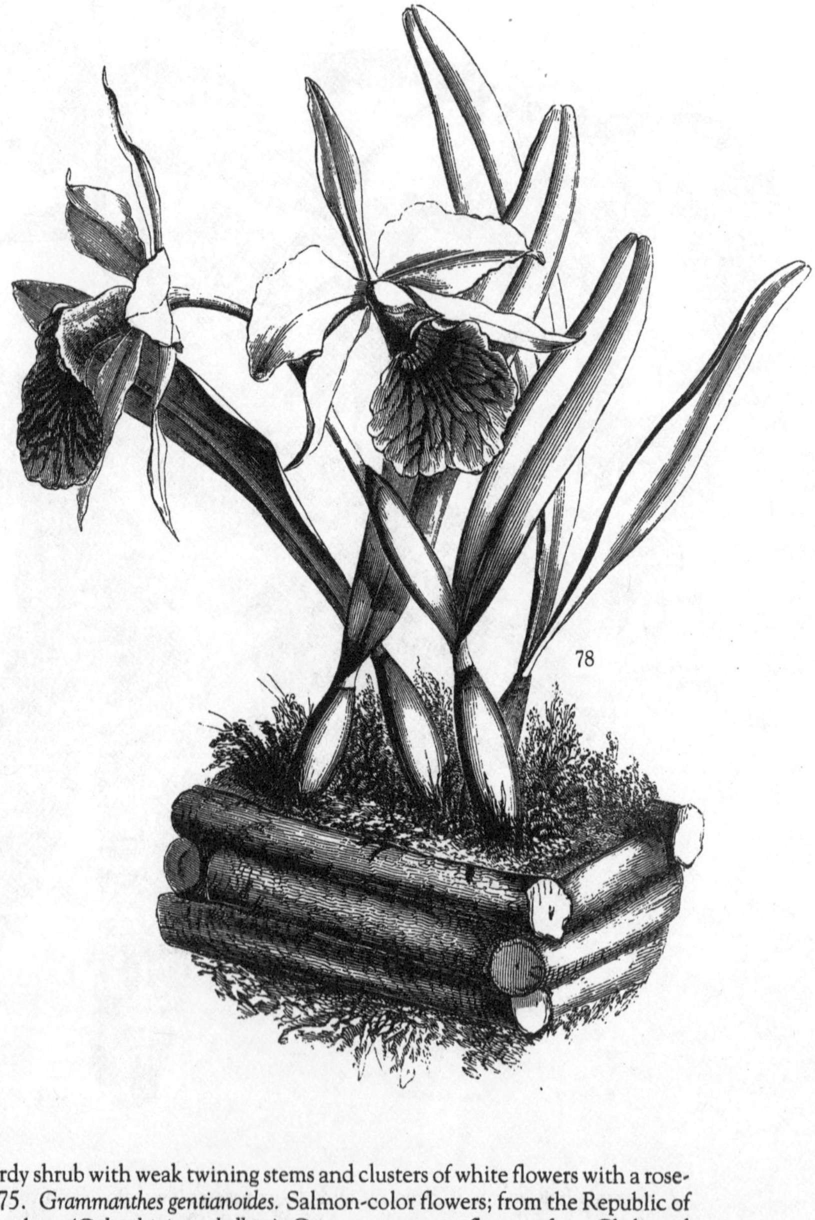

74. *Spiraea decumbens.* A hardy shrub with weak twining stems and clusters of white flowers with a rose-colored eye; from Europe. 75. *Grammanthes gentianoides.* Salmon-color flowers; from the Republic of South Africa. 76. Rock purslane (*Calandrinia umbellata*). Crimson-magenta flowers; from Chile and Peru. 77. *Eurybia alpina.* See Fig. 54. 78. *Laelia purpurata.* An orchid with pure white sepals and petals and deep purple limb; from Brazil.

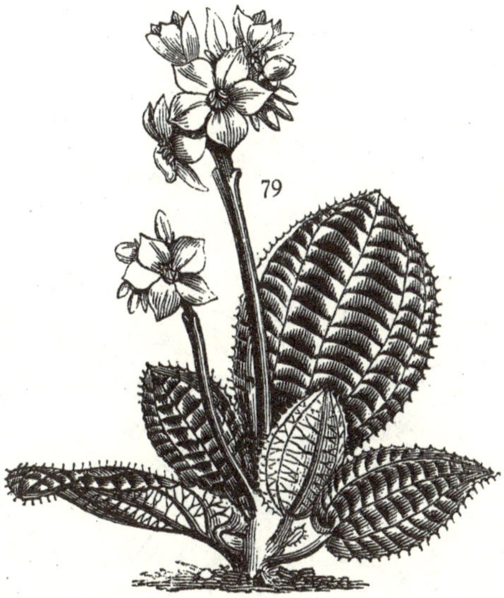

79

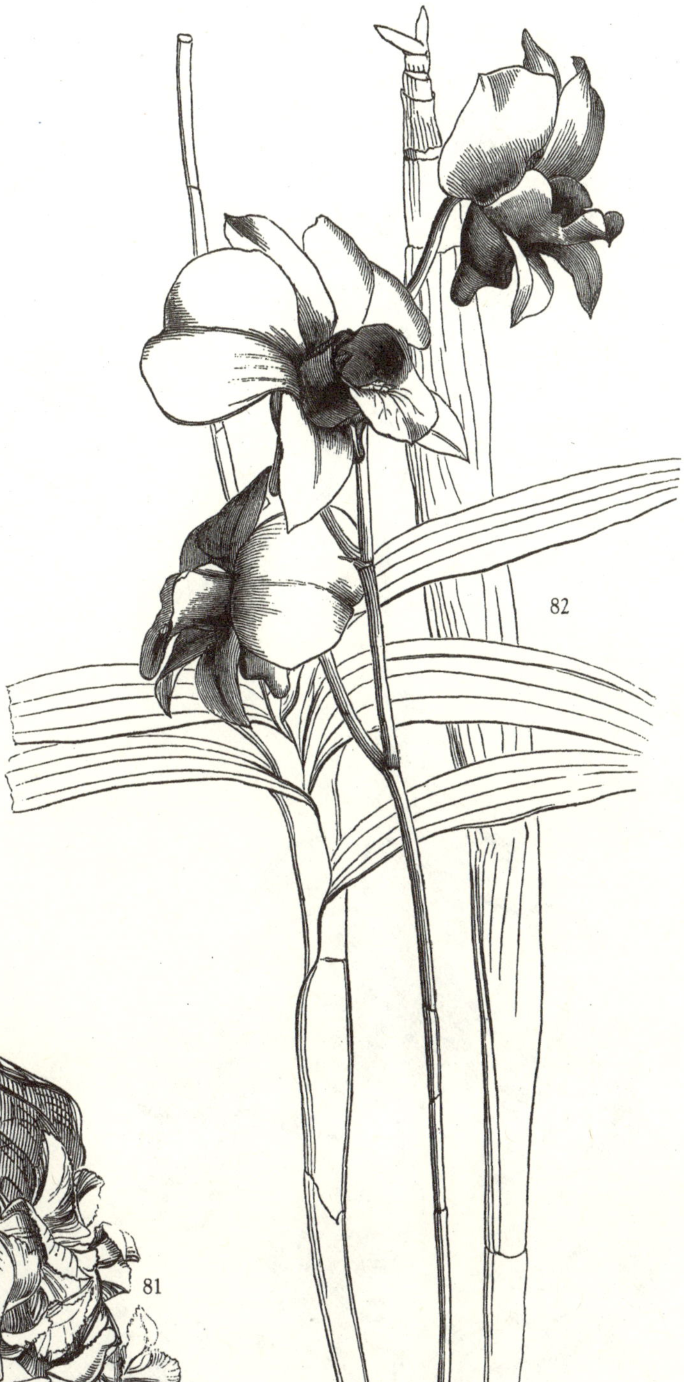

82

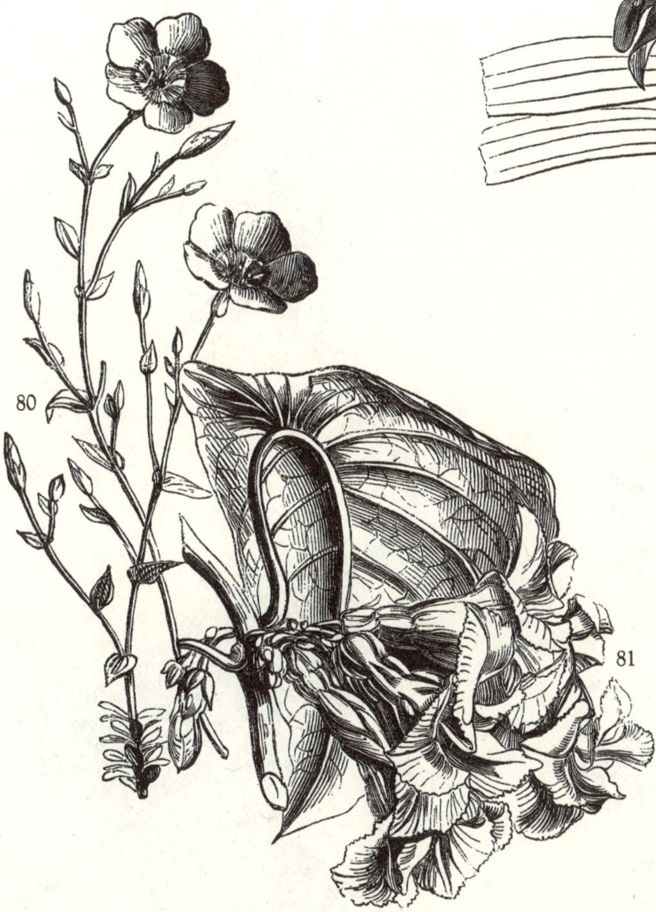

80

81

79. *Eriocnema marmoratum.* Leaves green, striped with white, flowers rose-colored; from Brazil. 80. *Linum grandiflorum.* A hardy annual with brilliant crimson flowers; from Algeria. 81. *Echites peltata.* A climbing plant with large, thick leaves and large, bright yellow, clustered flowers; from Brazil. 82. *Dendrobium bigibbum.* An orchid, flowers white with a purple blotch on each side of the crest of the lip; from northern Australia.

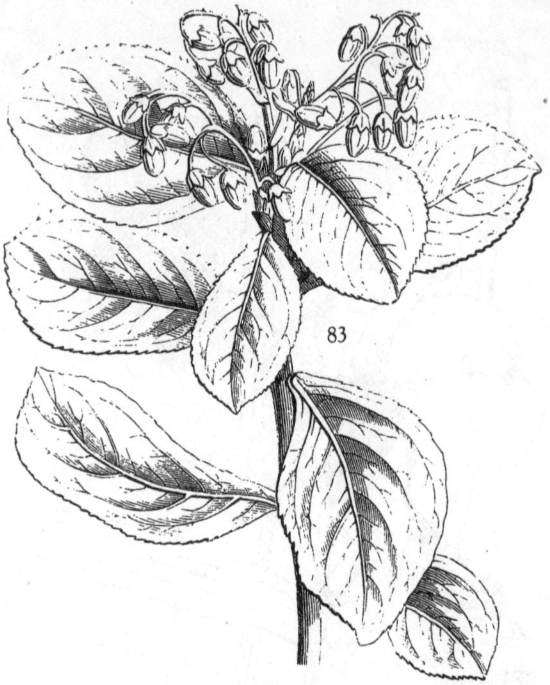

83

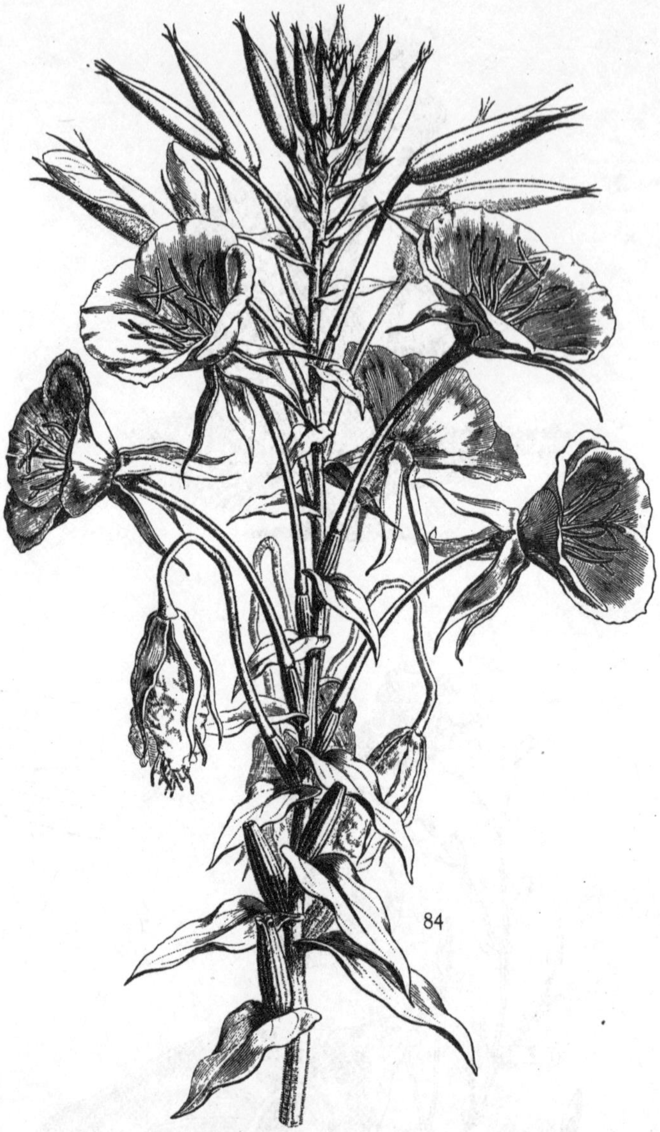

84

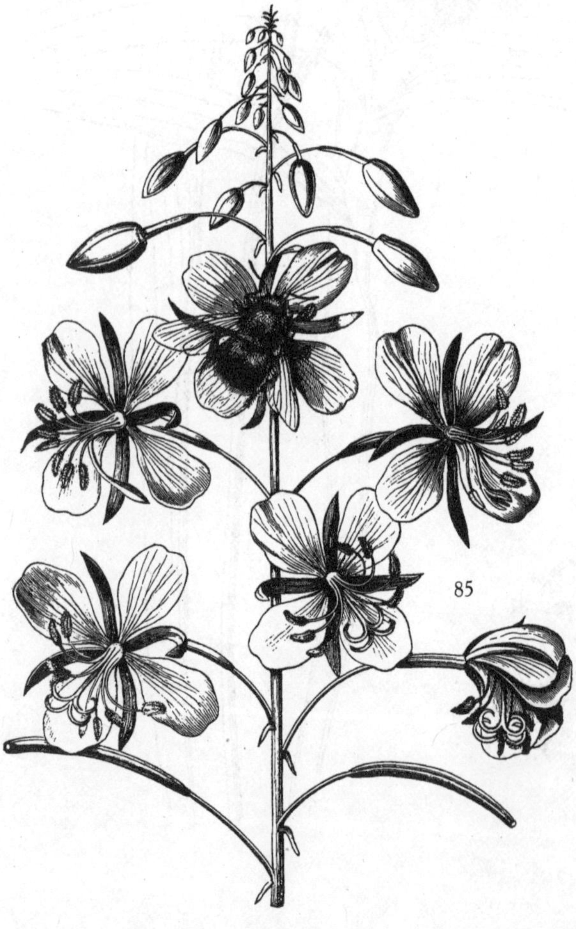

85

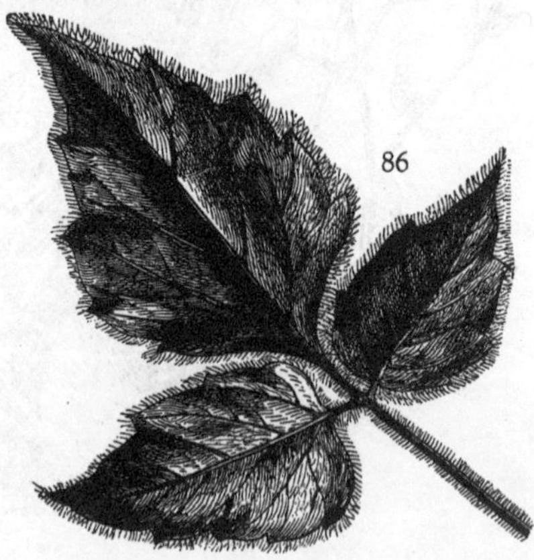

86

83. *Gaultheria lindeniana.* An evergreen shrub, one of the heathworts, with small white flowers; from the Andes. 84. Evening primrose (*Oenothera biennis*). From eastern North America. 85. *Epilobium angustifolium.* A willow herb, flowers rose to purple or white; from North America and Eurasia. 86. *Serjania gramatophora.* A leaf of a vine; from tropical and subtropical America.

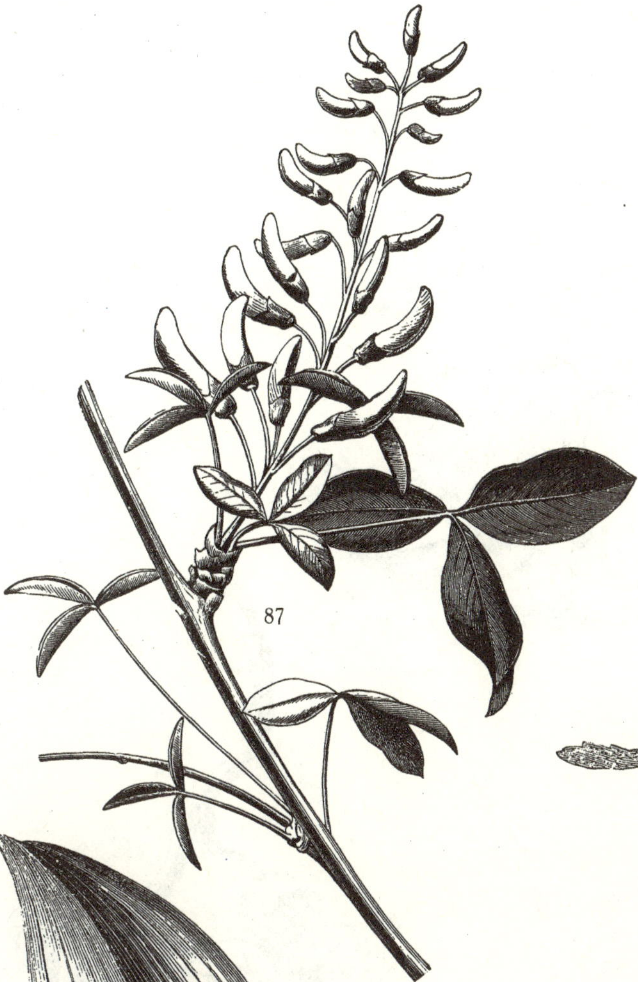

87

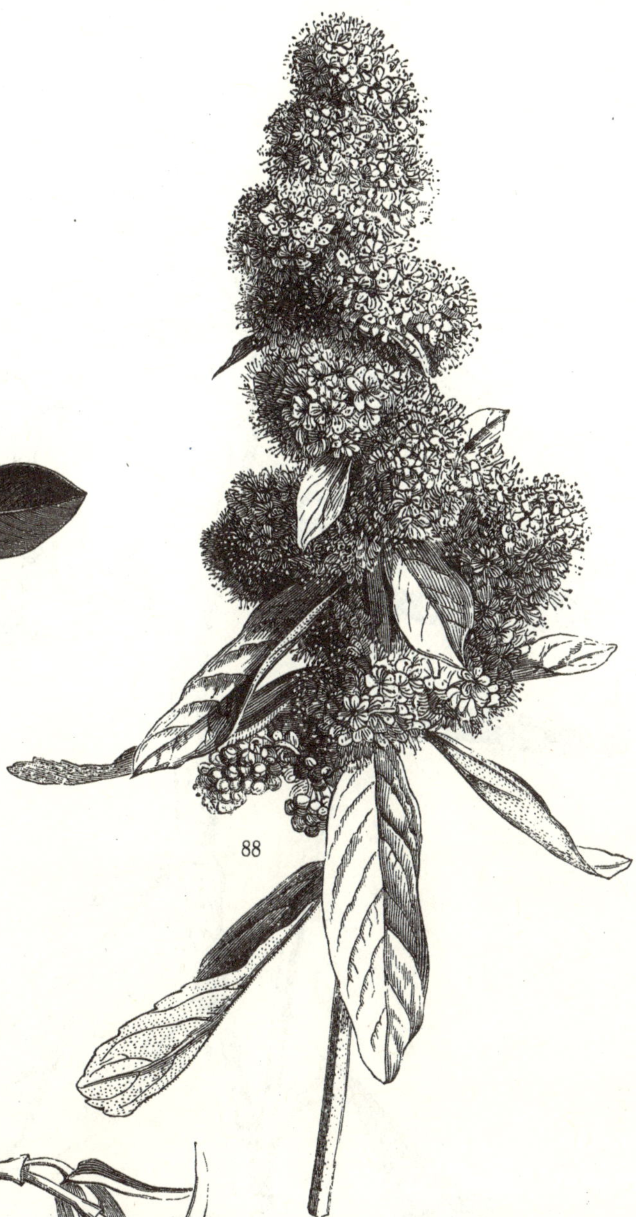

88

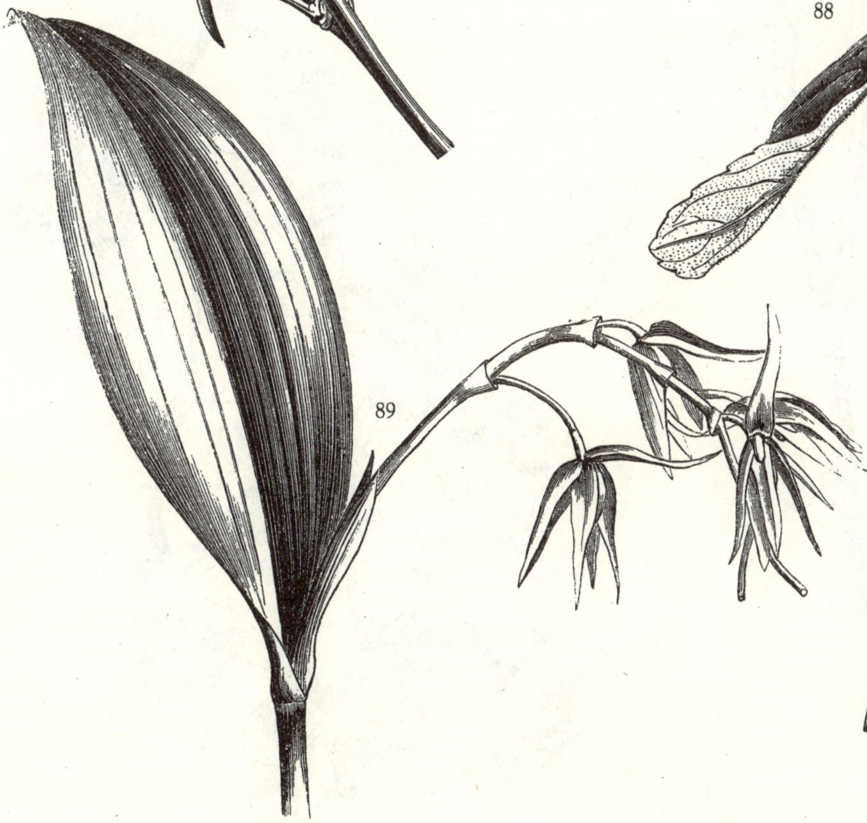

89

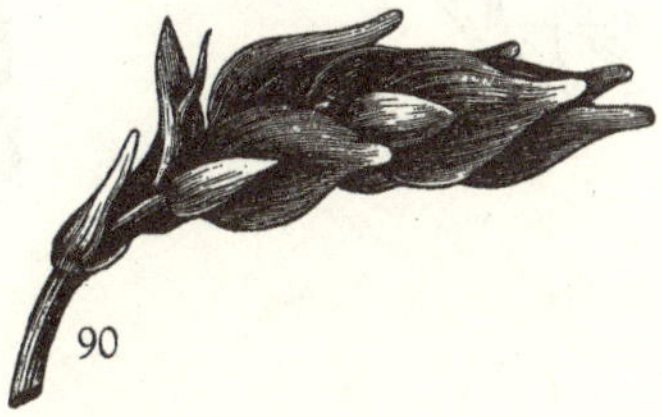

90

87. Cytisus *laburnum.* A laburnum with erect raceme, shown with the flowers closed; from Europe (see also Figs. 97 & 285). 88. *Spiraea douglasii.* A hardy shrub with deep rose-colored flowers; from Oregon. 89. *Pleurothallis pedunculata.* An orchid with dingy greenish flowers; from Venezuela. 90. Young shoot of *Ruscus hypoglossum.* See Fig. 20.

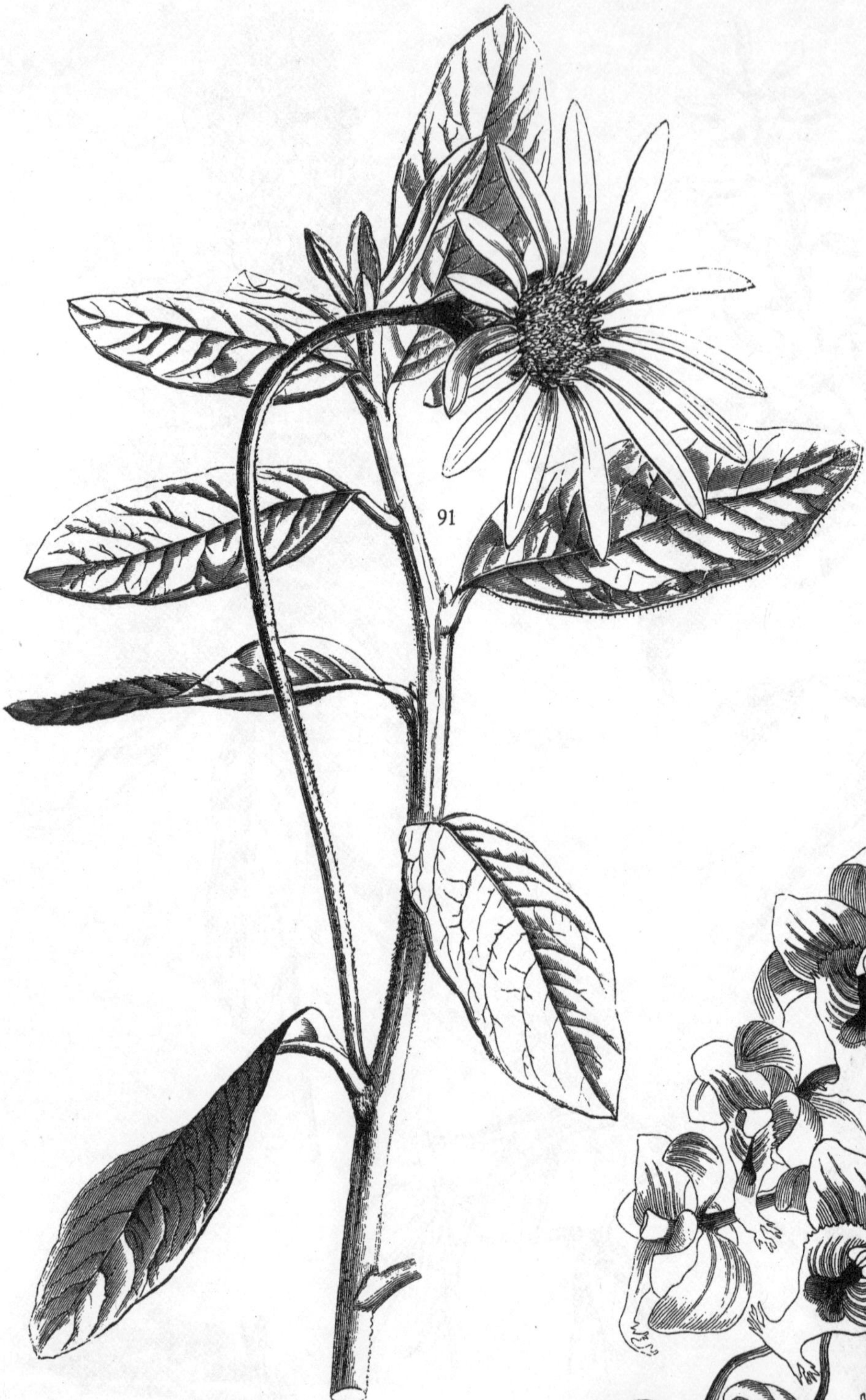

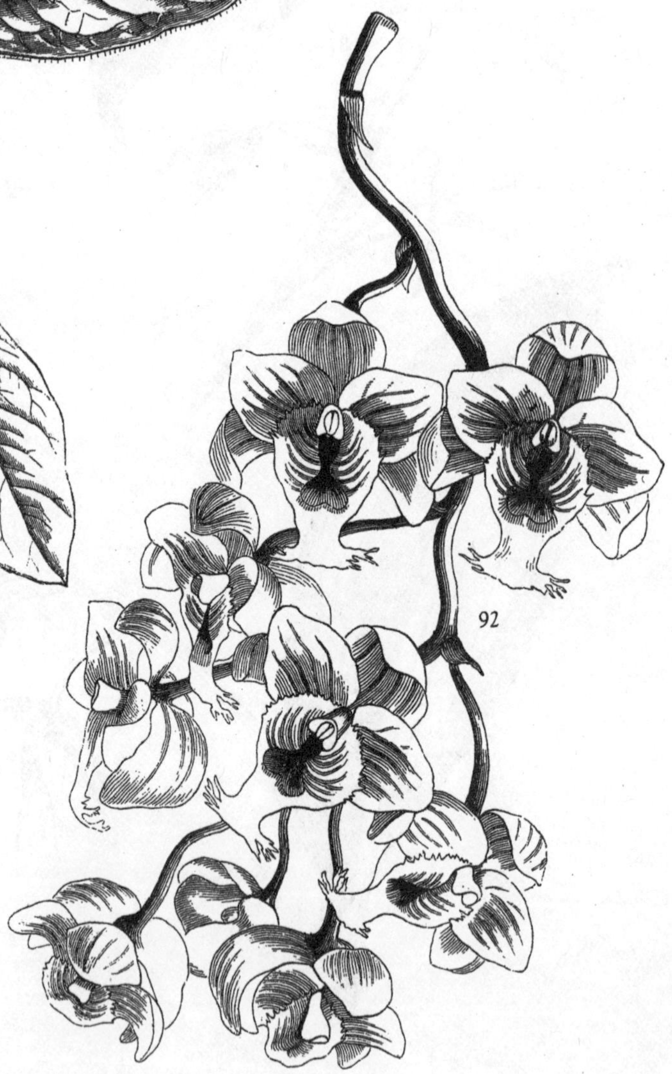

91. *Olearia pannosa.* An evergreen shrub with white flowers; from Australia. 92. *Catasetum warczewitzii.* A terrestrial orchid with pale flowers; from Central America, Colombia, Venezuela and Guiana.

93

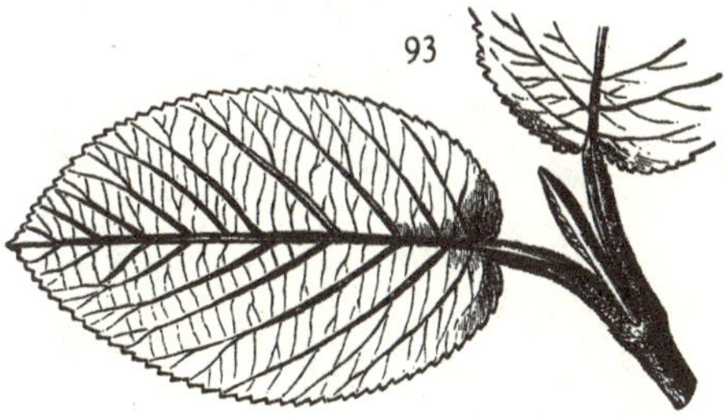

94

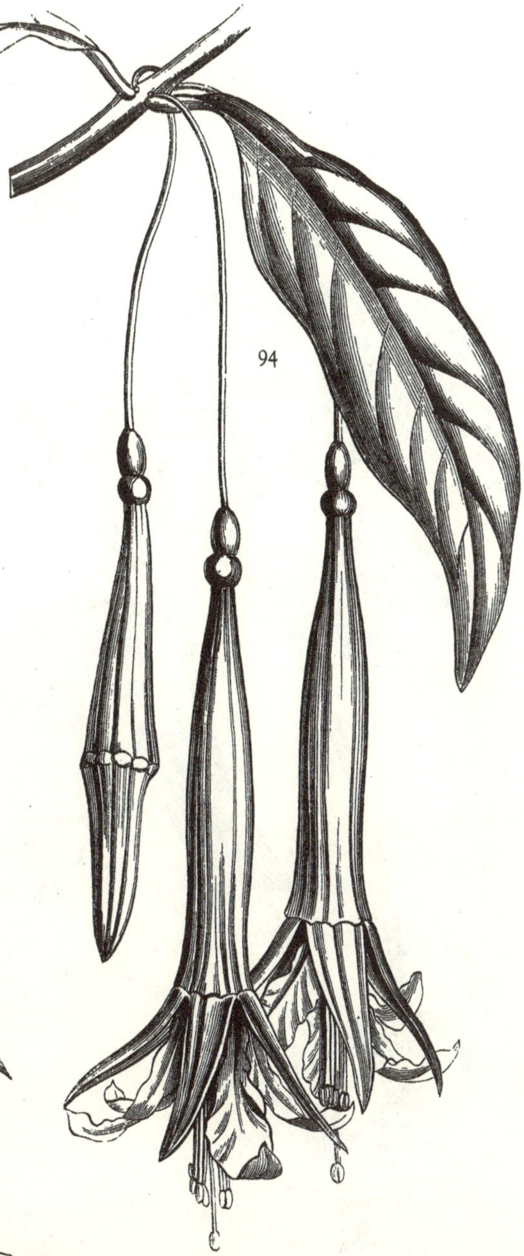

95

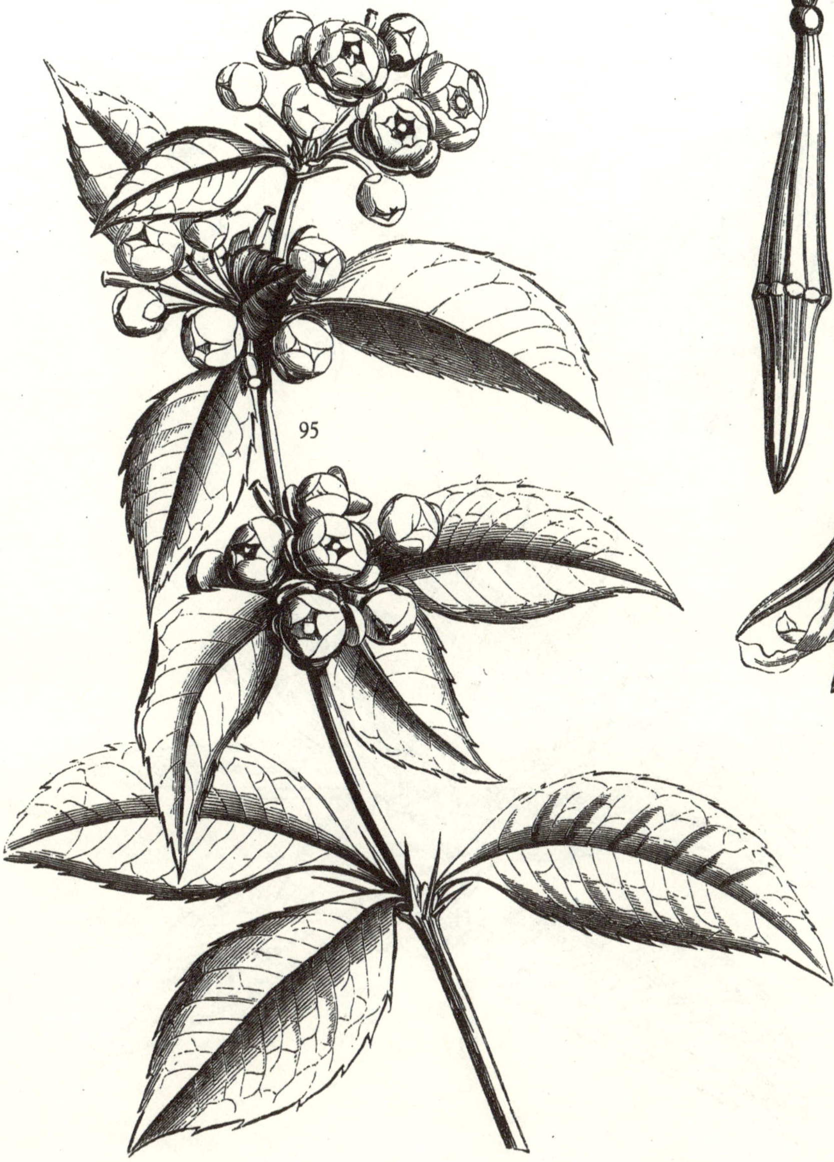

93. Unfolded leaf of the wayfaring tree (*Viburnum lantana*). From Europe and western Asia. 94. *Fuchsia venusta.* A shrub with long, solitary pendent salmon-colored flowers tipped with pink; from Peru. 95. *Berberis wallichiana.* An evergreen bush with large, deep yellow flowers; from the mountains of tropical Asia.

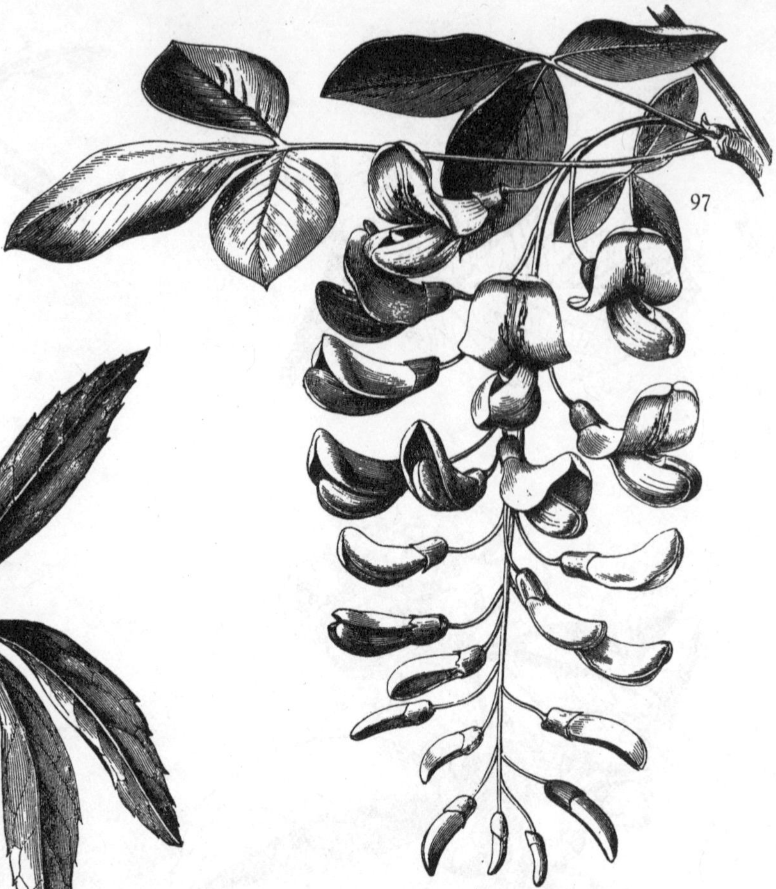
97

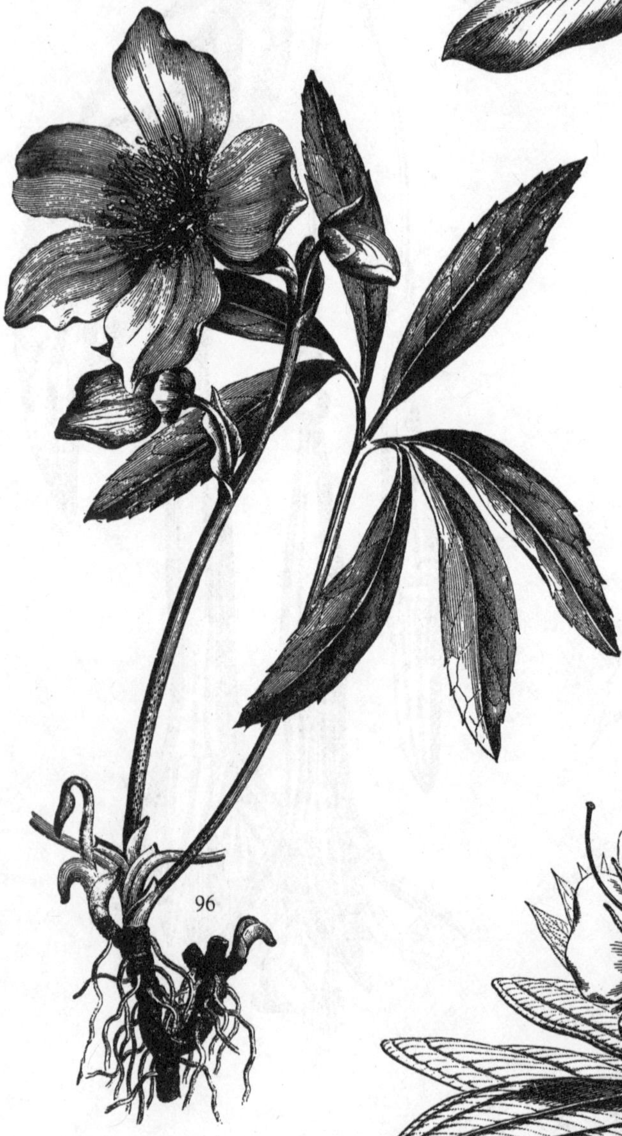
96

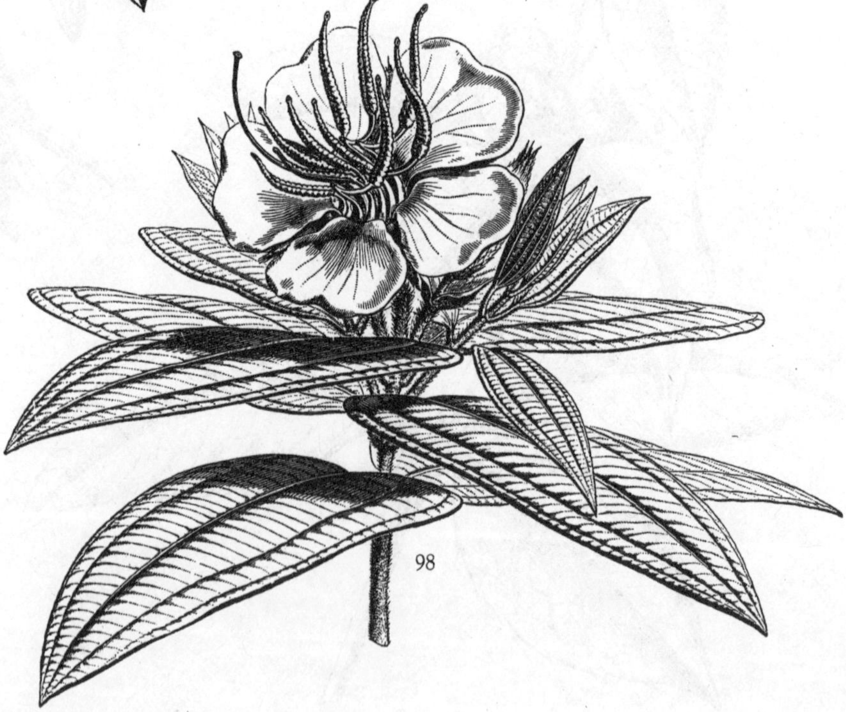
98

96. Christmas rose *(Helleborus niger)*. White, yellow, red, blue, violet or brown sepals; from Europe and Asia. 97. *Cytisus laburnum*. See Fig. 87. 98. Indian rhododendron (*Melastoma malabathricum*). A spreading shrub; from Asia, the Malay Archipelago, New Guinea and the Philippine Islands.

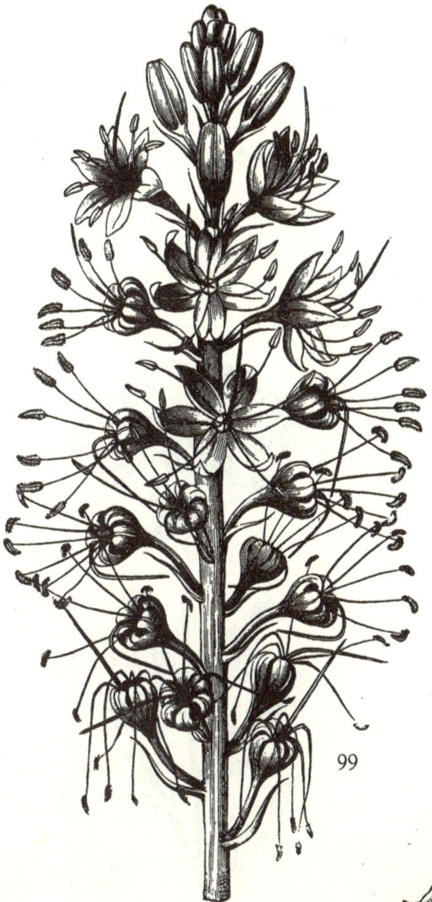

99

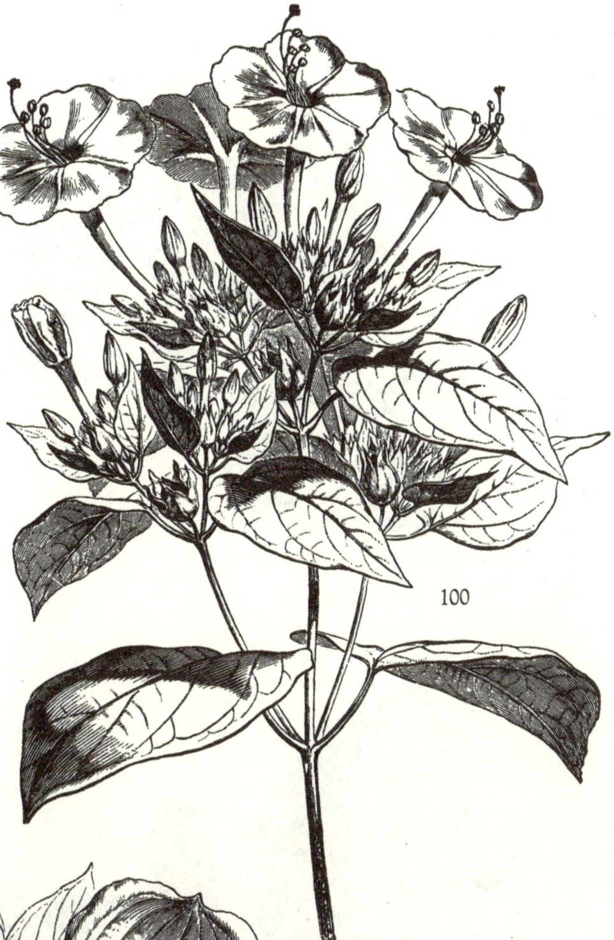

100

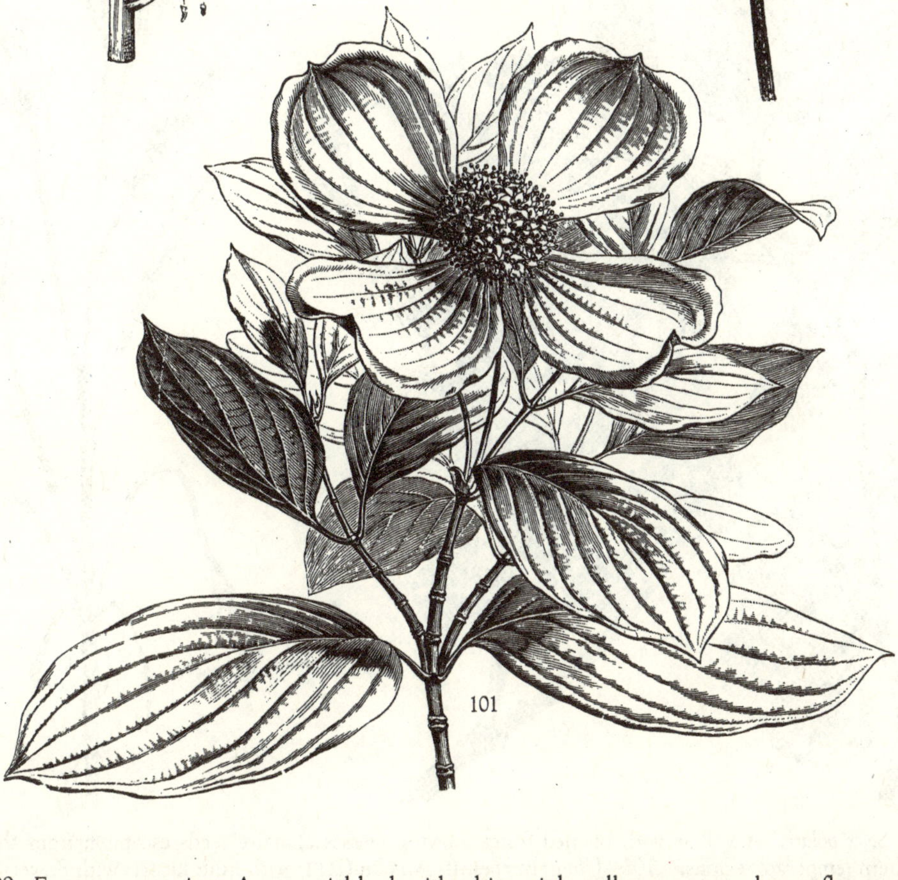

101

99. *Eremurus caucasicus.* A perennial herb with white, pink, yellow, orange or brown flowers; from western and central Asia. 100. Marvel-of-Peru *(Mirabilis jalapa).* Flowers red, pink, yellow or white, and often striped and mottled; from tropical America. 101. Flowering dogwood *(Cornus florida).* From North America.

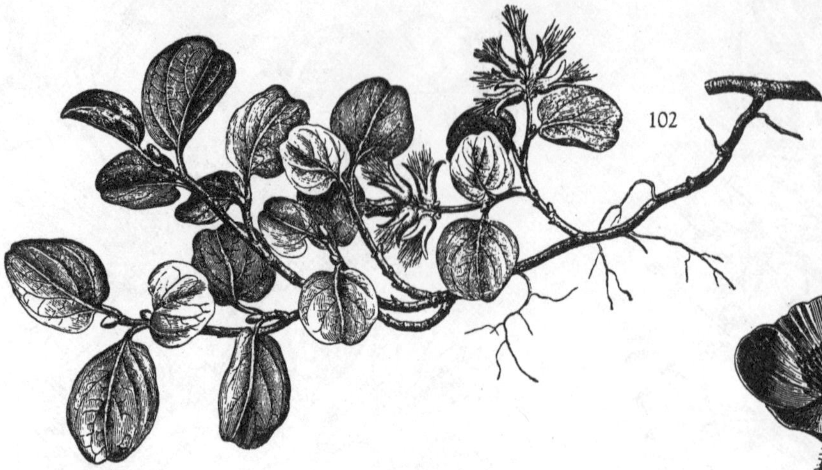

102

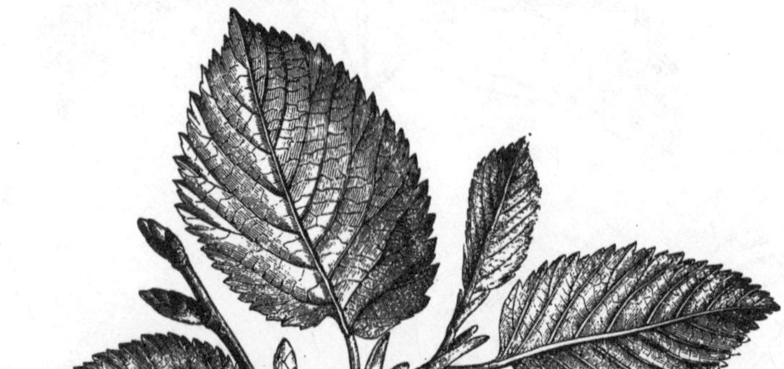

103

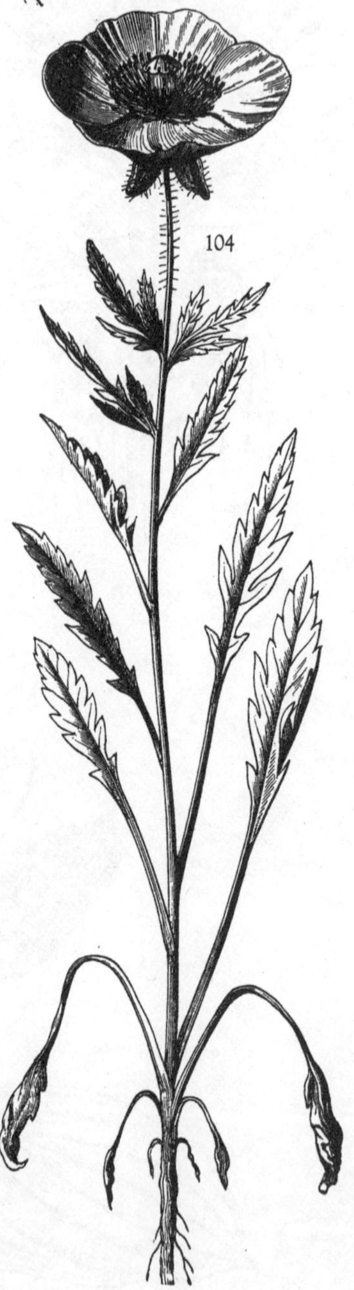

104

102. *Salix polaris.* A willow with opened fruits showing masses of hairy seeds escaping; from the northern temperate regions. 103. *Ulmus campestris.* An elm (LEFT: with fruit; RIGHT: with flowers); from North America. 104. *Papaver.* A poppy; flowers red, white, violet or yellow; from the Old World (see also Fig. 254).

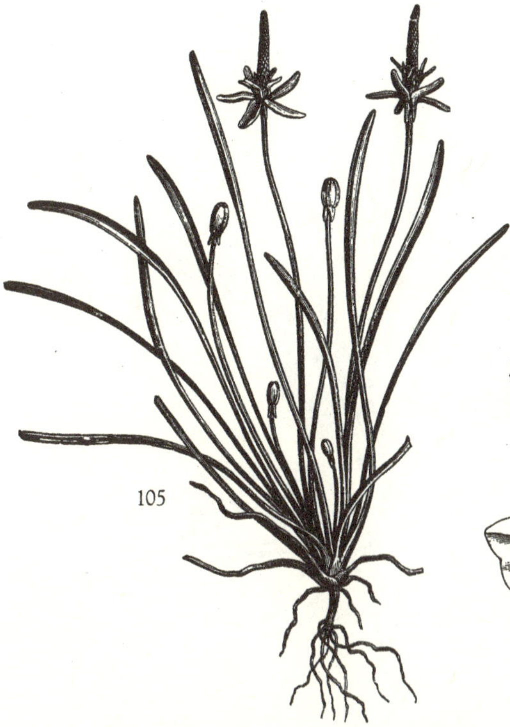

105

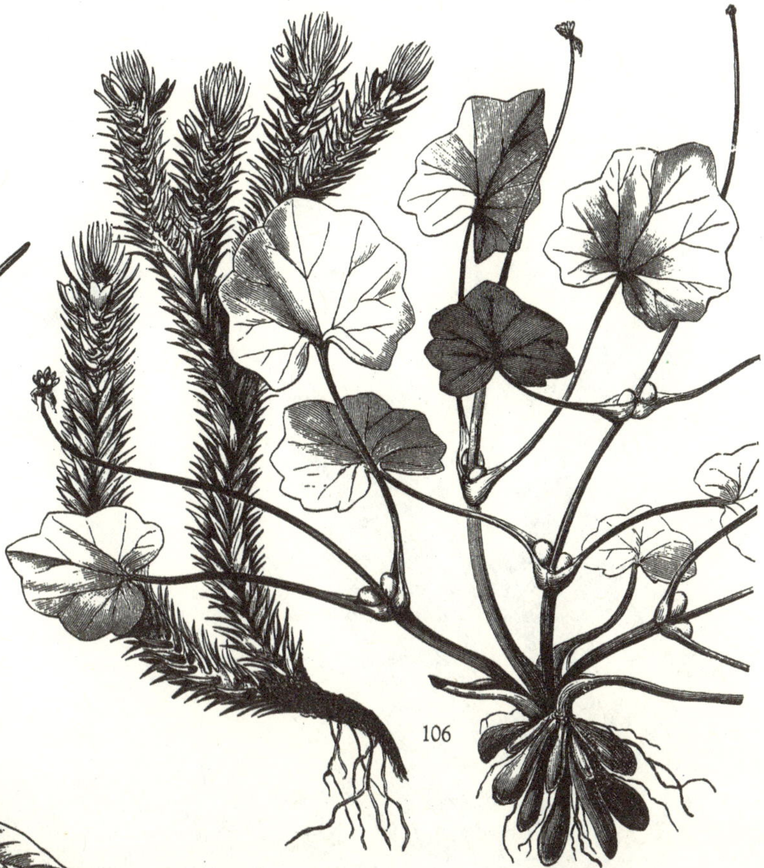

106

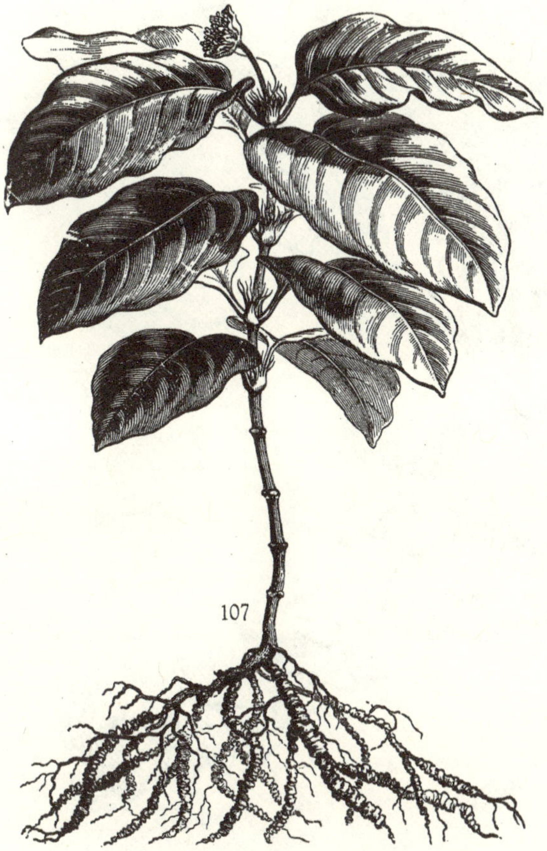

107

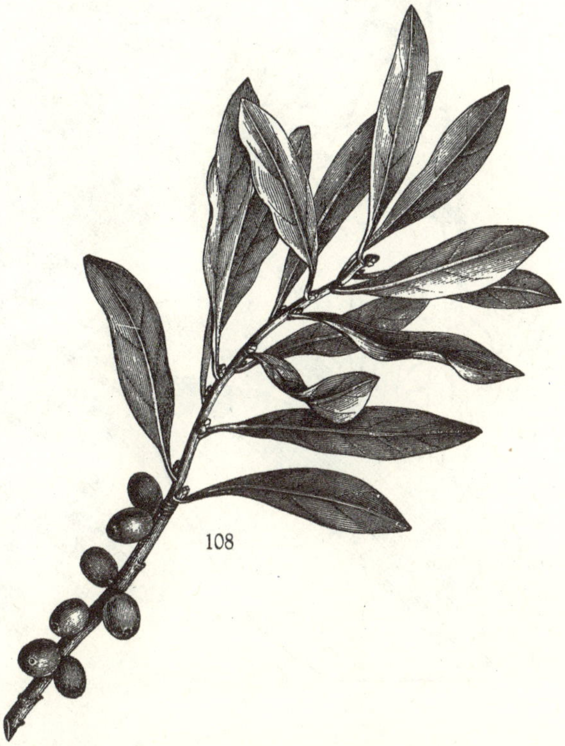

108

105. Mouse-tail *(Myosurus minimus)*. Yellow-green sepals and fruiting spikes. From Indiana and Kentucky to British Columbia, northern Mexico and Louisiana. 106. Lesser celandine *(Ranunculus ficaria)*. A perennial with golden-yellow flowers; from Europe and western Asia. 107. *Cephaëlis ipecacuanha.* A herbaceous perennial; from the tropics of the Americas, Africa and Asia. 108. A branch of mezereon *(Daphne mezereum)*. A deciduous shrub, with berries; from Europe and western Asia.

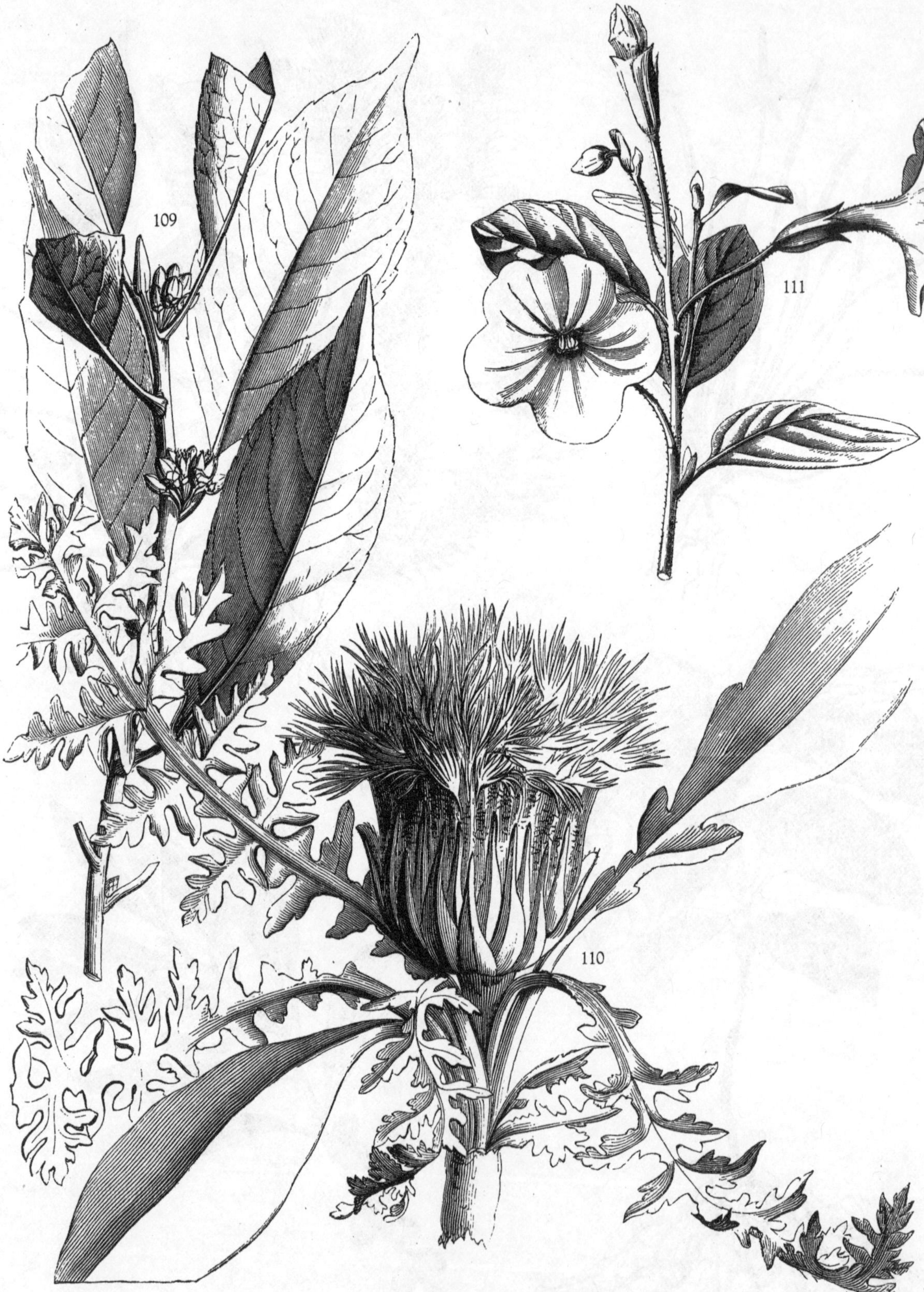

109. *Symplocos japonica.* A small evergreen shrub with flowers in small, pale yellow clusters; from Japan. 110. *Rhaponticum acaule.* A tap-rooted perennial; from northern Africa. 111. *Browallia jamiesoni.* A shrub with orange-yellow flowers; from Peru.

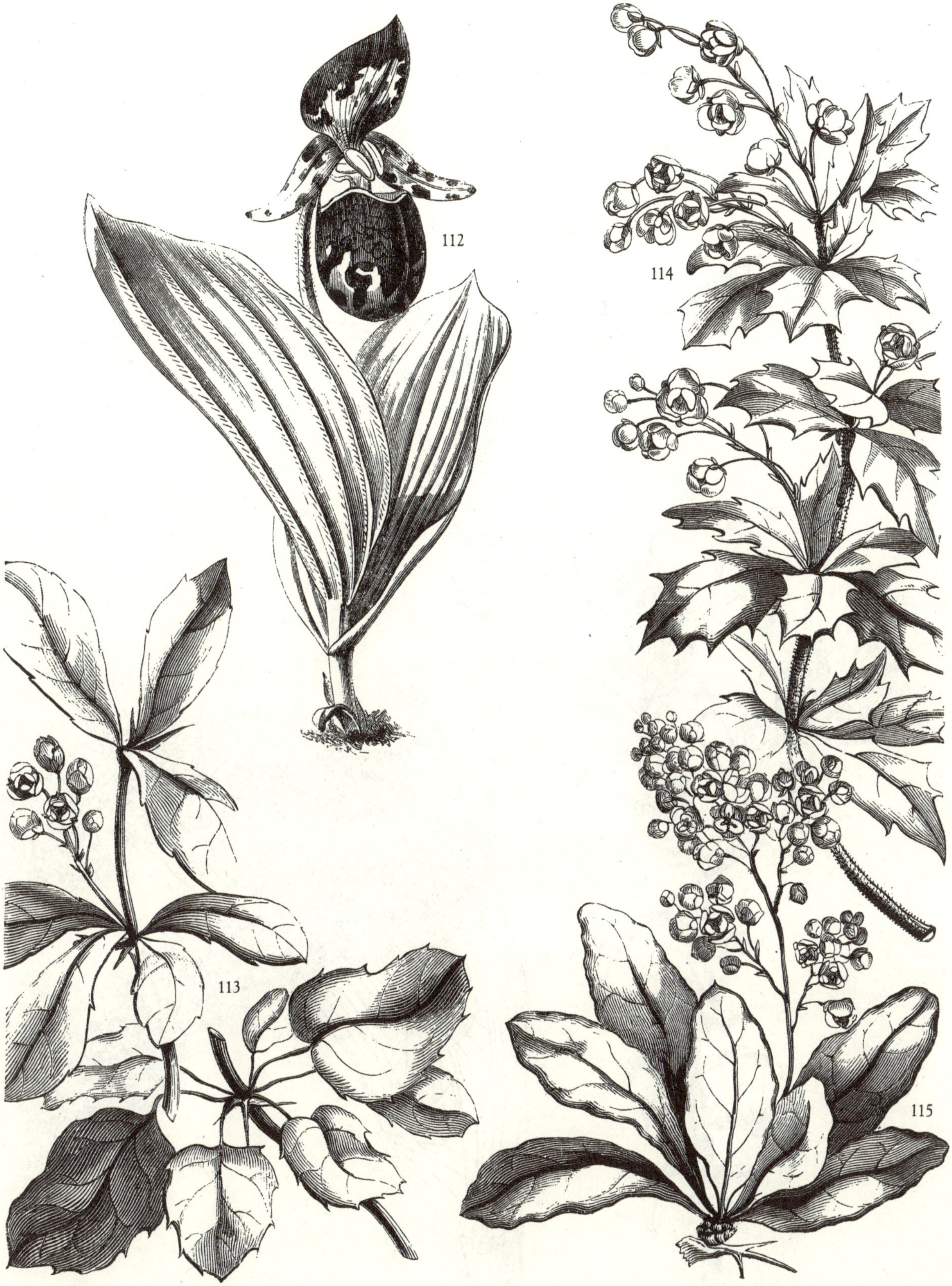

112. *Cypripedium guttatum.* A hardy terrestrial orchid with white flowers spotted purple; from northern Russia, Siberia and North America. 113. *Berberis tinctoria.* A hardy sub-evergreen shrub with dull green flowers; from India. 114. *Berberis darwinii.* A hardy evergreen bush; from Chile and Argentina. 115. *Berberis loxensis.* A hardy evergreen shrub; from South America.

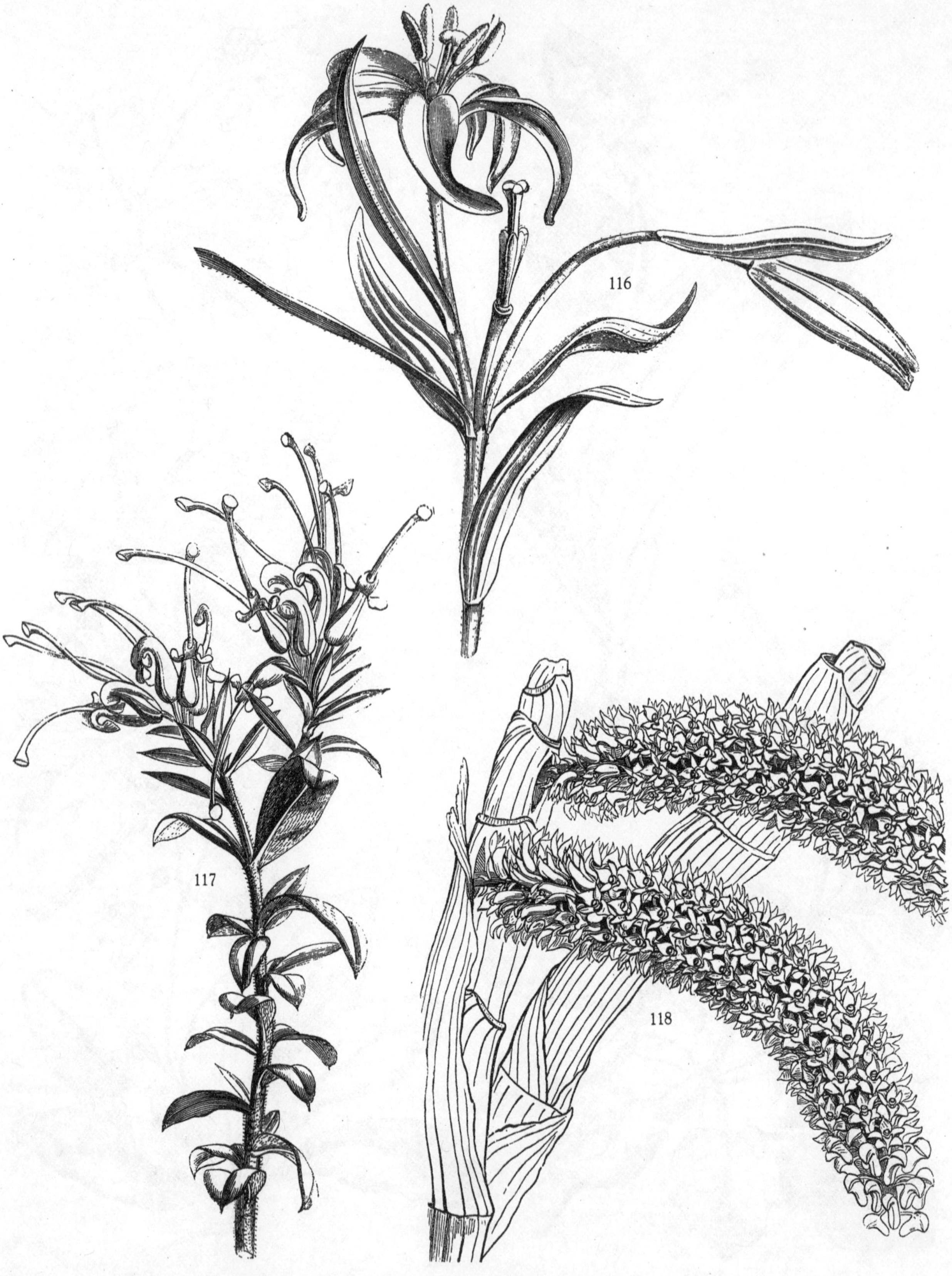

116. *Lilium sinicum.* A bulbous plant with scarlet flowers; from China. 117. Spider flower *(Grevillea rosea).* From Australia. 118. *Eria floribunda.* An orchid with long close spikes of white flowers; from Burma, the Malay Peninsula and the Philippine Islands.

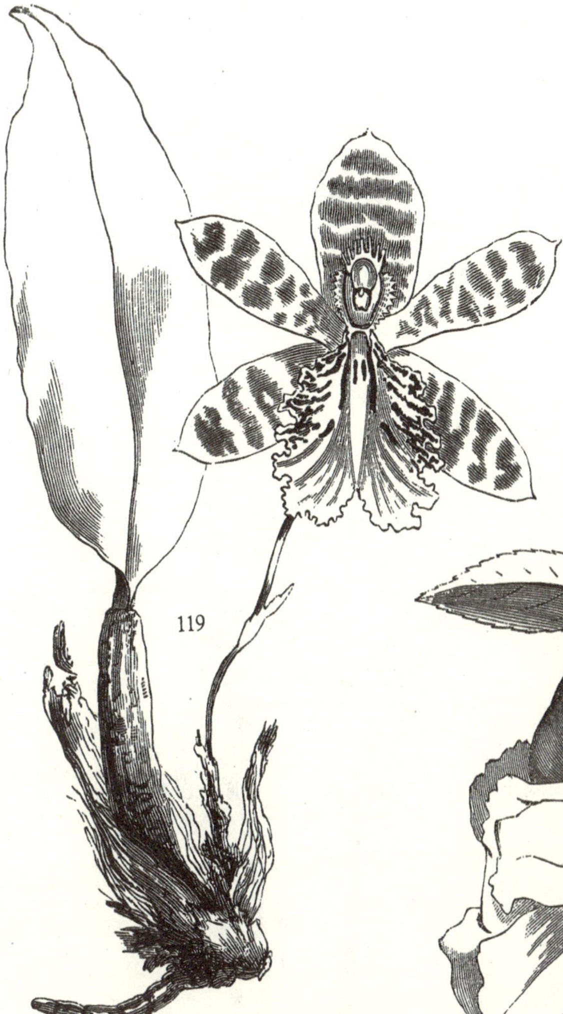

119

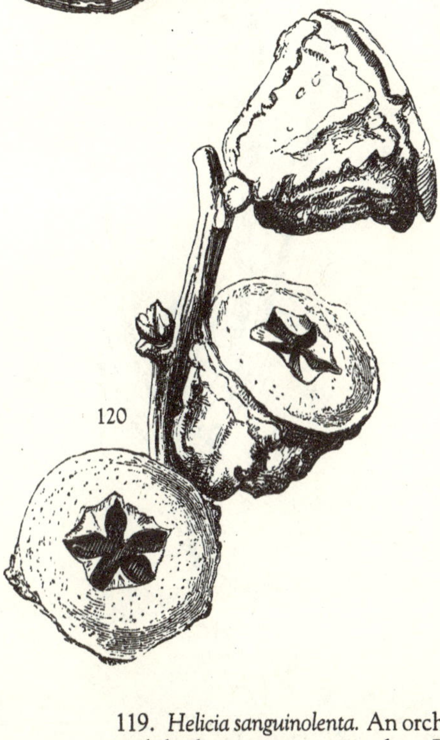

120

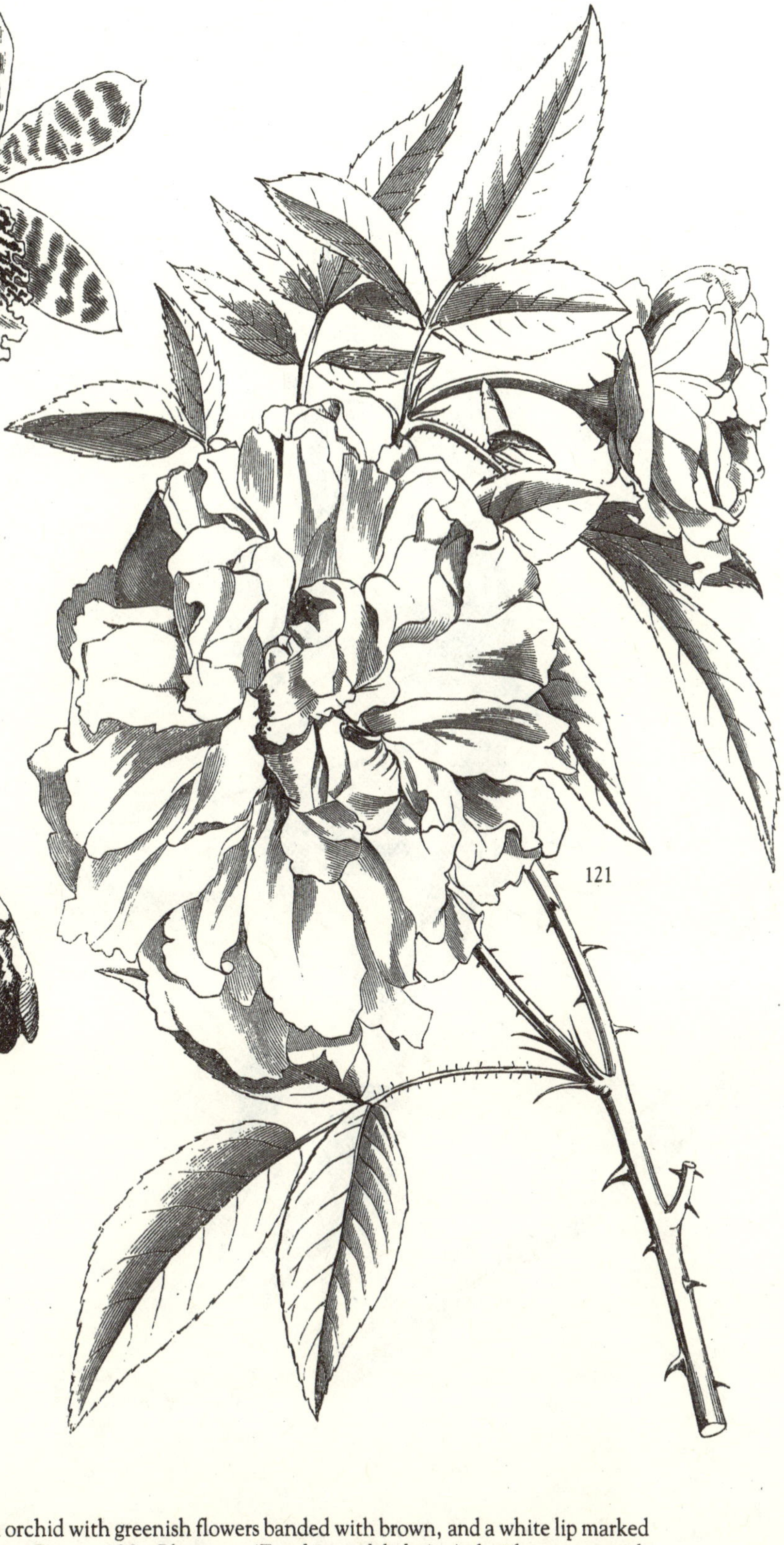

121

119. *Helicia sanguinolenta.* An orchid with greenish flowers banded with brown, and a white lip marked with broken crimson veins; from Peru. 120. Blue gum *(Eucalyptus globulus).* A deciduous tree with white flowers; from Tasmania. 121. *Rosa fortuniana.* A scrambling evergreen shrub with large solitary flowers; from China.

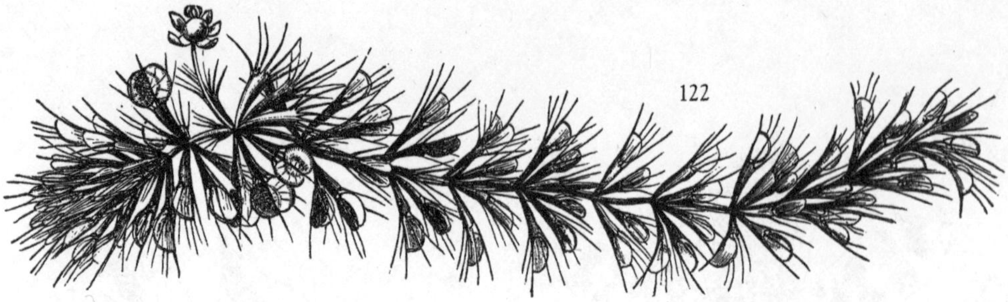

122

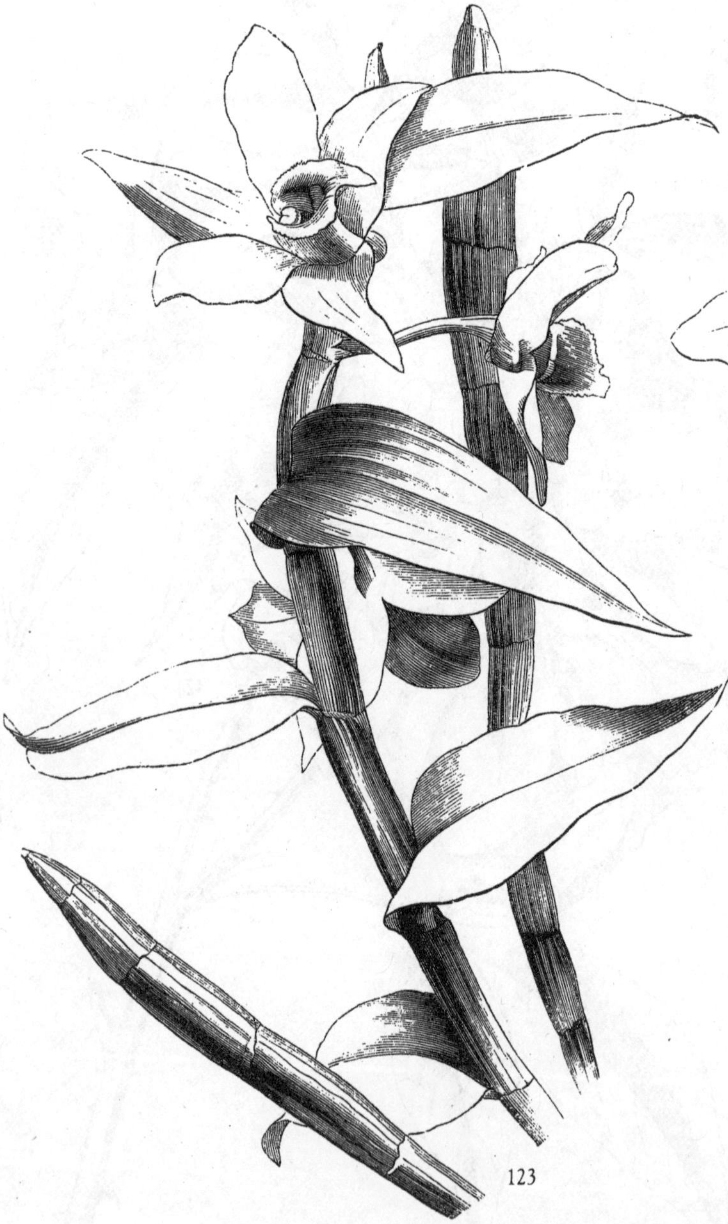

123

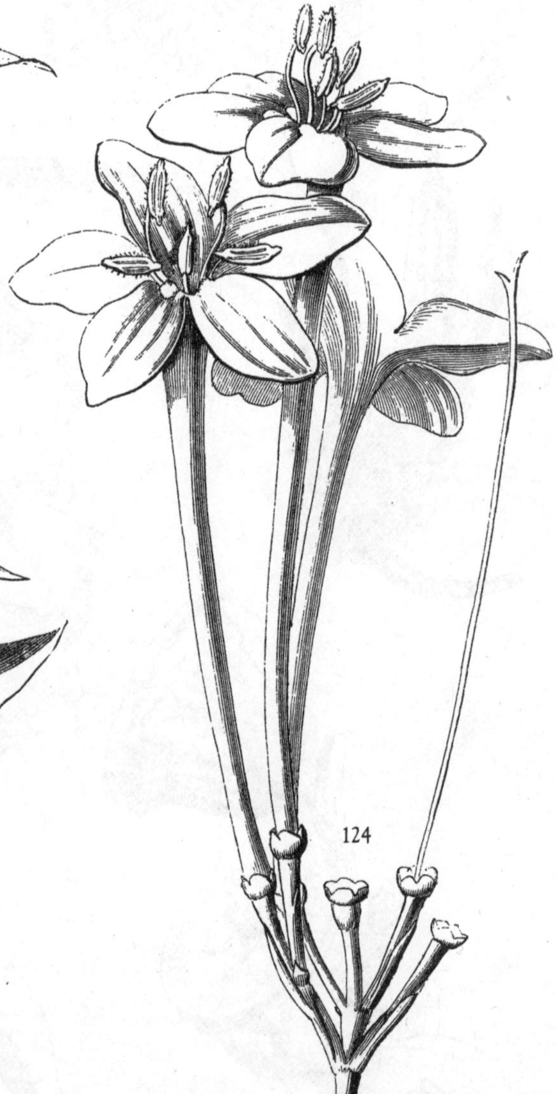

124

122. *Aldrovandia vesiculosa.* A floating aquatic with greenish-white flowers; from Central Europe and Asia. 123. *Dendrobium album.* An orchid with white flowers; from Asia, Australia and the Pacific Islands. 124. *Posoqueria formosa.* A shrub with large white flowers; from tropical America.

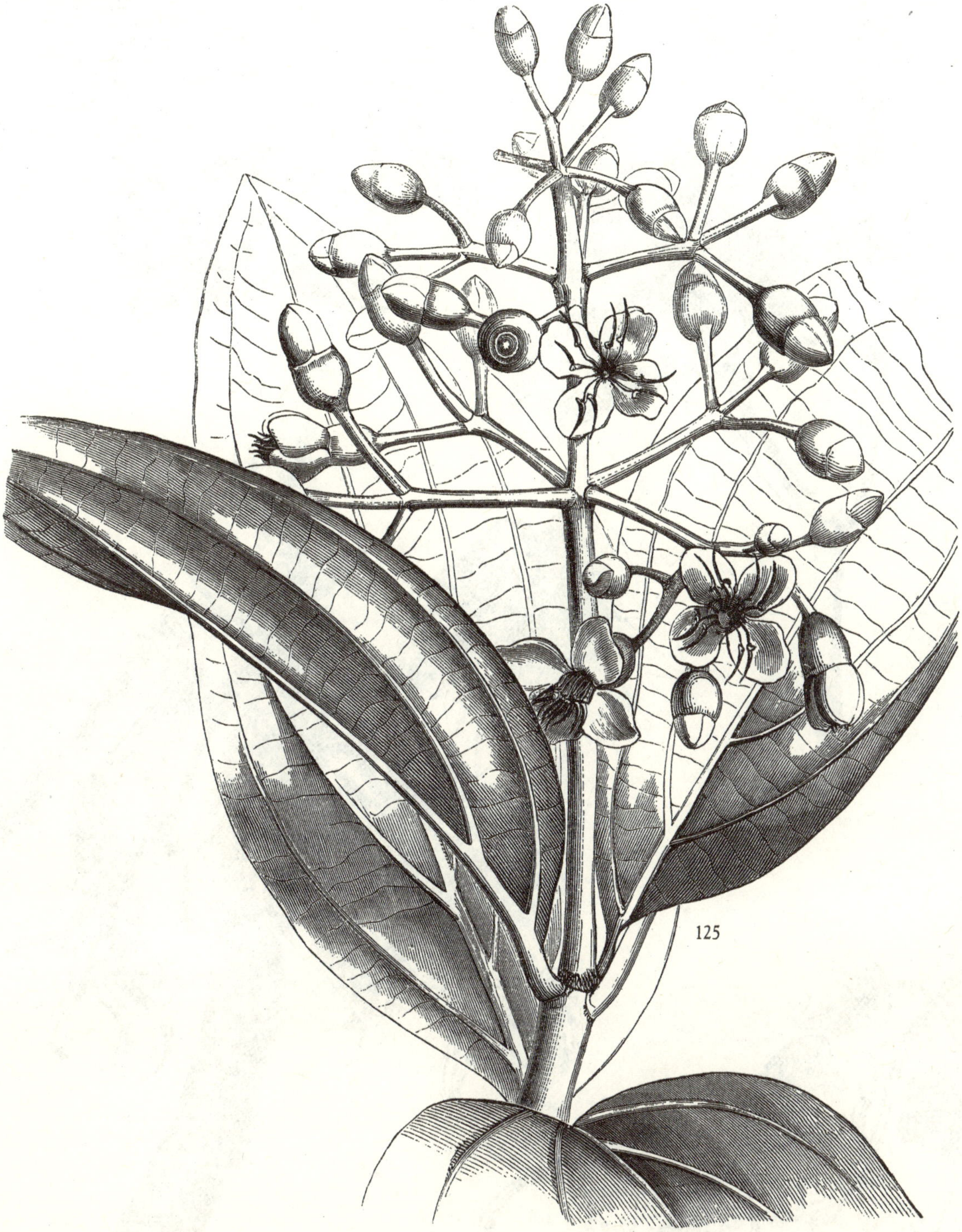

125

125. *Medinilla sieboldiana.* A white-flowered shrub; from Java.

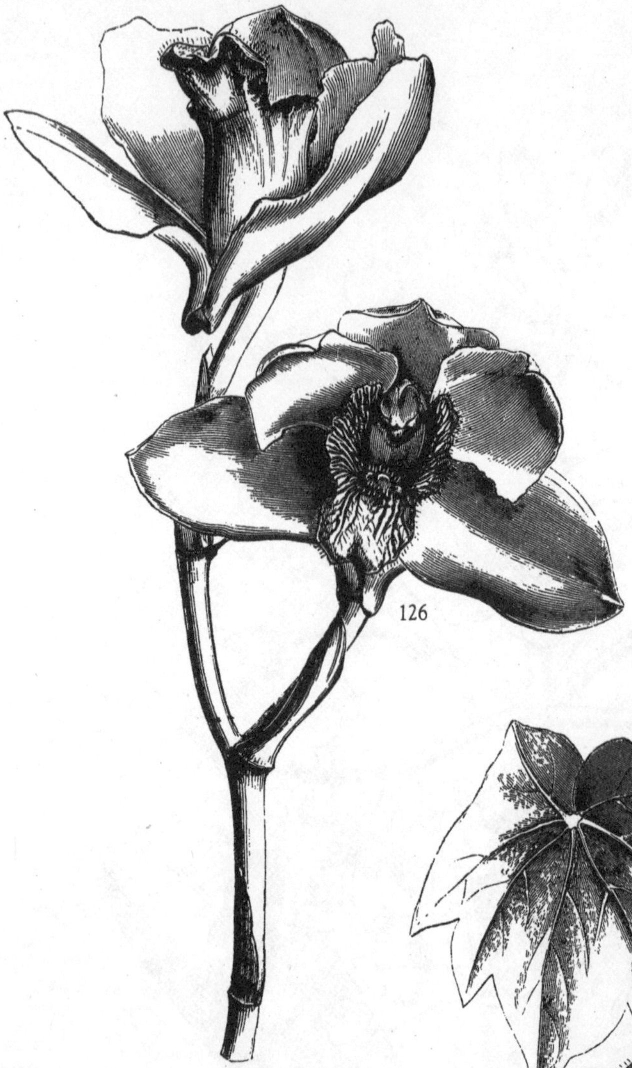

126

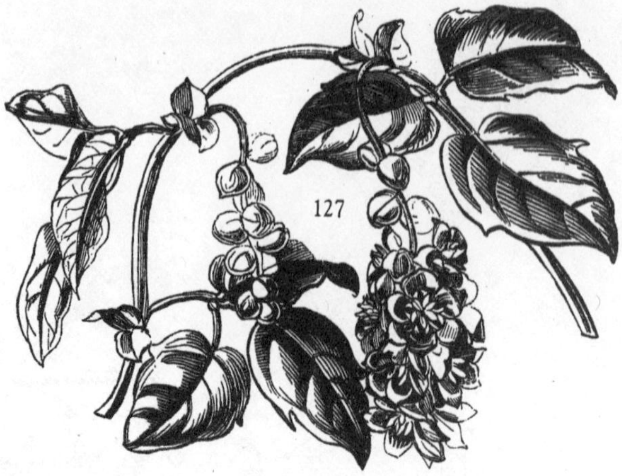

127

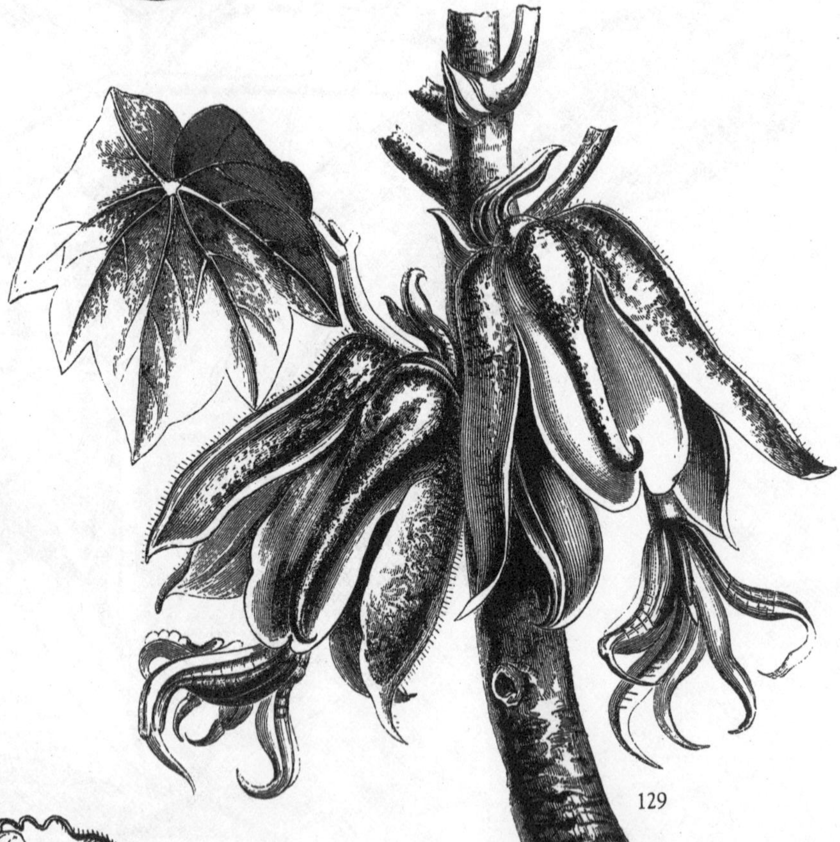

129

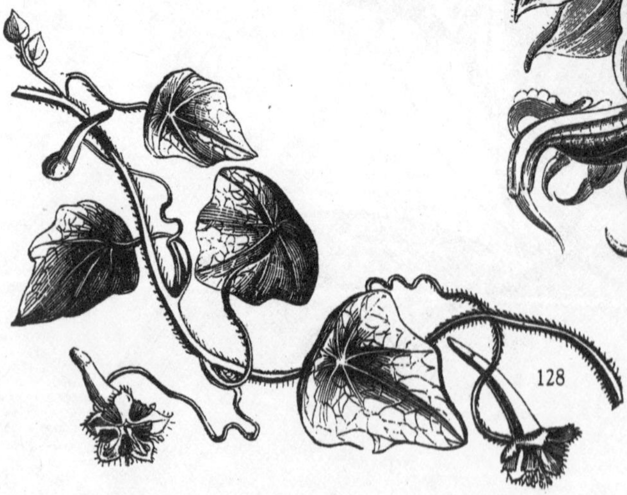

128

126. *Maxillaria harrisoniae.* An orchid with large waxy pale yellow flowers and a rich rose-colored hairy lip; from tropical America. 127. *Lardizabala biternata.* A hardy evergreen climbing shrub with dark purple flowers; from Chile. 128. *Tropaeolum deckerianum.* A nasturtium with blue, green and scarlet flowers; from Mexico and South America. 129. *Cheirostemon platanoides.* A large tree with broad plane-like leaves and brown bell-shaped flowers; from Guatemala.

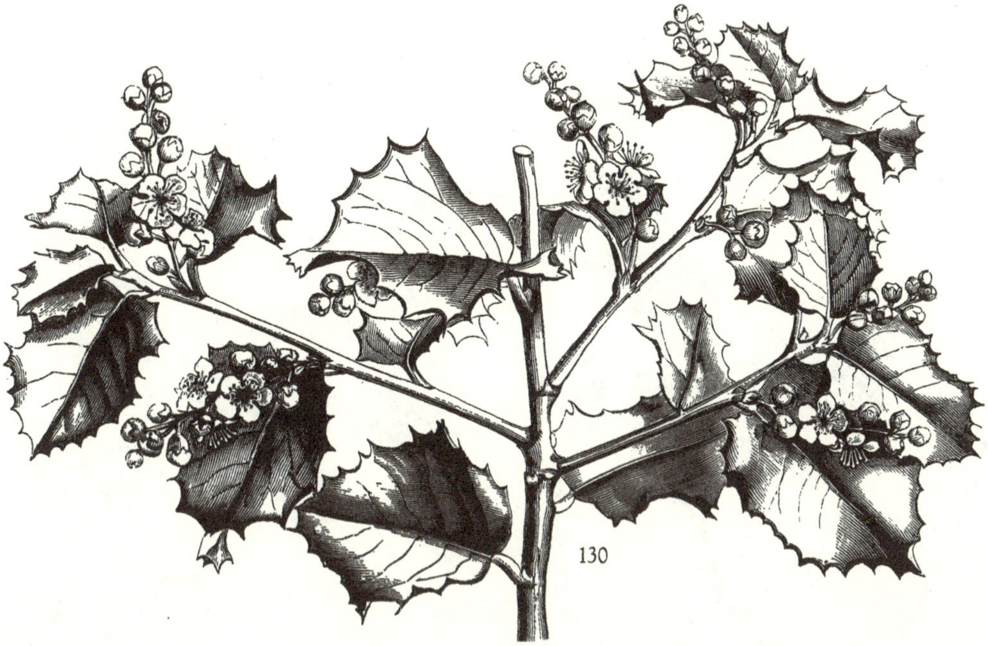

130

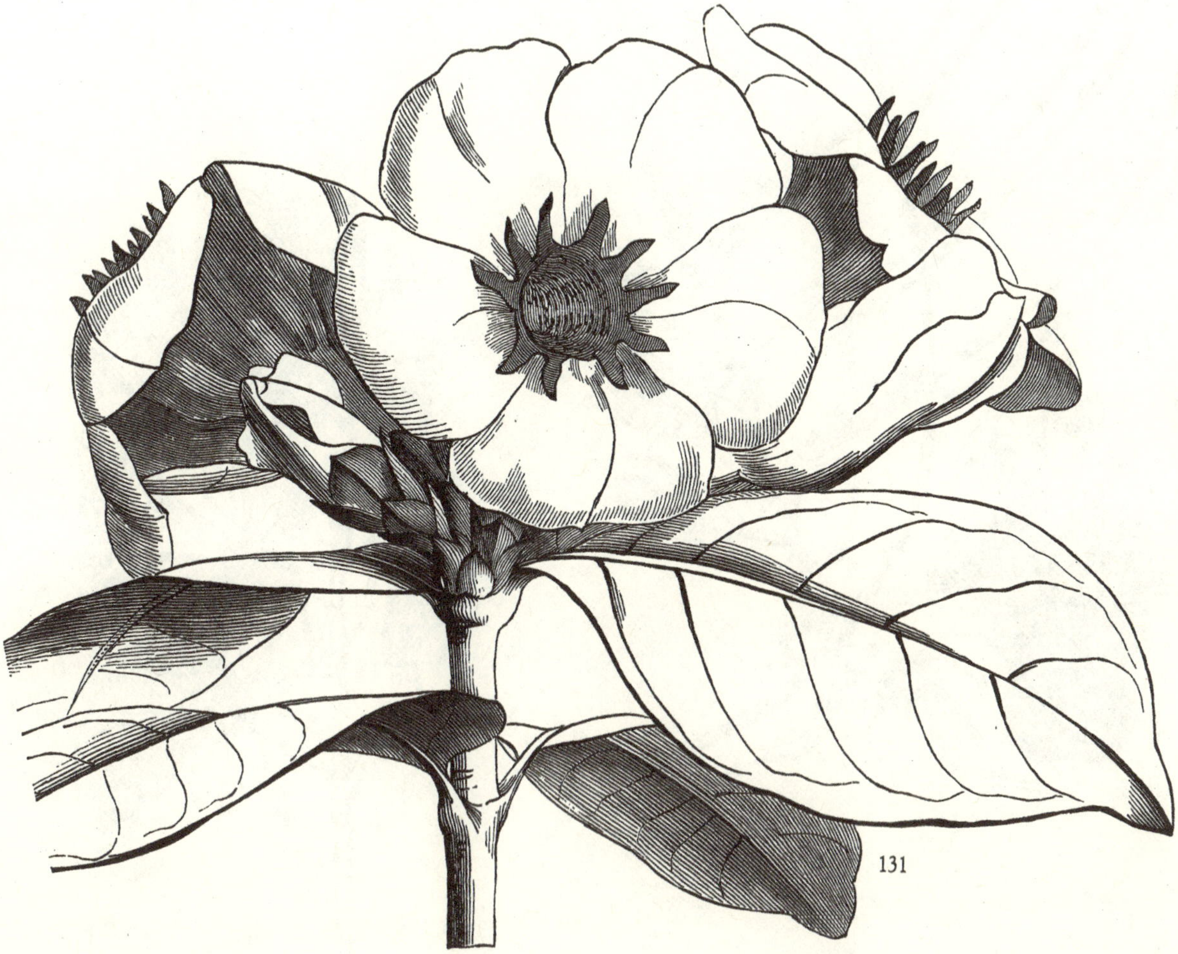

131

130. *Cerasus ilicifolia.* A hardy evergreen bush or small tree with white flowers; from California.
131. *Roupellia grata.* A climbing plant with large, coarse flowers; from Sierra Leone.

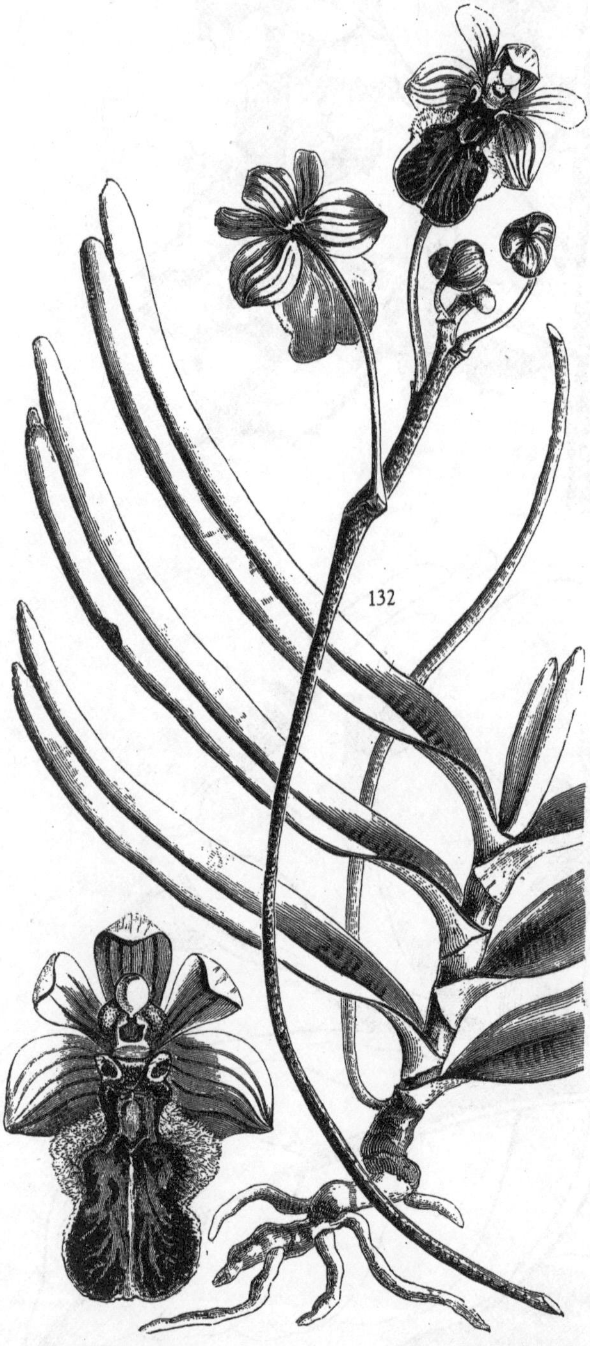
132

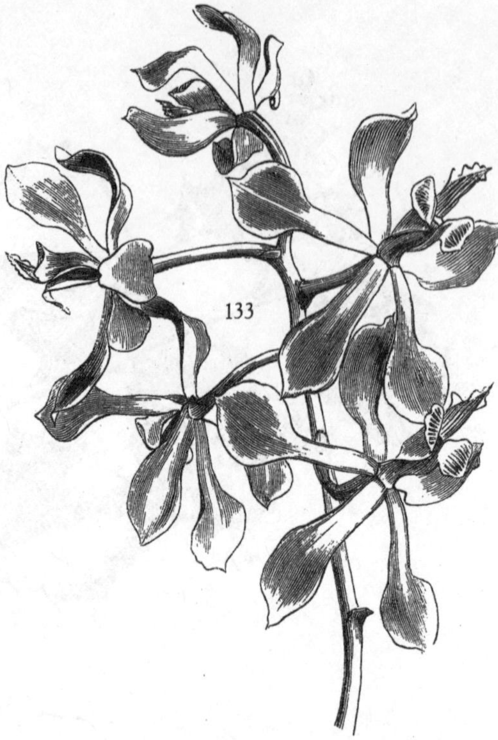
133

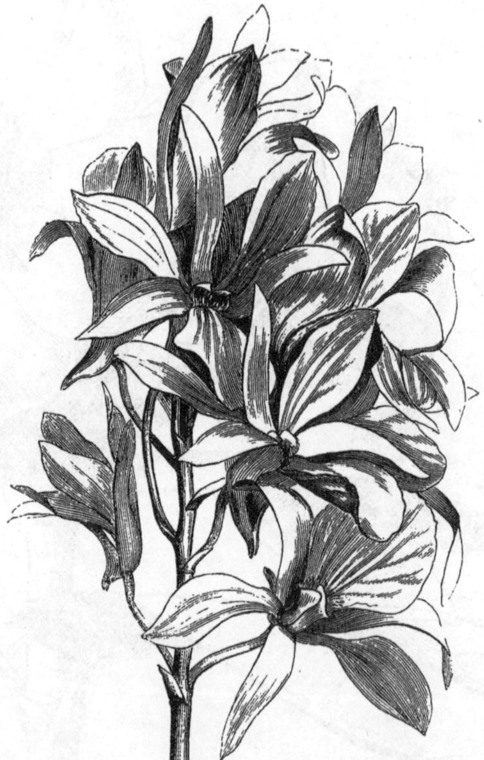
134

132. *Vanda peduncularis.* An orchid with brown and purple bee-like flowers; from Ceylon. 133. *Epidendrum replicatum.* An orchid with yellowish flowers stained with brown, and a white and pink lip; from Cuba. 134. *Dendrobium barbatulum.* An orchid with white flowers; from Burma.

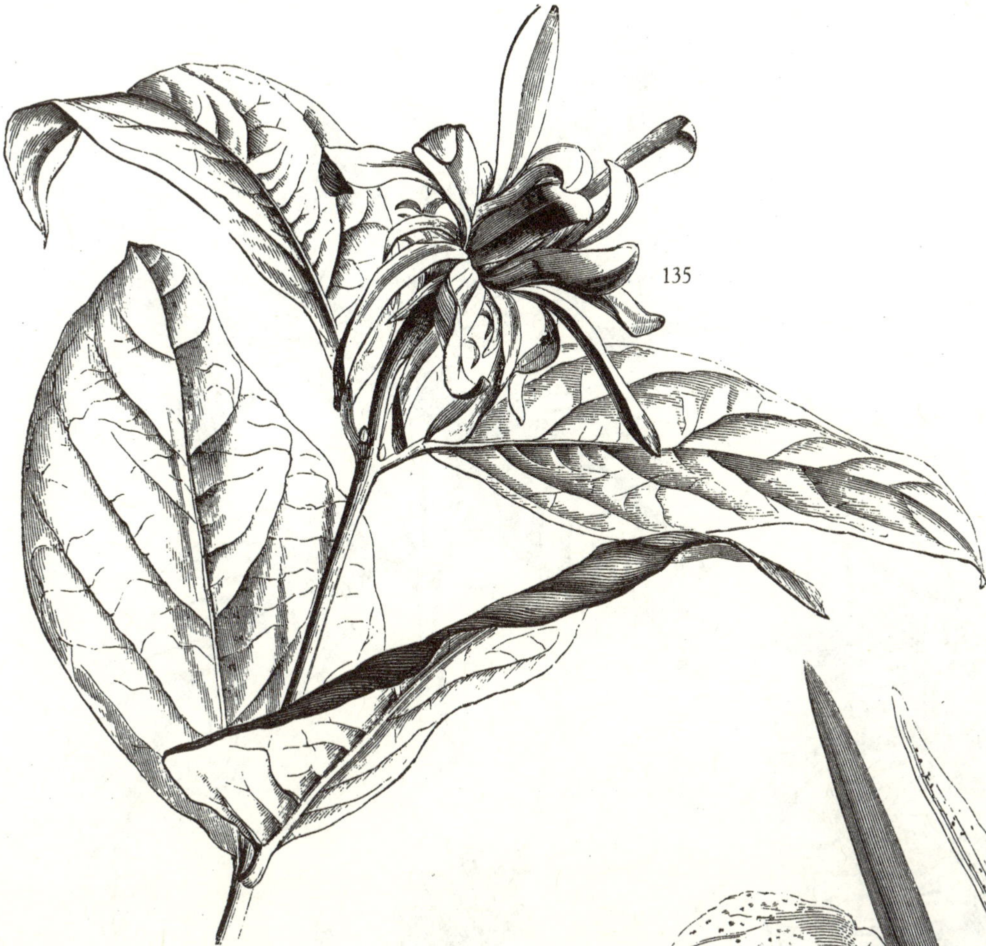

135

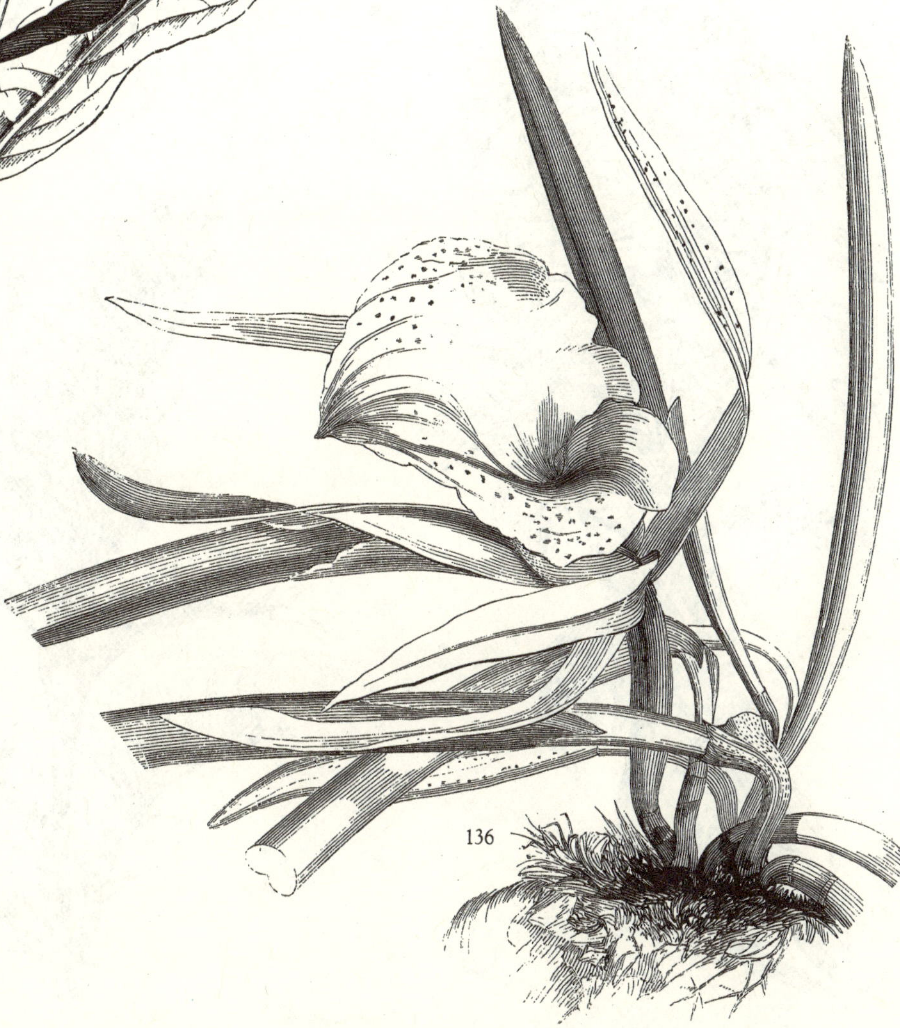

136

135. *Calycanthus occidentalis.* A hardy deciduous shrub with brown flowers; from California.
136. *Brassavola acaulis.* An orchid with cream-color flowers; from Costa Rica and Panama.

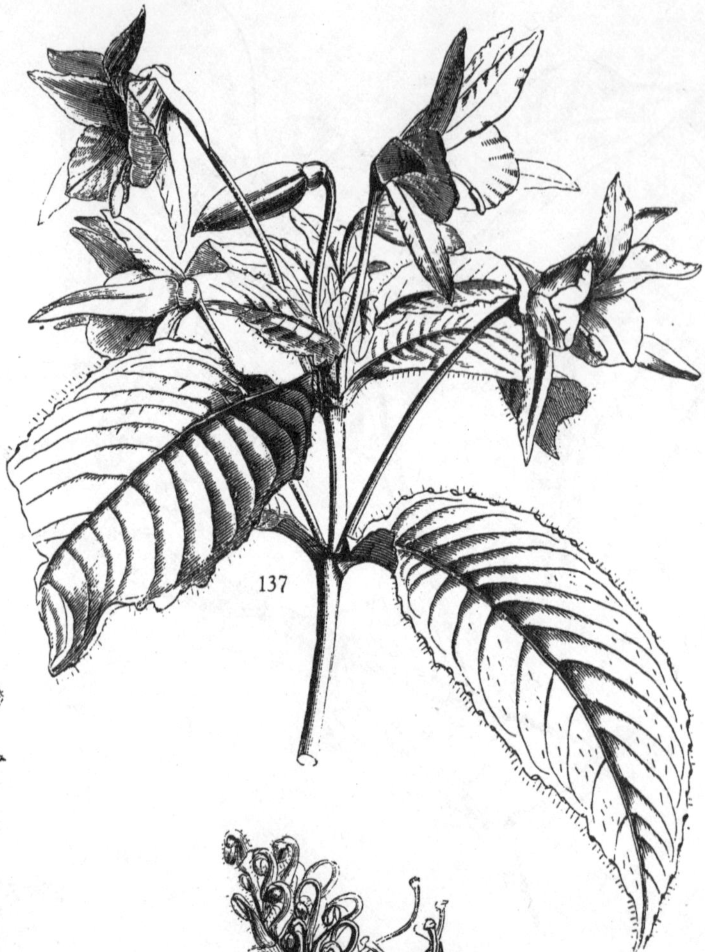

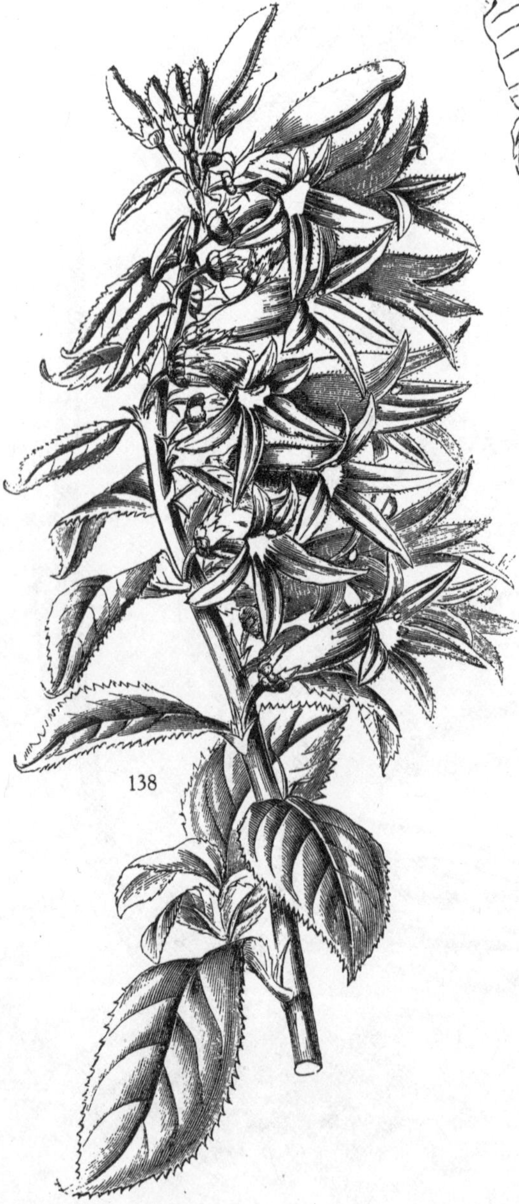

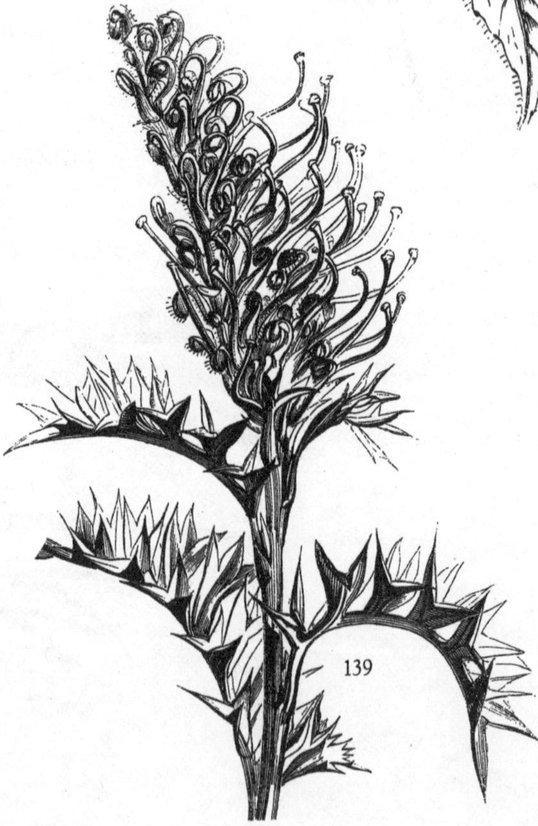

137. *Lopezia macrophylla.* A showy half-hardy perennial with deep rose flowers; from Guatemala.
138. *Siphocampylus amoenus.* A shrub with rich orange-red flowers; from the mountains of Brazil.
139. *Grevillea acanthifolia.* A half-hardy evergreen with purple flowers; from Australia.

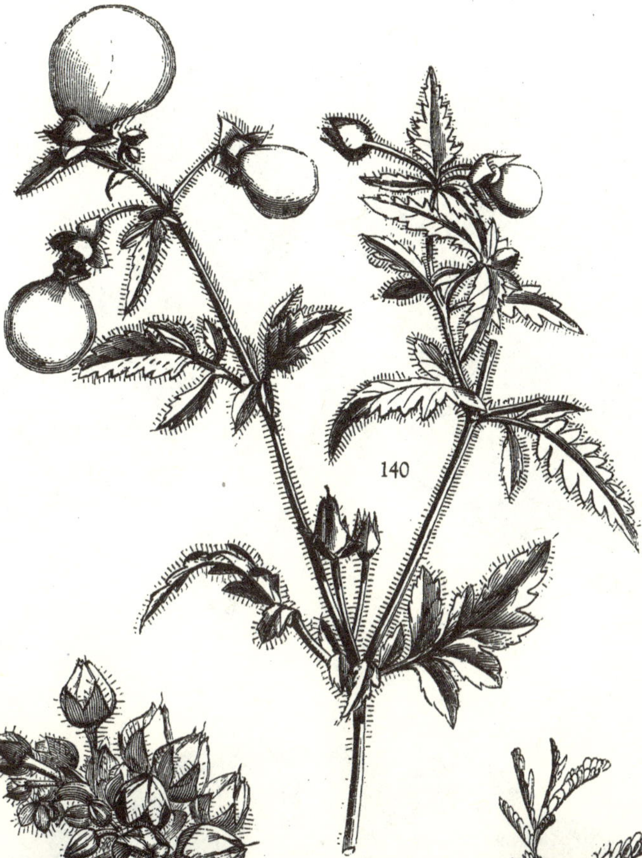

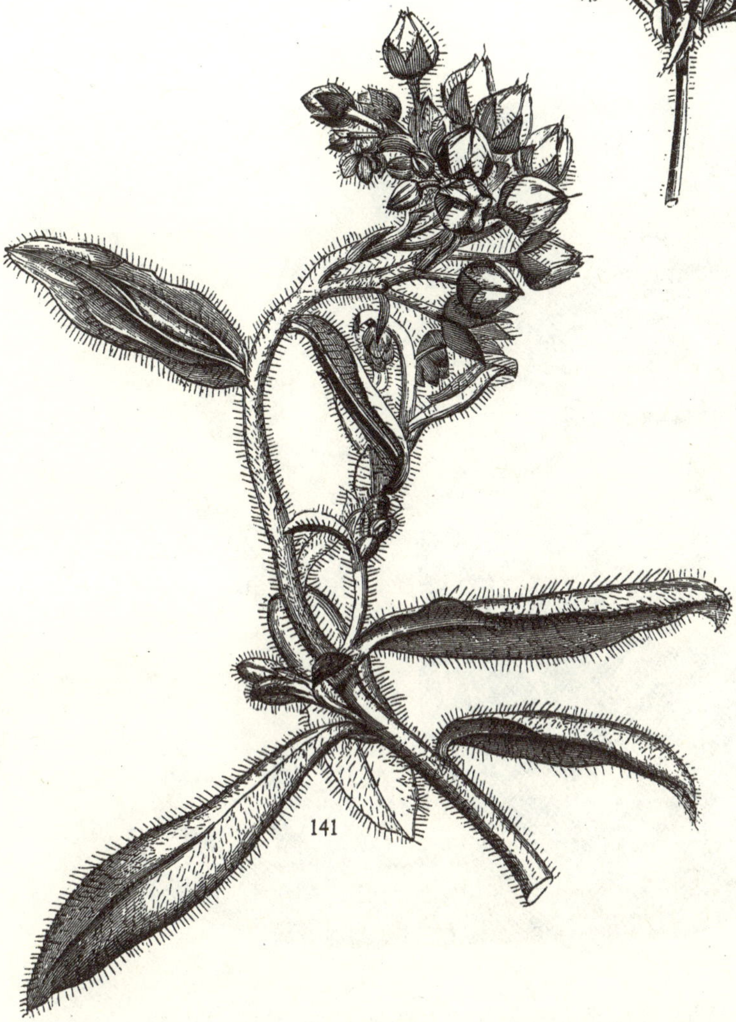

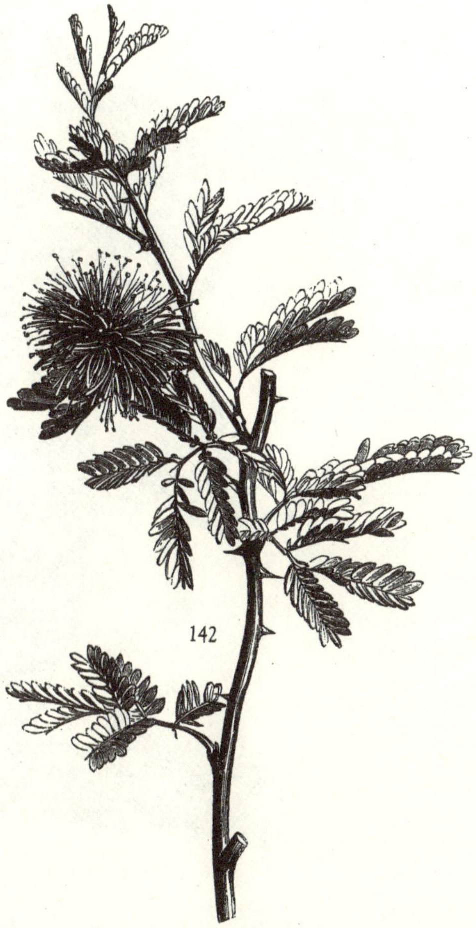

140. *Calceolaria chelidonioides.* A half-hardy annual with yellow flowers; from Peru. 141. *Maharanga emodi.* A hardy perennial with pale rose-color flowers; from Nepal. 142. *Mimosa uruguensis.* A half-hardy spiny shrub with brick-red flowers; from Uruguay.

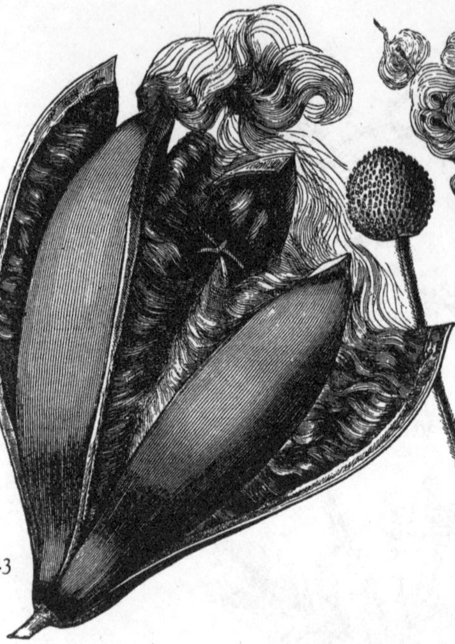

143

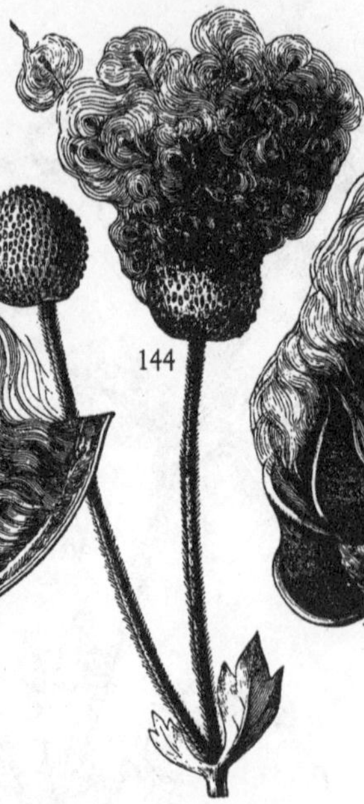

144

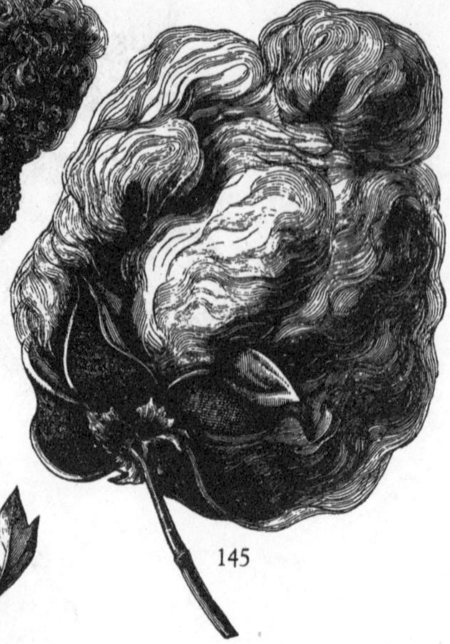

145

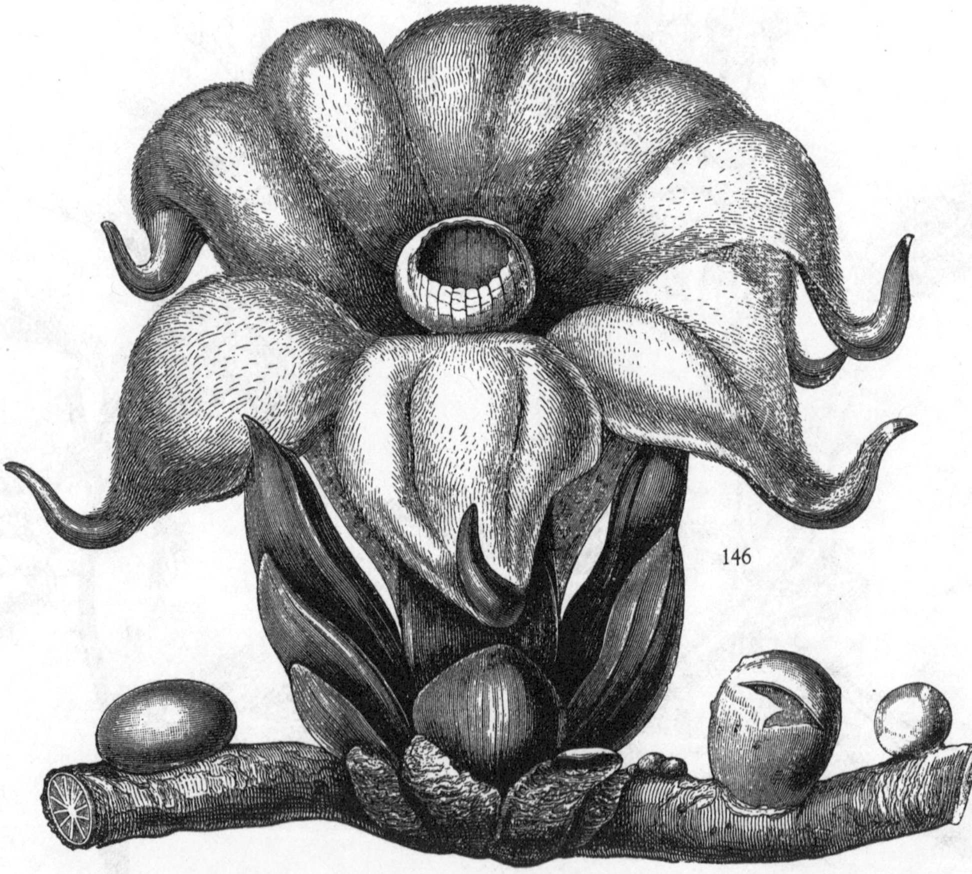

146

143. Red-silk-cotton tree *(Bombax).* Wind-dispersed seeds; from tropical Asia, Africa and Australia. 144. Lily-of-the-field *(Anemone sylvestris).* From Europe and Siberia. 145. *Gossypium barbadense.* A species of cotton; from tropical America. 146. *Brugmansia zipellii.* A shrub; from the Andes.

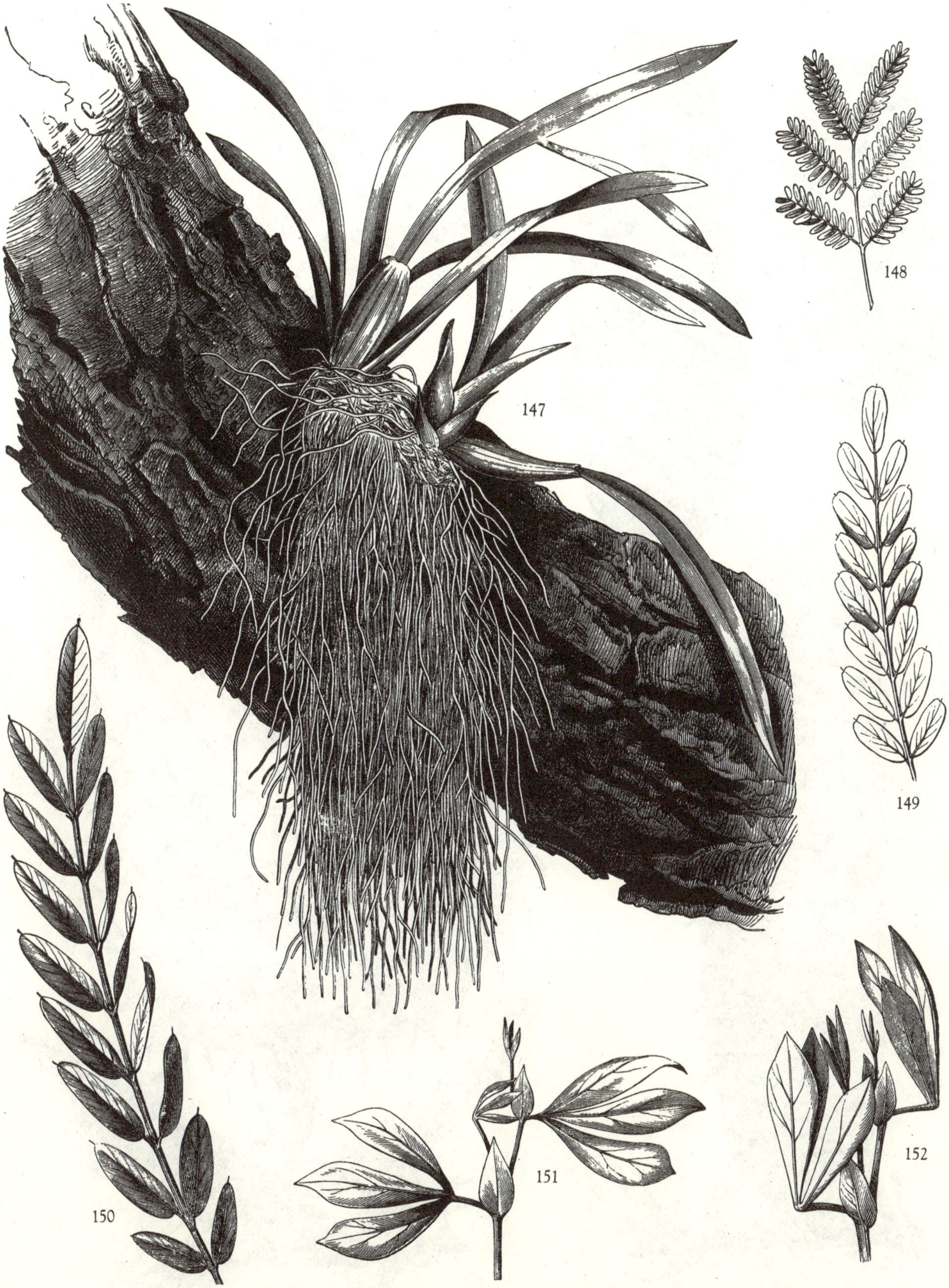

147

148

149

150

151

152

147. Aerial roots of an orchid on the branch of a tree. 148. A leaf of the cat's-claw mimosa (*Mimosa lindheimeri*). A prickly shrub with pinkish flowers; from Texas, New Mexico and Arizona. 149. A leaf of crown vetch (*Coronilla varia*). A straggling herb with purple, pink or yellow flowers; from Europe. 150. A leaf of false indigo (*Amorpha fruticosa*) in day position; from North America (see also Fig. 281). 151. A leaf of winged pea (*Tetragonolobus siliquosus*) in day position. A perennial herb with large, solitary pale yellow flowers; from North America. 152. A leaf of *Tetragonolobus siliquosus* in night position.

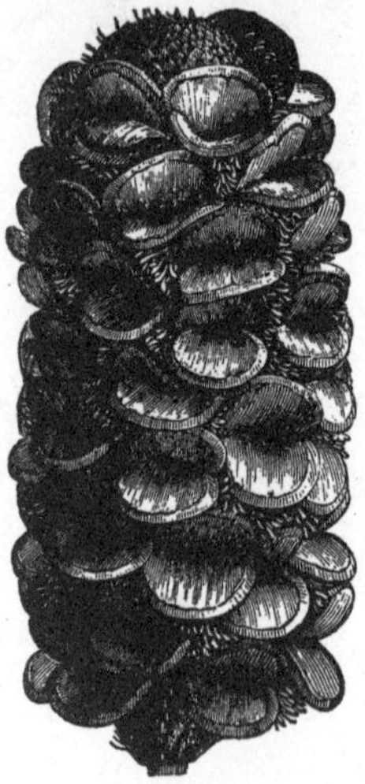

153

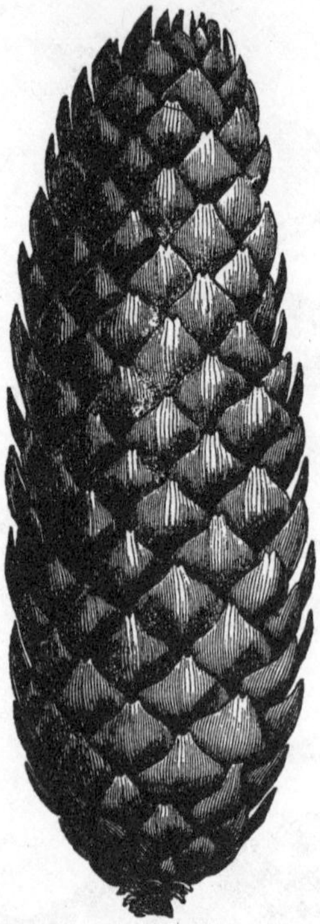

154

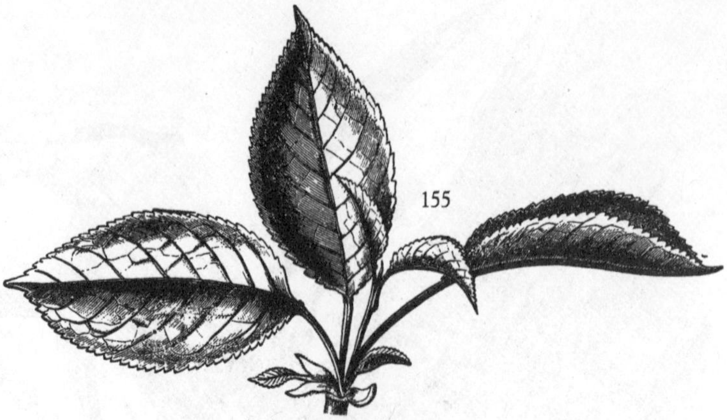

155

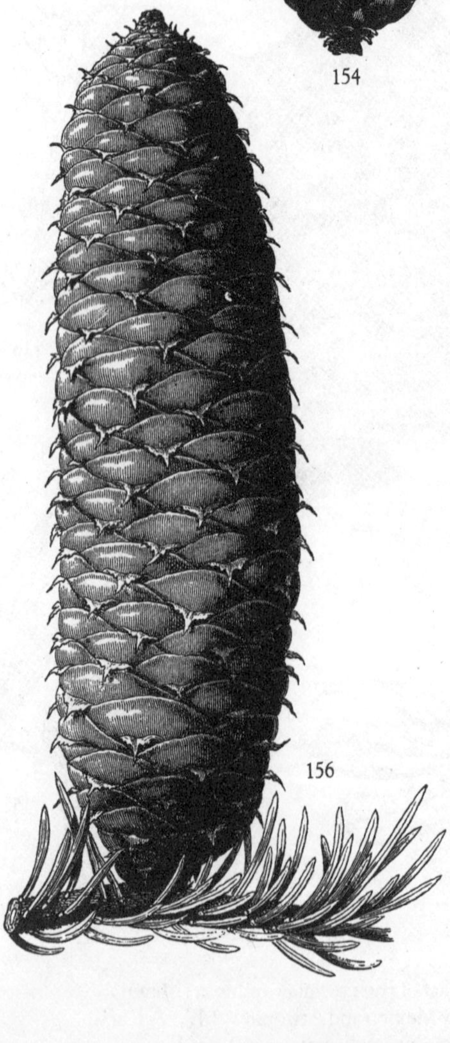

156

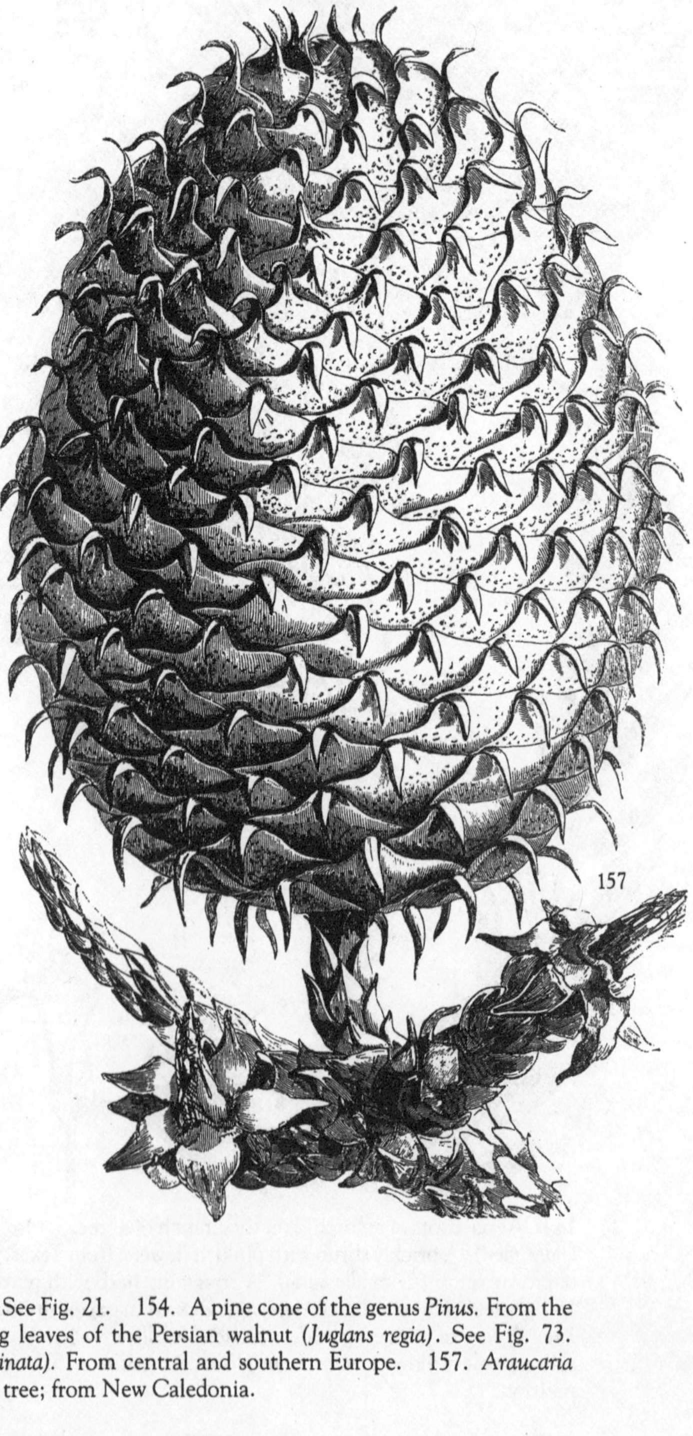

157

153. A fruiting spike of *Banksia ericifolia.* See Fig. 21. 154. A pine cone of the genus *Pinus.* From the Northern Hemisphere. 155. Unfolding leaves of the Persian walnut *(Juglans regia).* See Fig. 73. 156. A cone of the silver fir *(Abies pectinata).* From central and southern Europe. 157. *Araucaria cookii.* A very large evergreen coniferous tree; from New Caledonia.

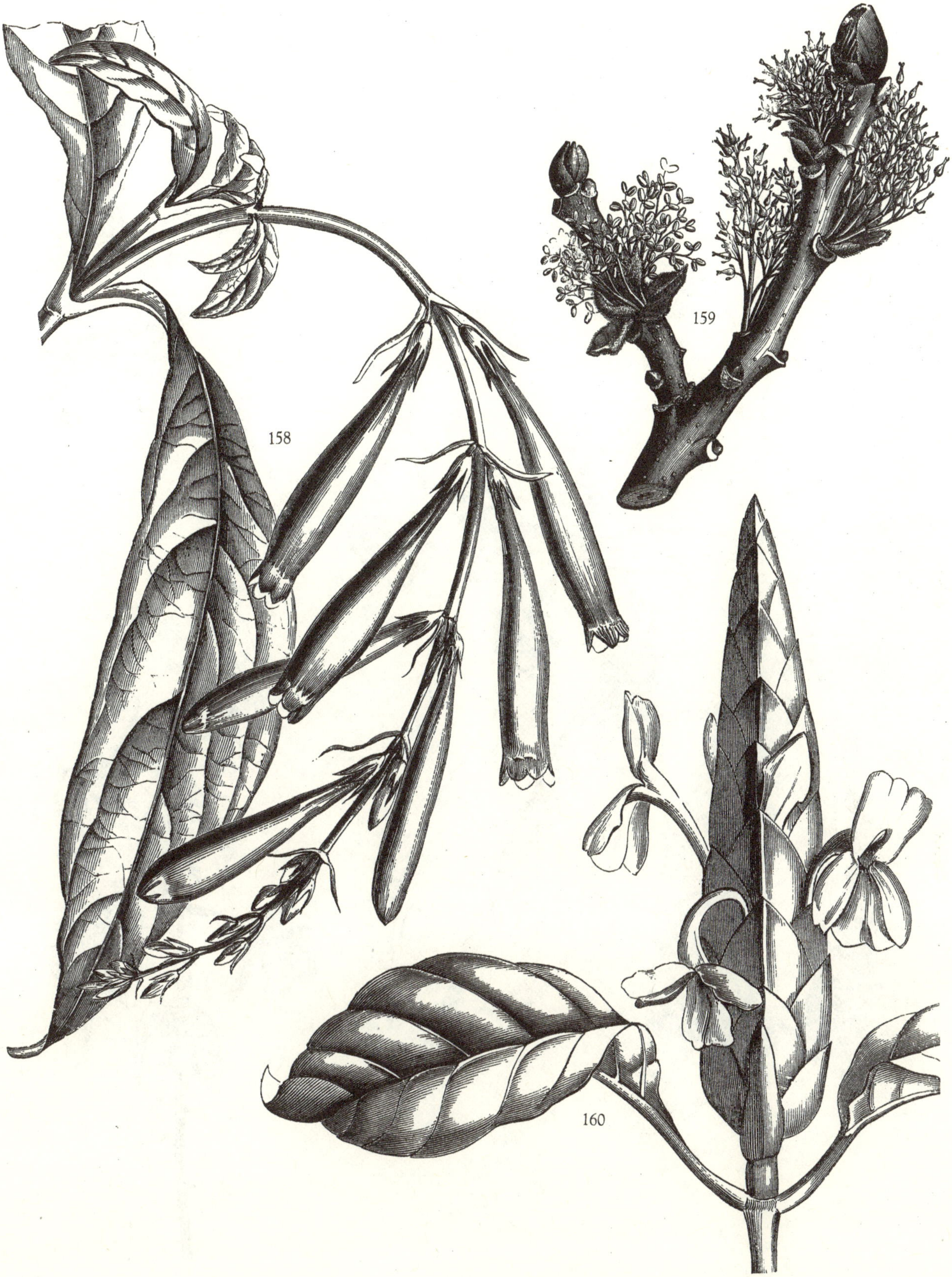

158. *Thyrsacanthus rutilans.* A shrub with rich crimson flowers; from the tropical regions of America. 159. A small bifurcating branch of the ash *(Fraxinus excelsior).* The left-hand limb of the fork is bearing male flowers, the right-hand limb is bearing hermaphrodite flowers; from Europe and Asia Minor. 160. *Strobilorachis glabra.* A shrub with green cones and pale yellow flowers; from Brazil.

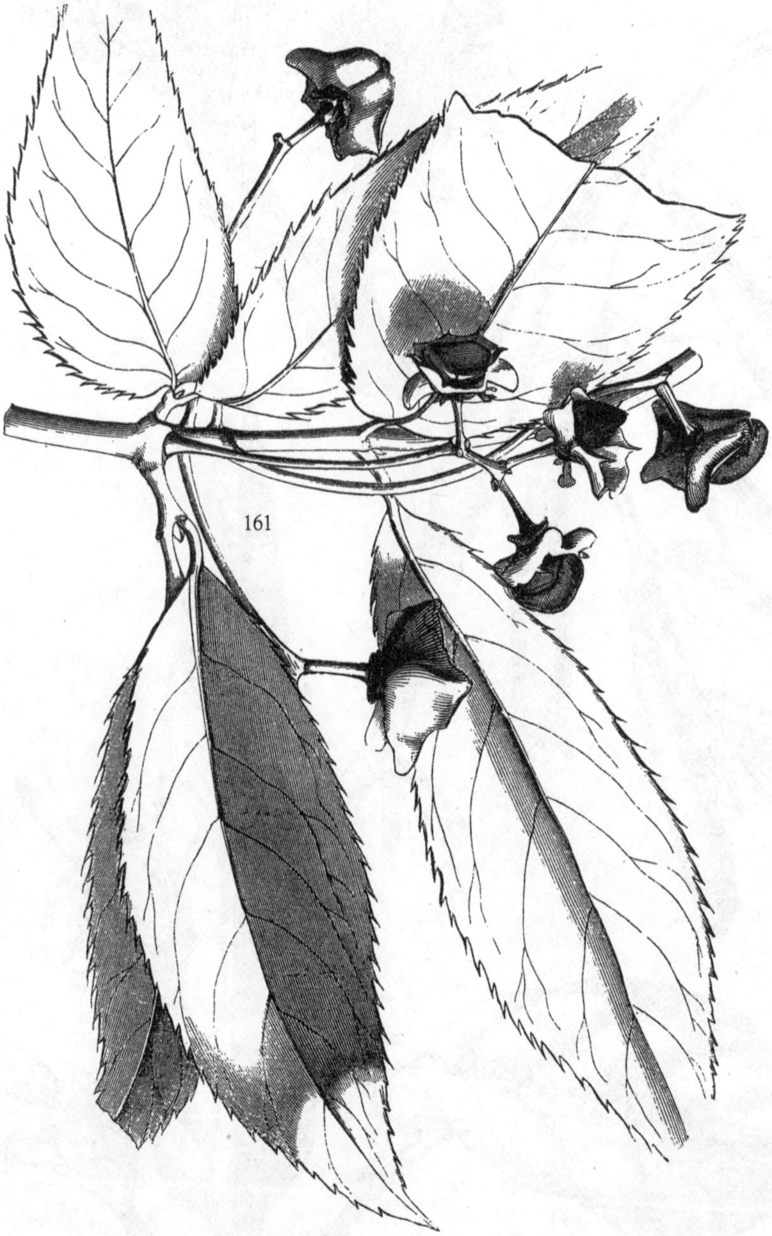

161

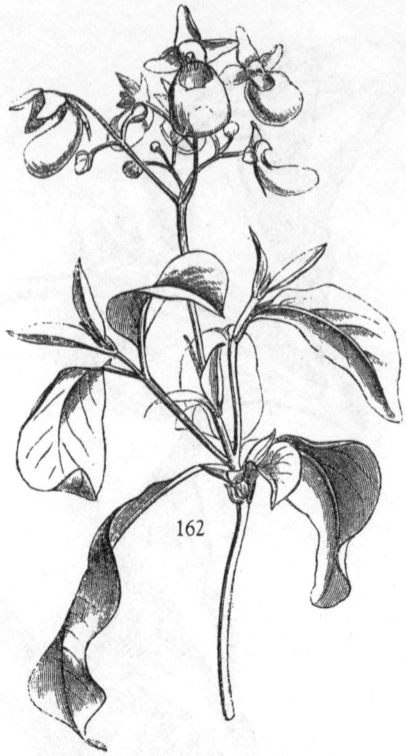

162

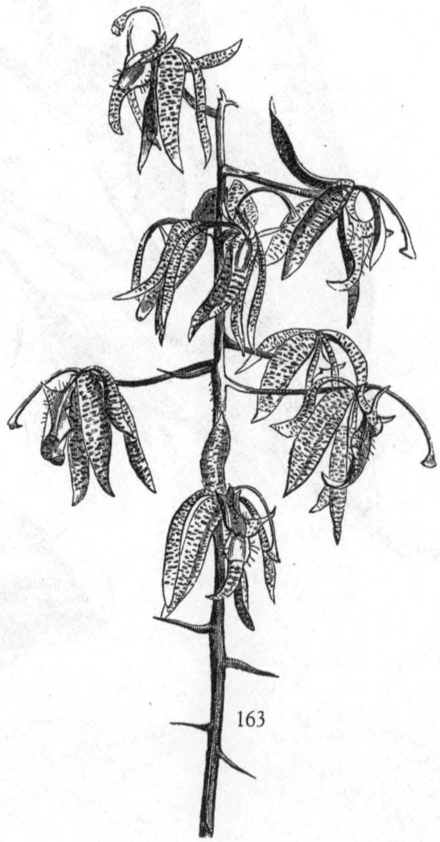

163

161. *Euonymus fimbriatus.* An evergreen bush with green flowers; from the Himalayas. 162. *Calceolaria tetragona.* See Fig. 30. 163. *Cycnoches musciferum.* An orchid with pale flowers spotted with brown; from Colombia.

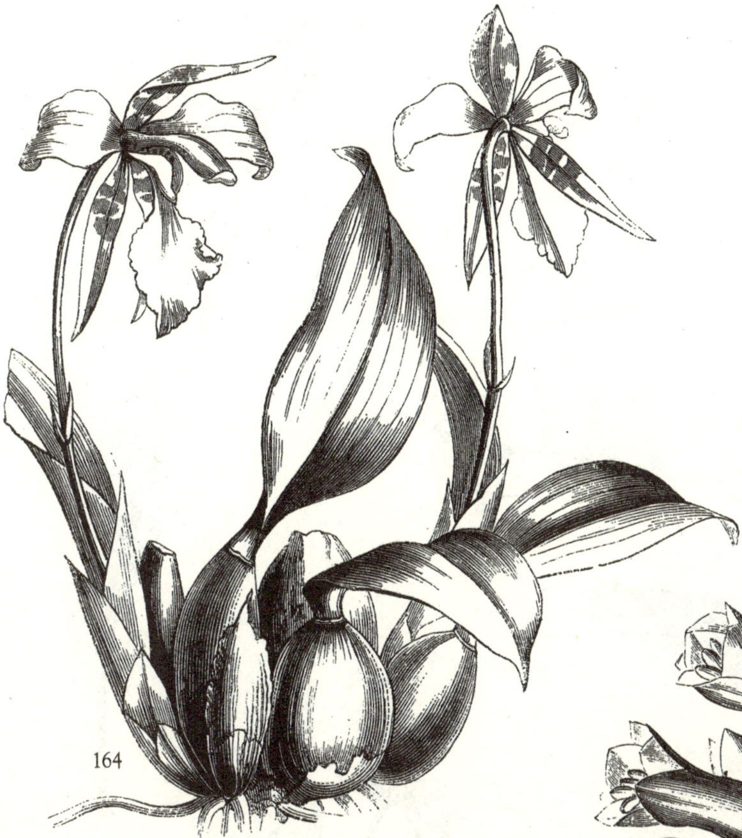

164

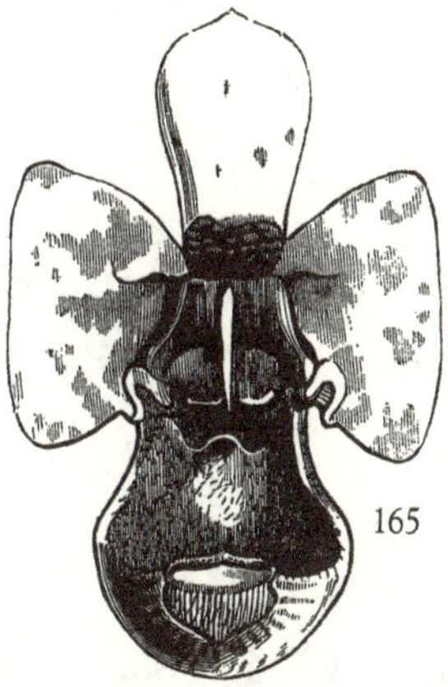

165

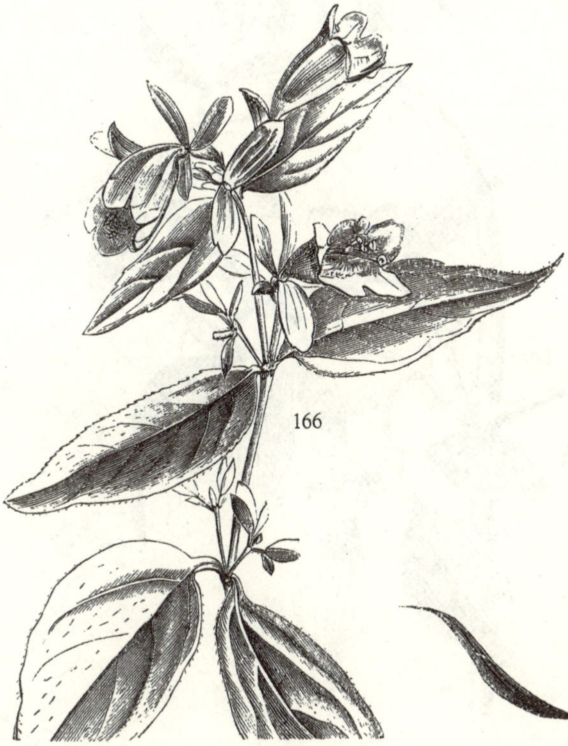

166

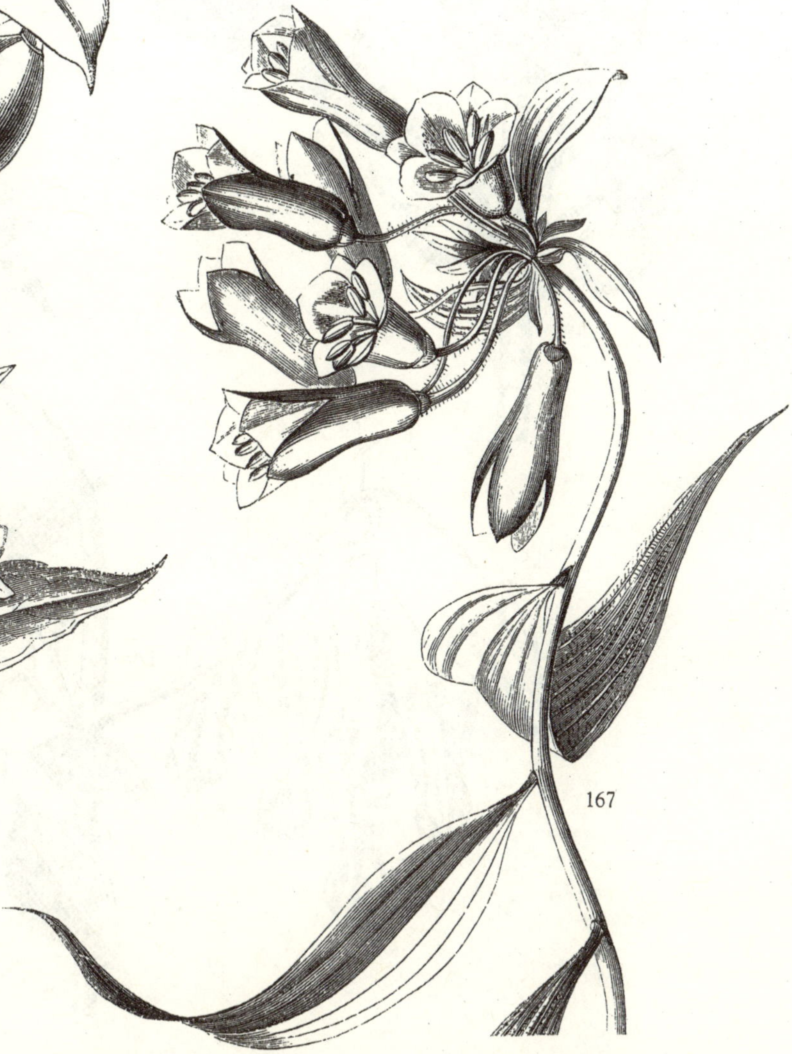

167

164. *Odontoglossum ehrenbergii.* An orchid with delicate white flowers spotted with brown on the sepals; from Mexico and Guatemala. 165. *Acineta densa.* An orchid with yellowish flowers spotted with crimson; from Costa Rica, Panama and Colombia. 166. *Abelia uniflora.* A small evergreen shrub with pinkish-white flowers, orange in throat; from the north of China. 167. *Bomarea acutifolia.* A twining herbaceous plant with dull red flowers; from Mexico.

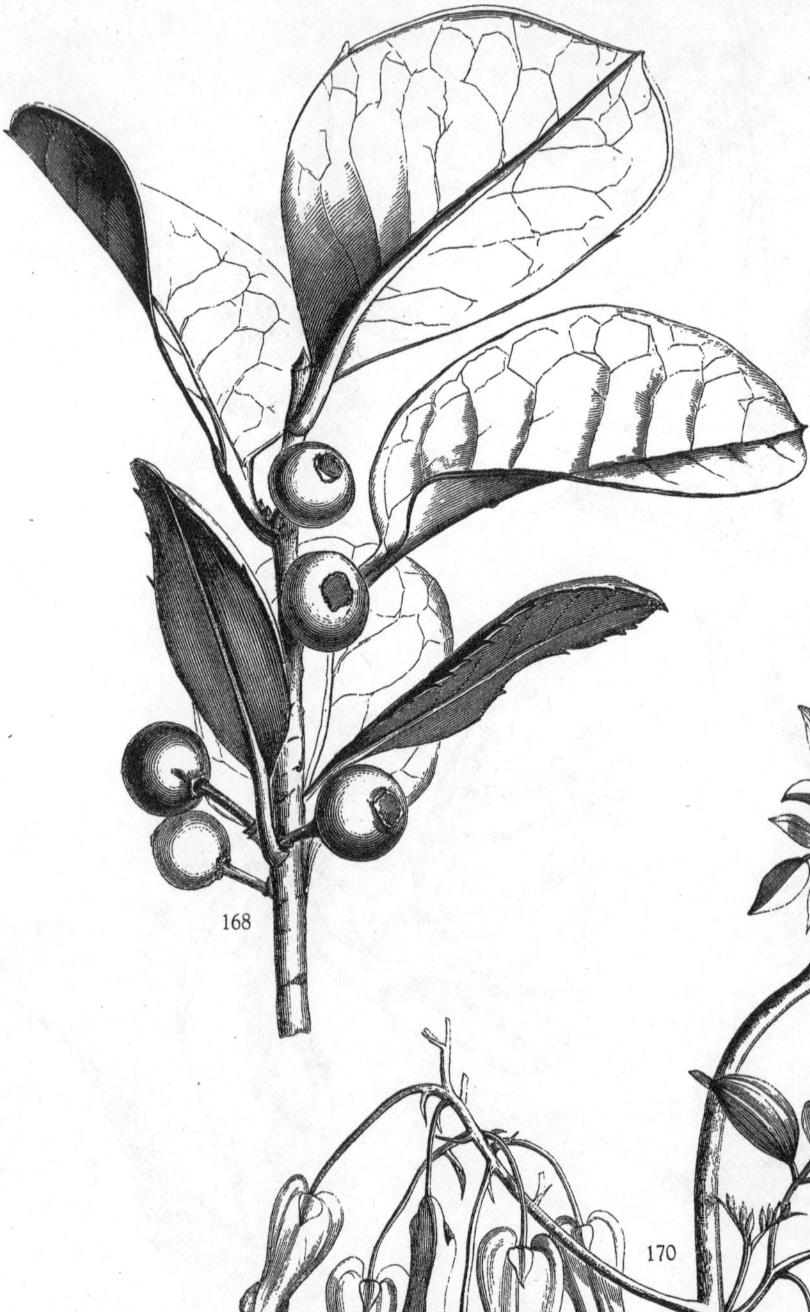

168

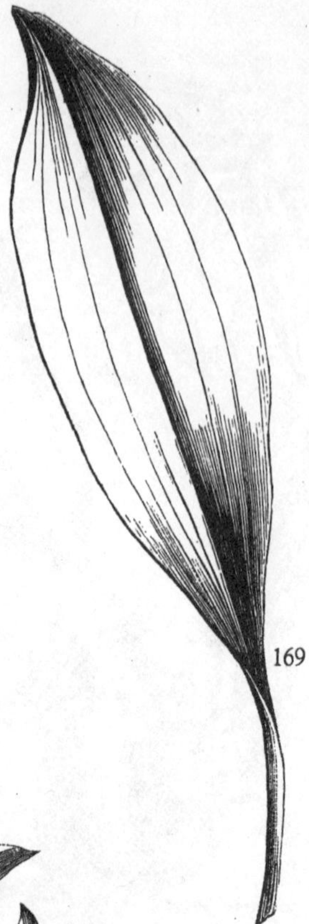

169

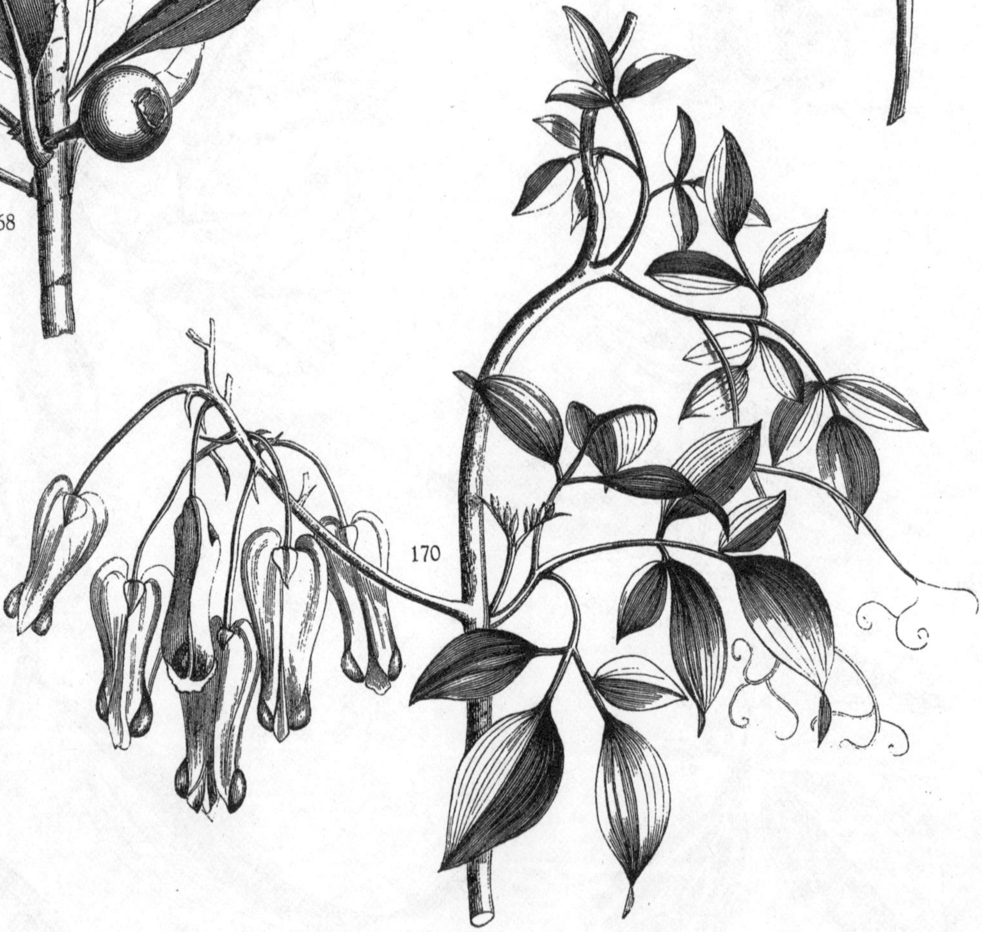

170

168. *Ilex perado.* An evergreen tree with broad flat foliage and bright red fruit; from the Canary and Madeira Islands. 169. *Schlimmia jasminodora.* An orchid with white flowers; from Central America (see also Fig. 177). 170. *Dactylicapnos thalictrifolia.* A climbing hardy perennial with large yellow flowers; from Nepal.

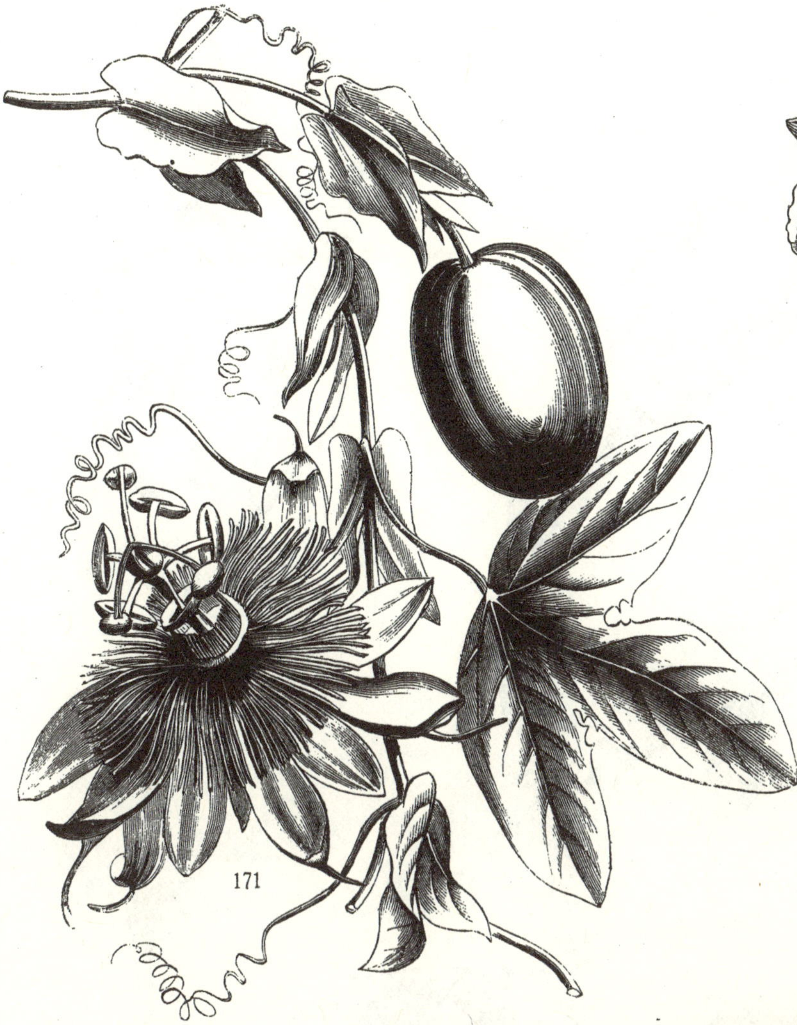

171

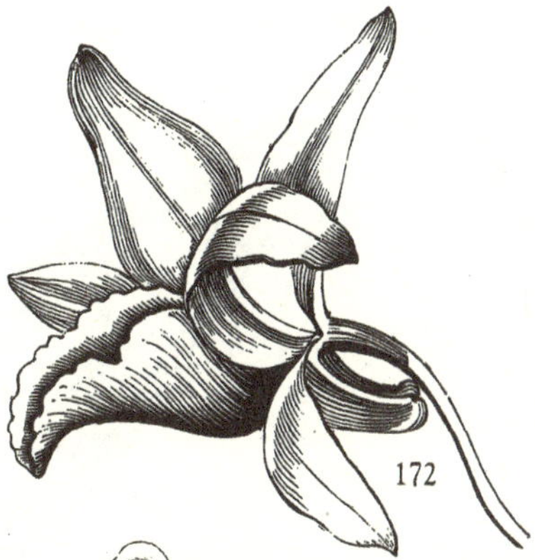

172

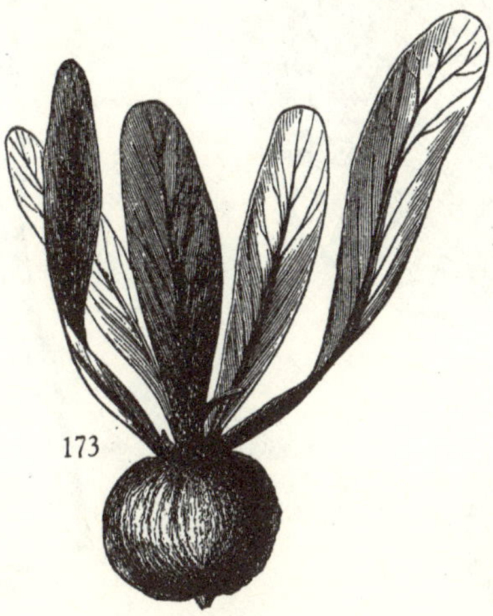

173

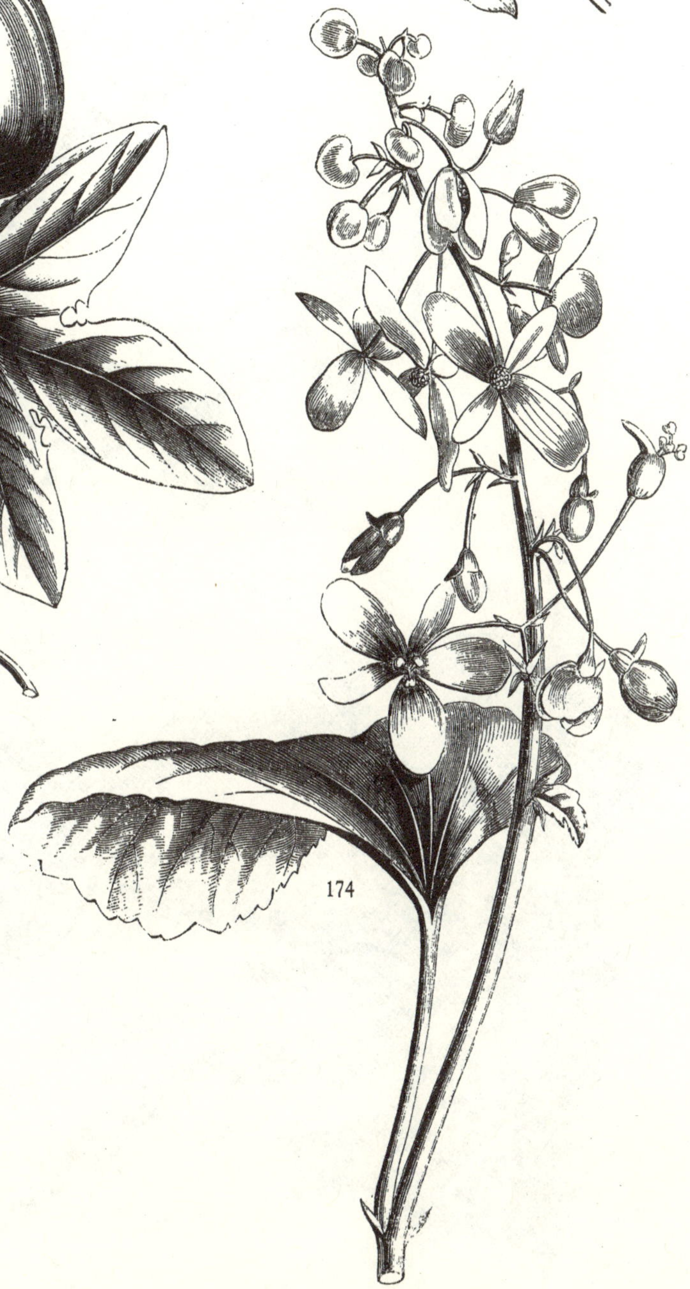

174

171. *Passiflora alba.* A vine with white flowers; from the tropical Americas. 172. Flower and magnified lip of the green-centered dendrobe (*Dendrobium mesochlorum*). An orchid from tropical and subtropical Asia, Australia and the Pacific Islands. 173. The fruit of *Dryobalanops*, a resin-producing tree; from Sumatra and Borneo. 174. *Begonia monoptera.* A tuberous perennial with pure white flowers; from Mexico.

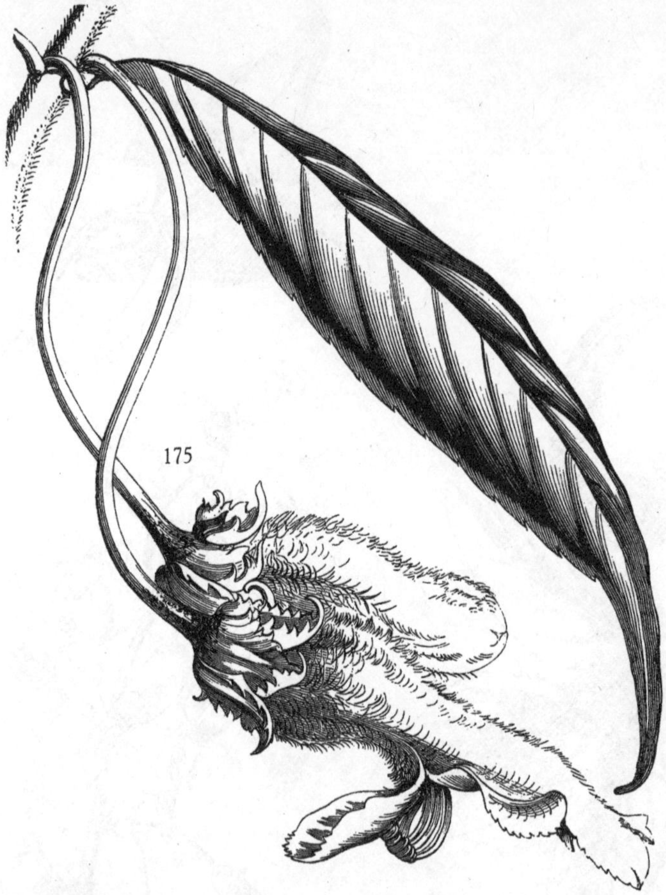

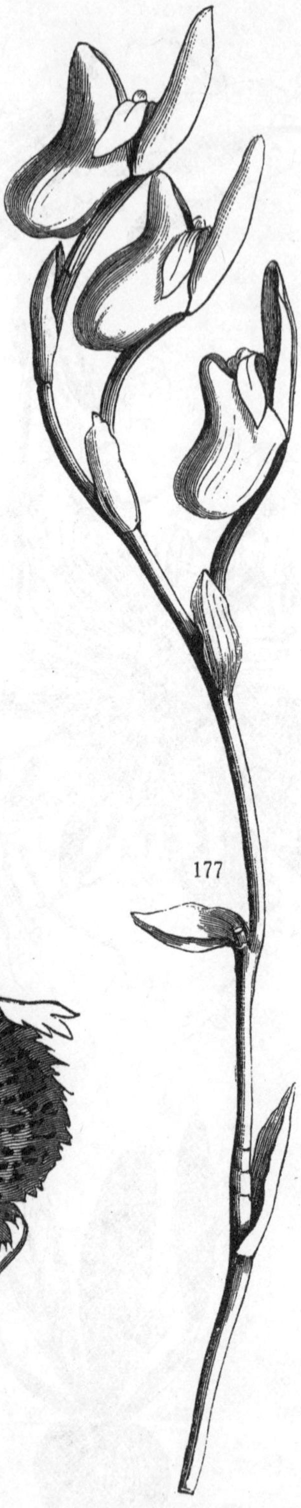

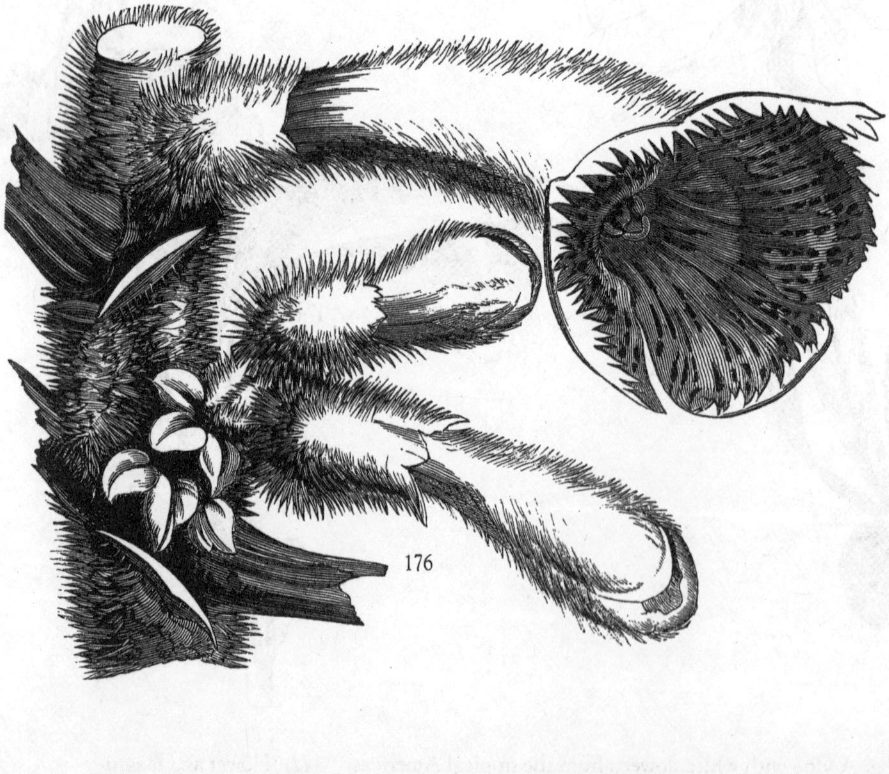

175. *Columnea aurantiaca.* A climbing vine with large, rich orange-colored flowers; from Colombia and Panama. 176. *Arctocalyx endlicherianus.* A vine with a shaggy brownish-black stem and long yellow flowers; from Mexico. 177. *Schlimmia jasminodora.* See Fig. 169.

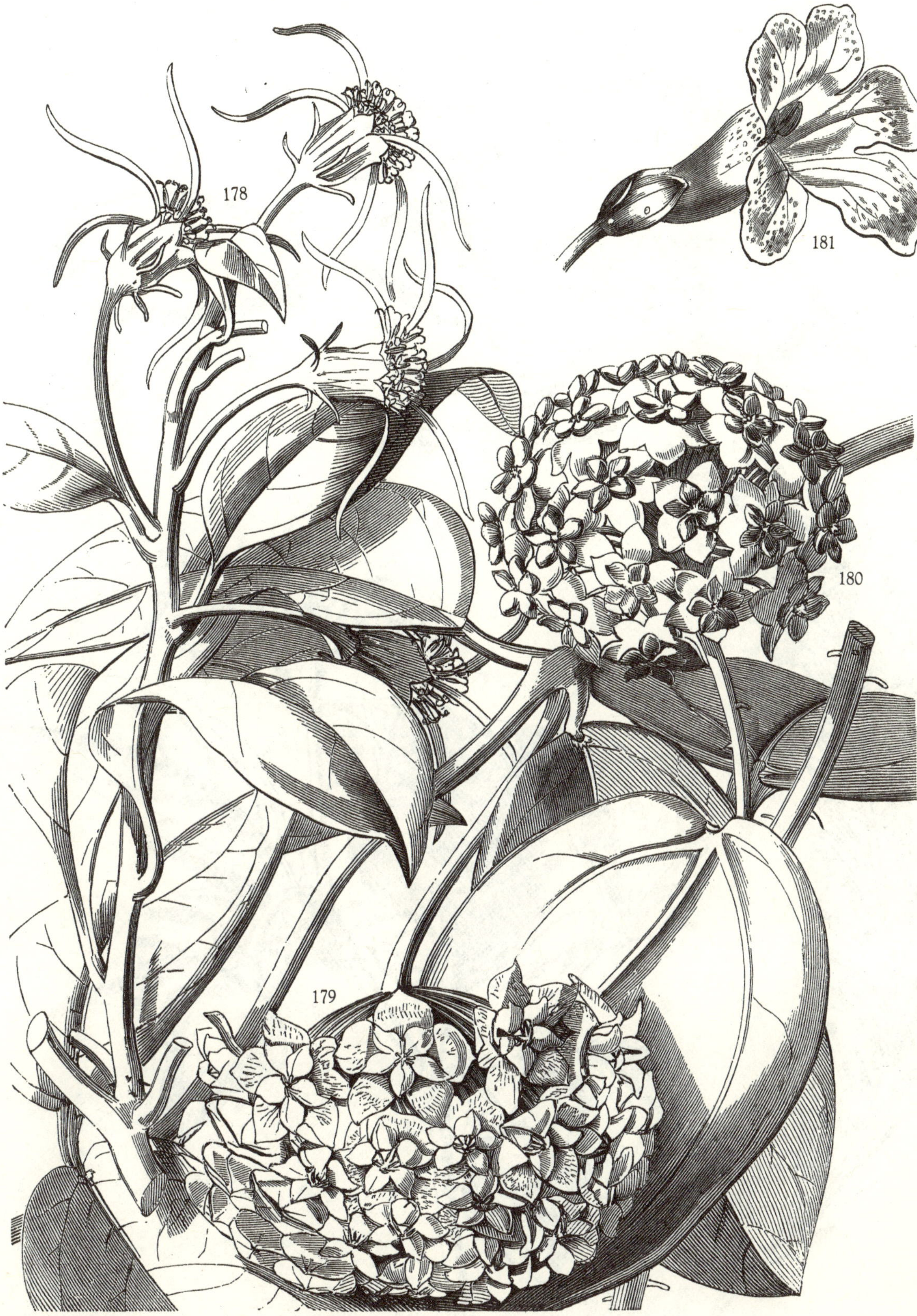

178. *Gynoxys fragrans.* A perennial plant with yellow flowers; from Guatemala. 179. *Hoya coriacea.* A climbing shrub with yellowish flowers; from Java. 180. *Hoya purpureo-fusca.* A twining plant with small umbels of richly tinted purple and gray flowers; from Java. 181. *Spathodea laevis.* A tree with white flowers streaked with rose; from Sierra Leone.

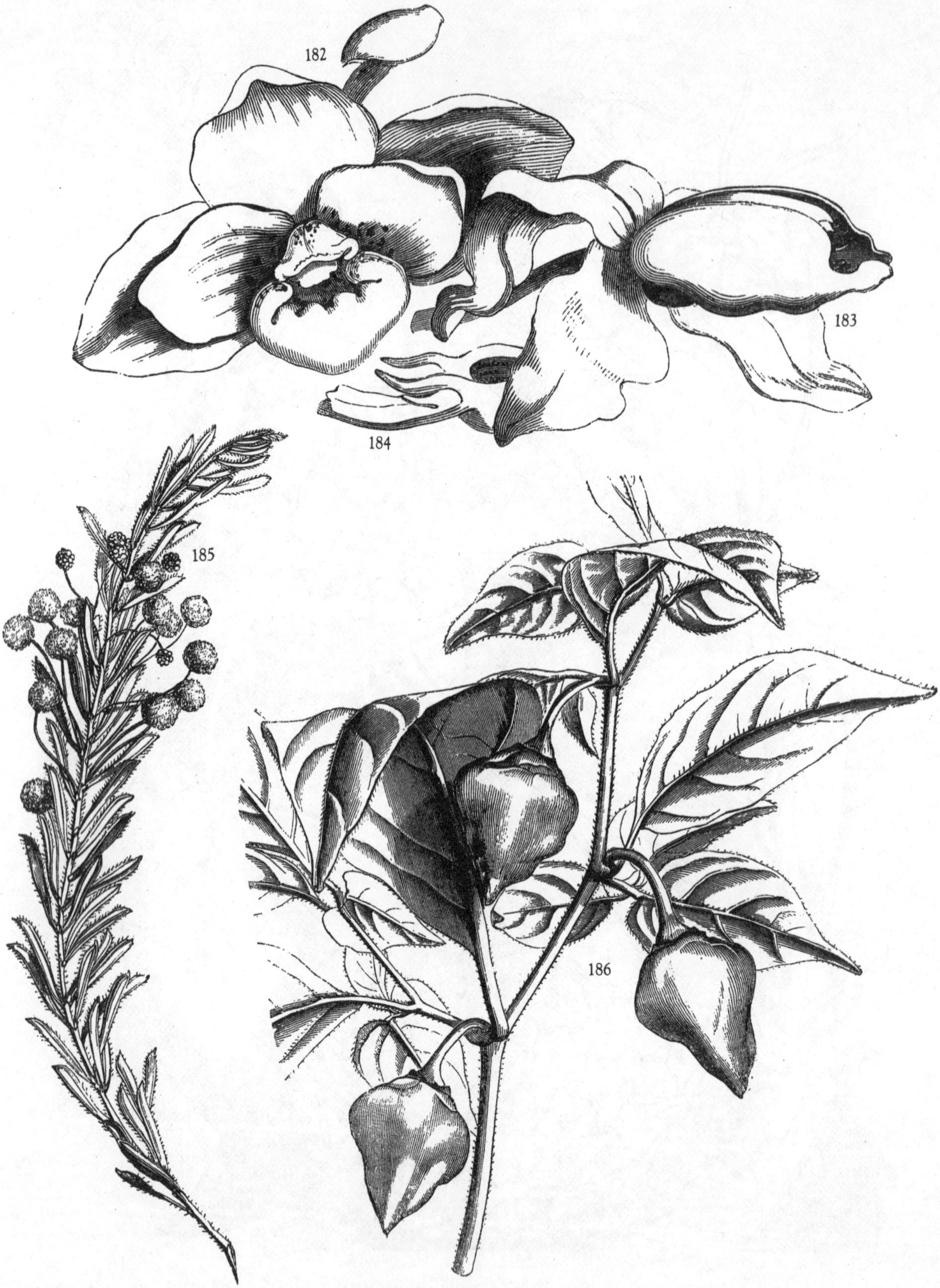

182. *Stanhopea ecornuta.* An orchid, flowers white, with the base of the lip yellow; from Guatemala and Honduras. 183. *Stanhopea tricornis.* An orchid with yellow petals; from Colombia and Ecuador. 184. A portion of the lip of the previous orchid. 185. *Acacia lineata.* A shrub with heads of yellow flowers; from Australia. 186. *Capsicum cereolum.* A pepper with yellow waxy fruit; from South America.

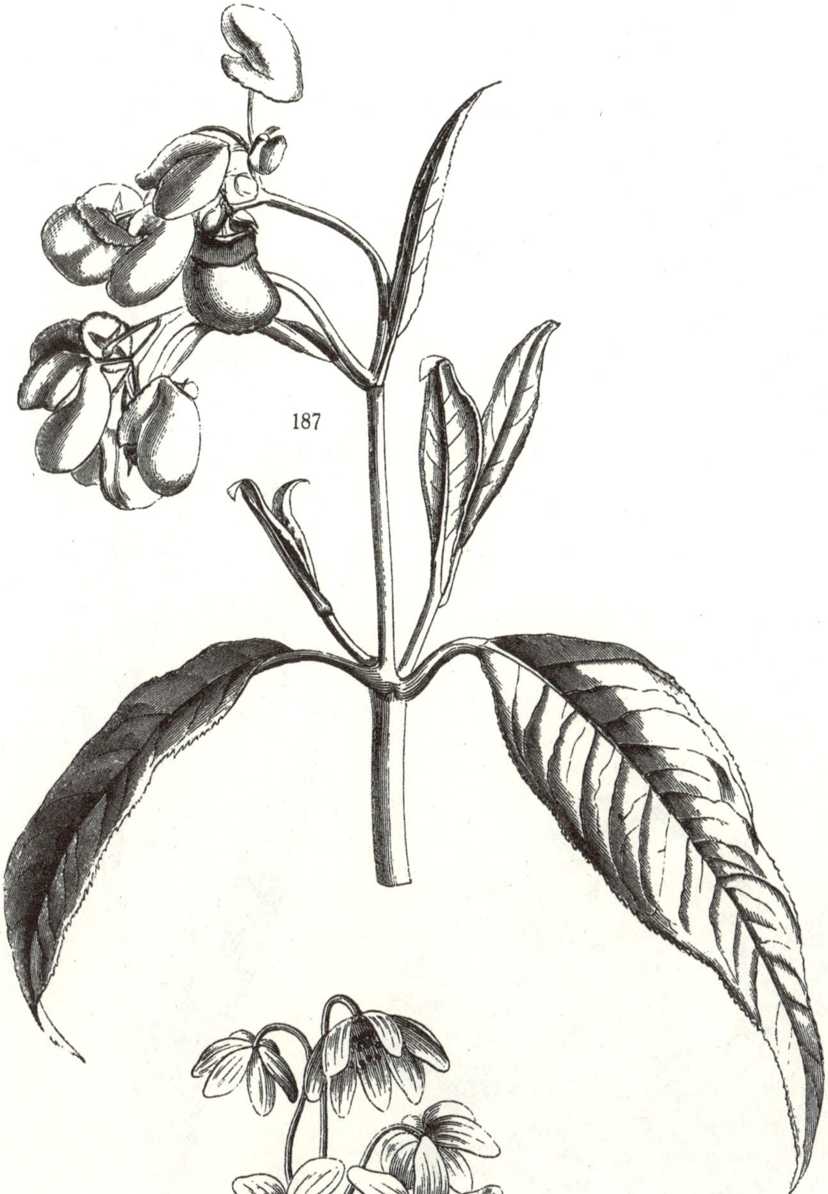

187

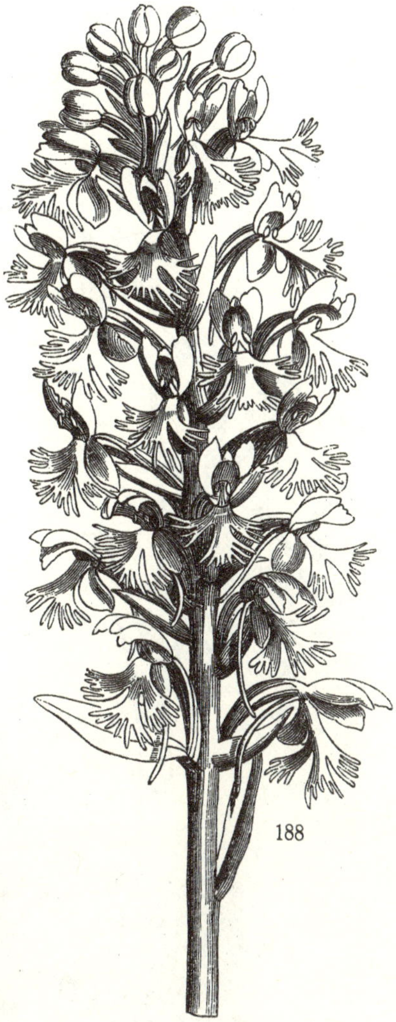

188

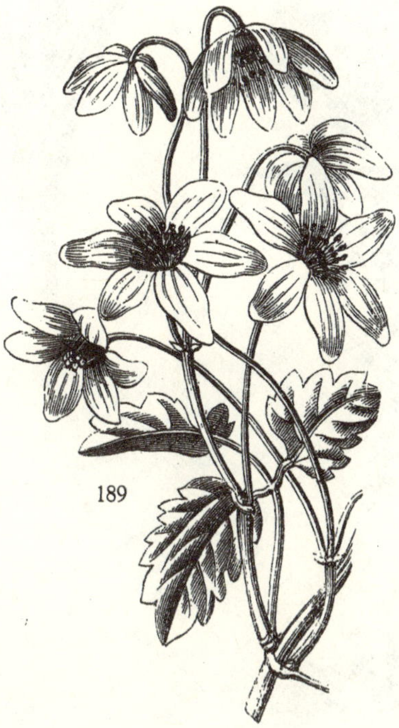

189

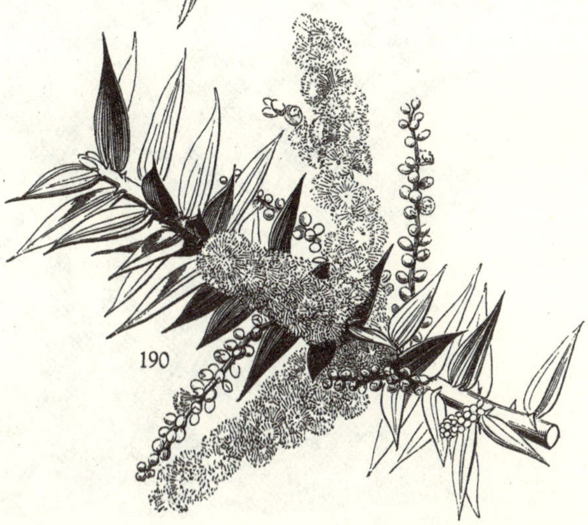

190

187. *Calceolaria stricta.* A half-hardy shrub with pale yellow flowers; from Peru. 188. *Platanthera incisa.* A hardy herbaceous orchid with cylindrical spikes of purple flowers; from North America. 189. *Clematis indivisa.* A climbing plant, flowers large and pure white, with crimson anthers; from New Zealand. 190. *Acacia oxycedrus.* A bush with flowers in bright yellow spikes; from southeastern Australia.

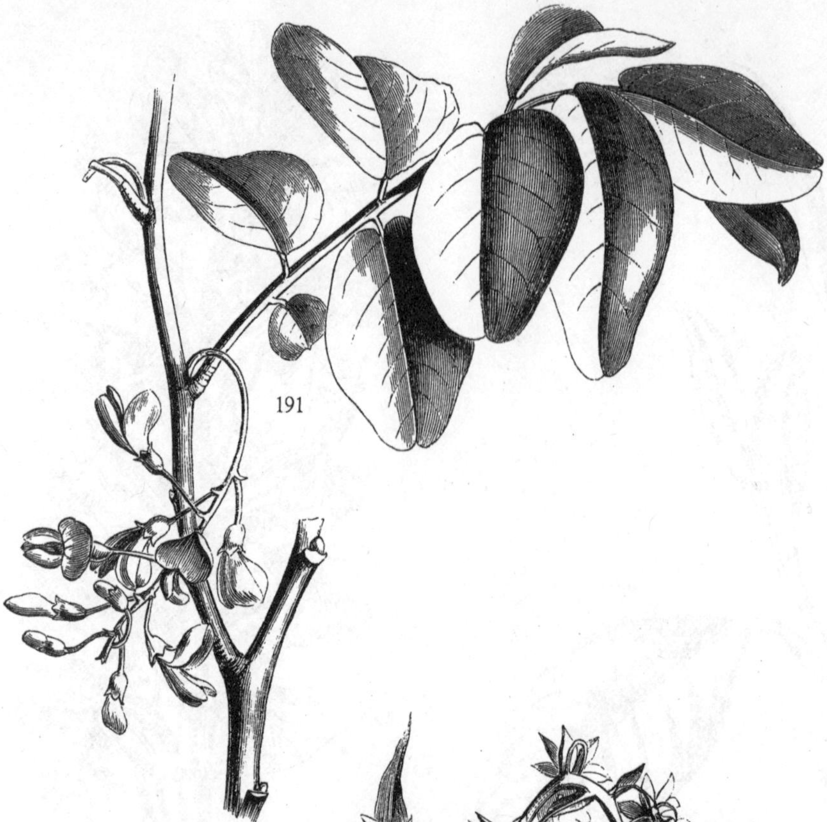

191

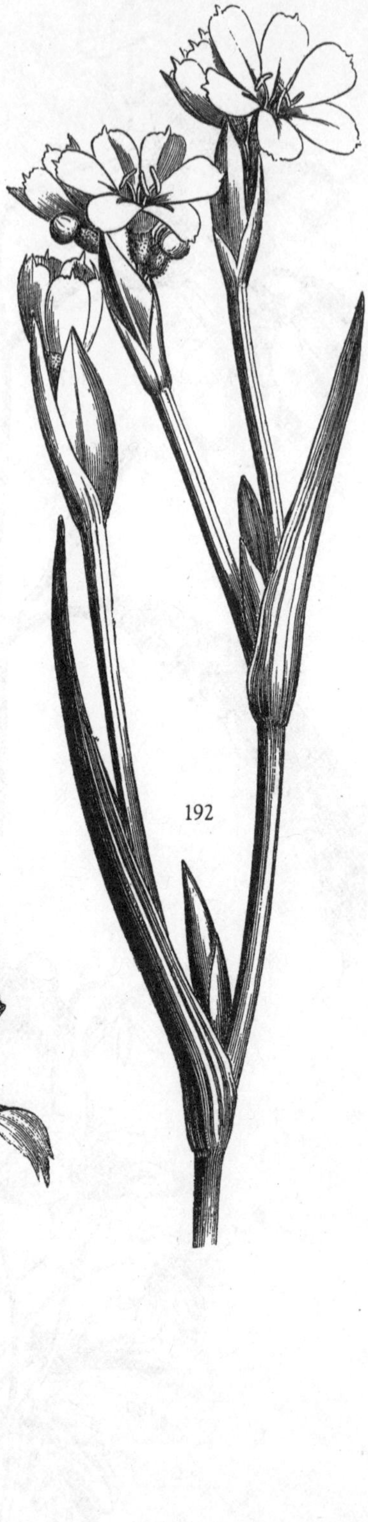

192

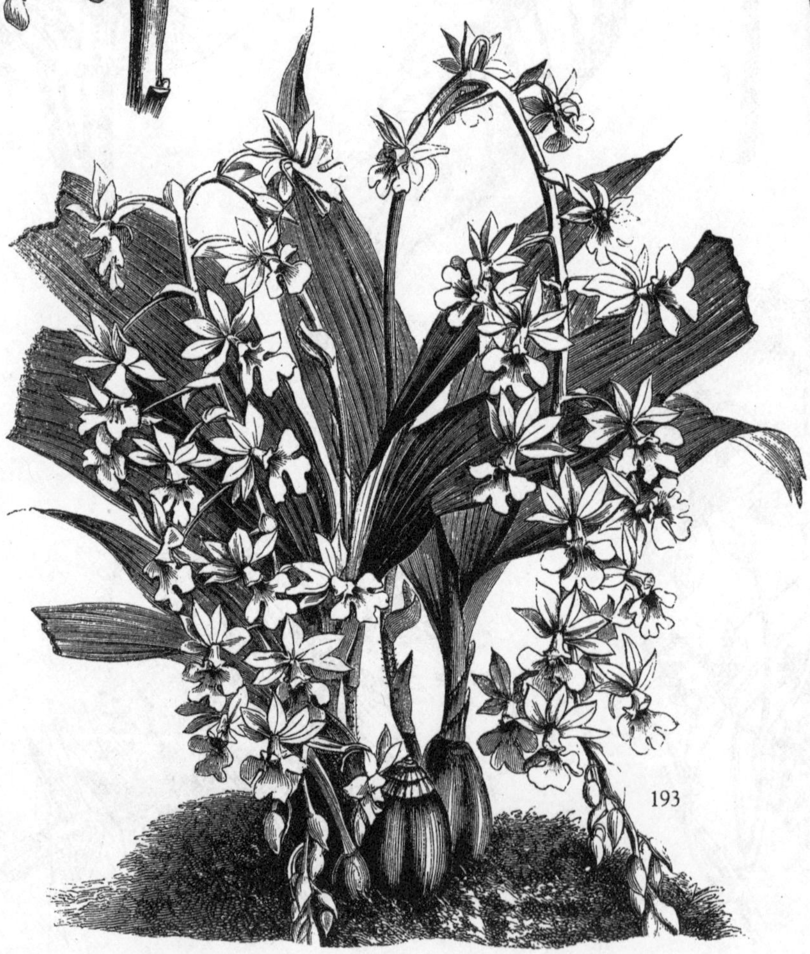

193

191. *Lennea robinioides.* A tree with purple flowers; from Mexico. 192. *Sisyrinchium majale.* A half-hardy perennial, flowers yellow with a brown eye; from Chile. 193. *Calanthe vestita.* See Fig. 45.

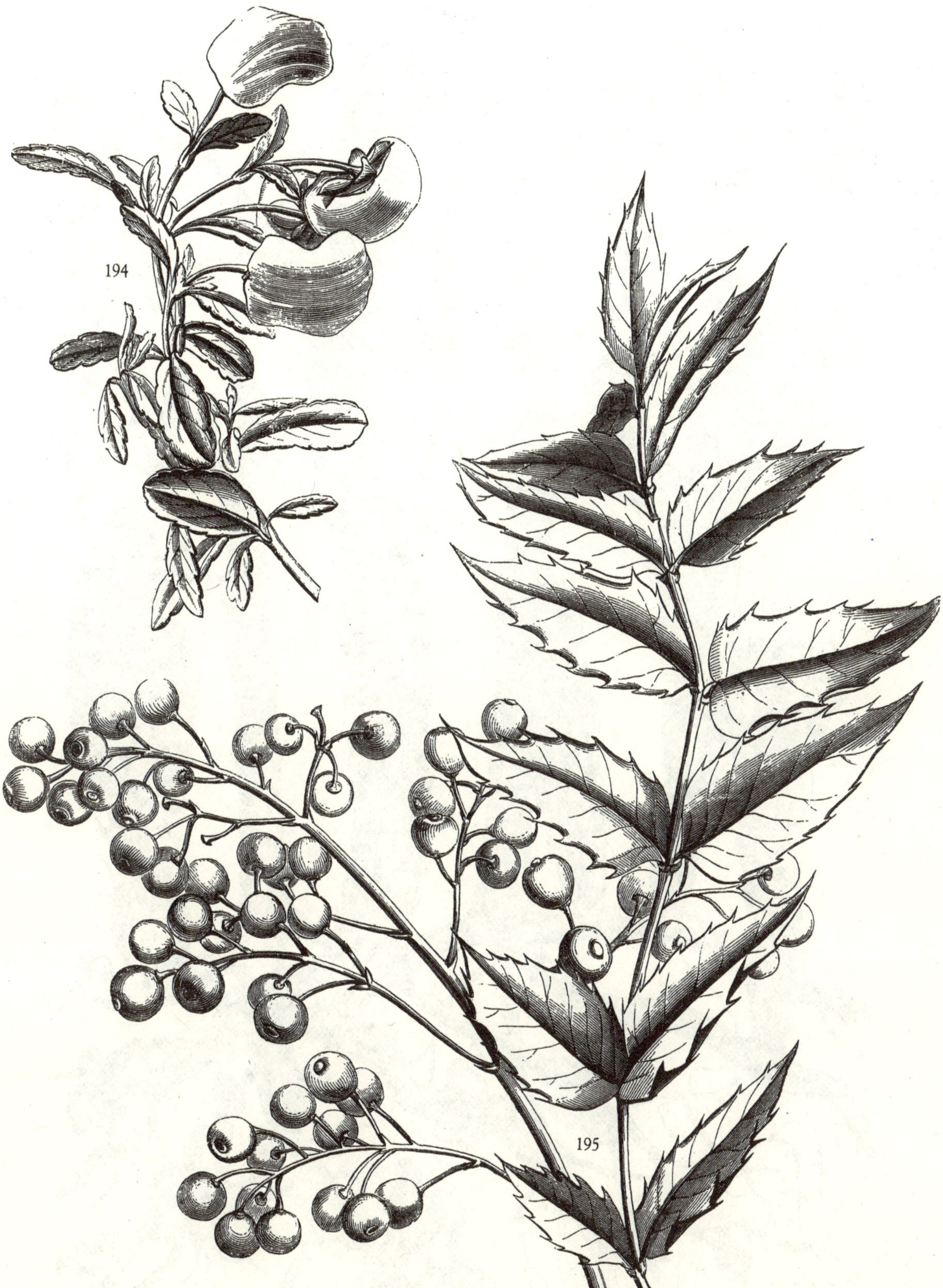

194. *Calceolaria cuneiformis.* A shrub with pale lemon-colored flowers; from Bolivia. 195. *Berberis pallida.* An evergreen bush, flowers yellow, berries black; from Mexico.

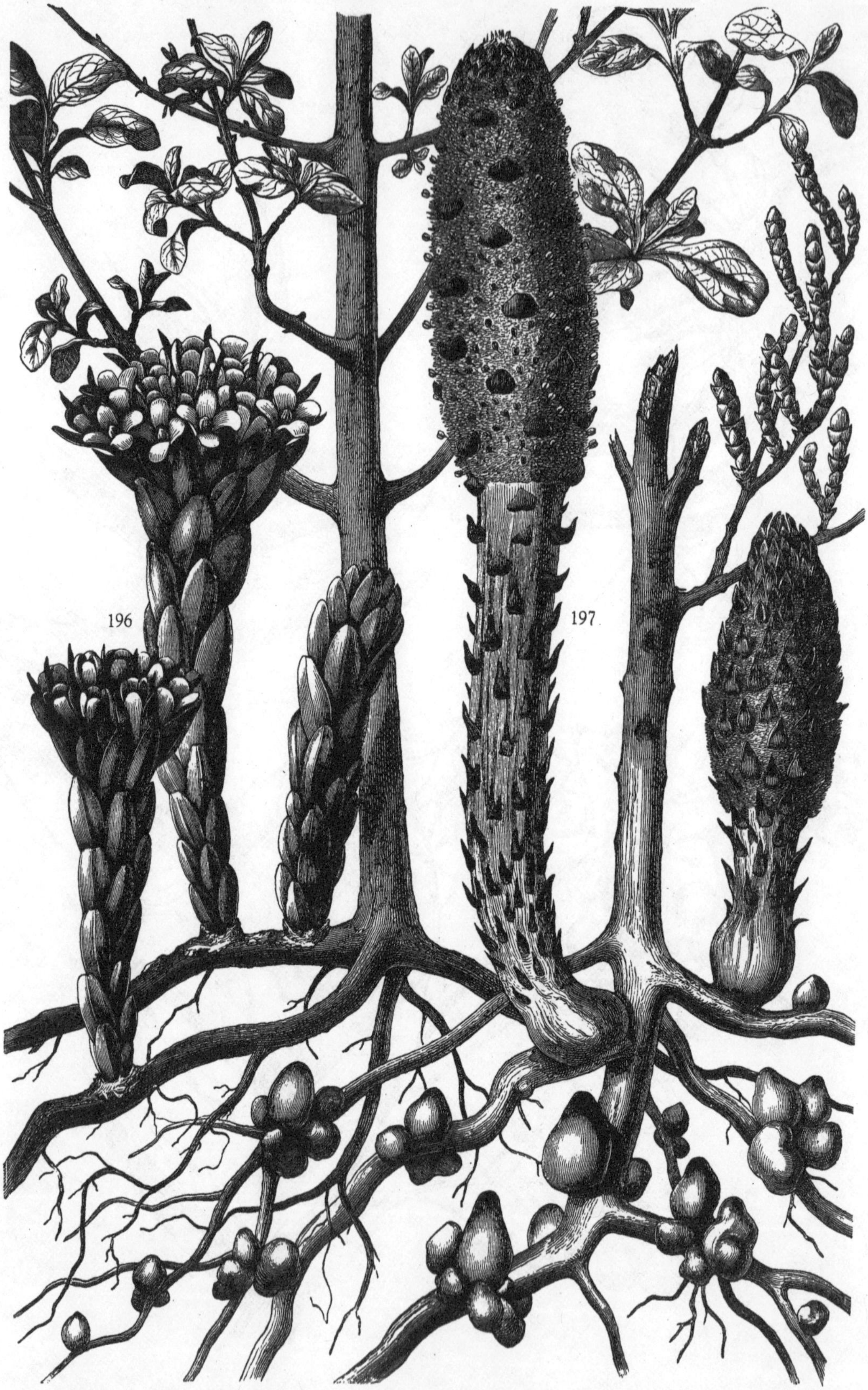

196. *Cytinus hypocistus.* A parasite with white flowers; from the Mediterranean basin.
197. *Cynomorium coccineum.* A parasite; from southern Europe.

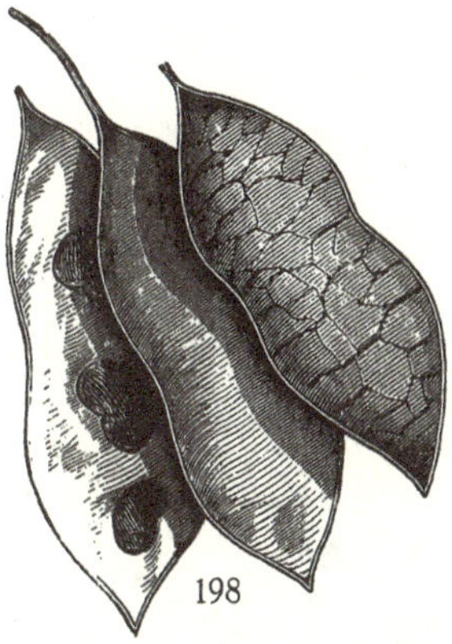

198

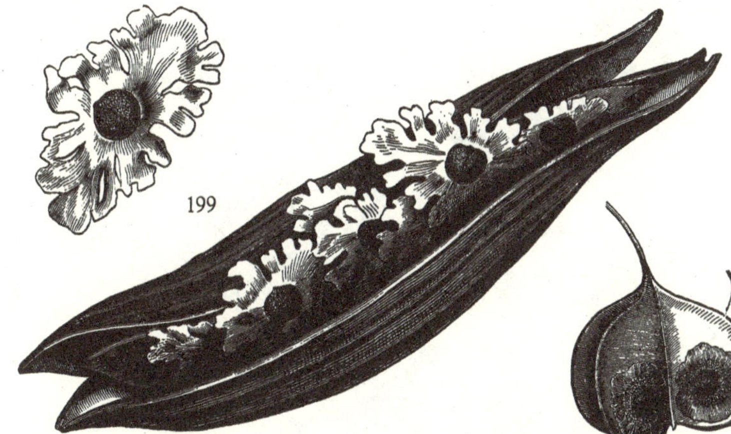

199

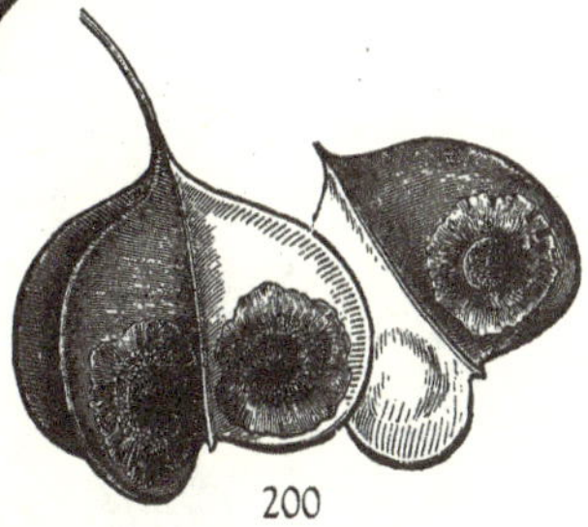

200

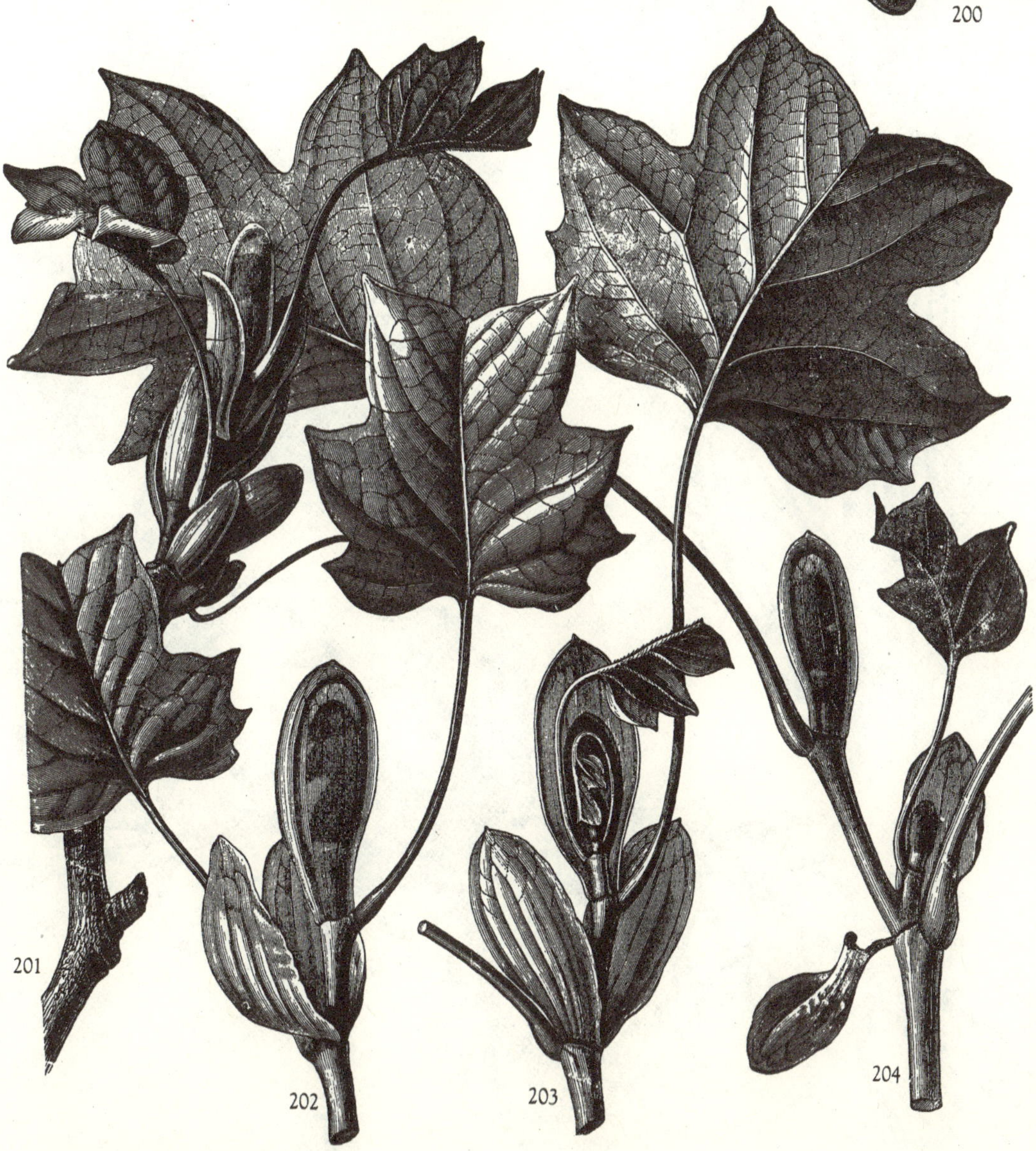

201

202

203

204

198. The fruit of *Lunaria rediviva.* The two valves of the fruit have become detached and the seeds are fastened to the inside of each valve; flowers white to purple; from Europe. 199. The opened capsule of a *Bigonia* from which winged seeds are being carried off by the wind. 200. The capsule of a yam *(Dioscorea)* after the freeing of the pollen. 201–204. A leaf unfolding from the tulip tree *(Liriodendron tulipifera).* From North America. In sequence: a twig at the end of which the leaves are beginning to unfold; end of the same twig, the leaves being further expanded; the anterior boat-shaped stipule artificially removed from the upper bud; one of the stipules about to fall off.

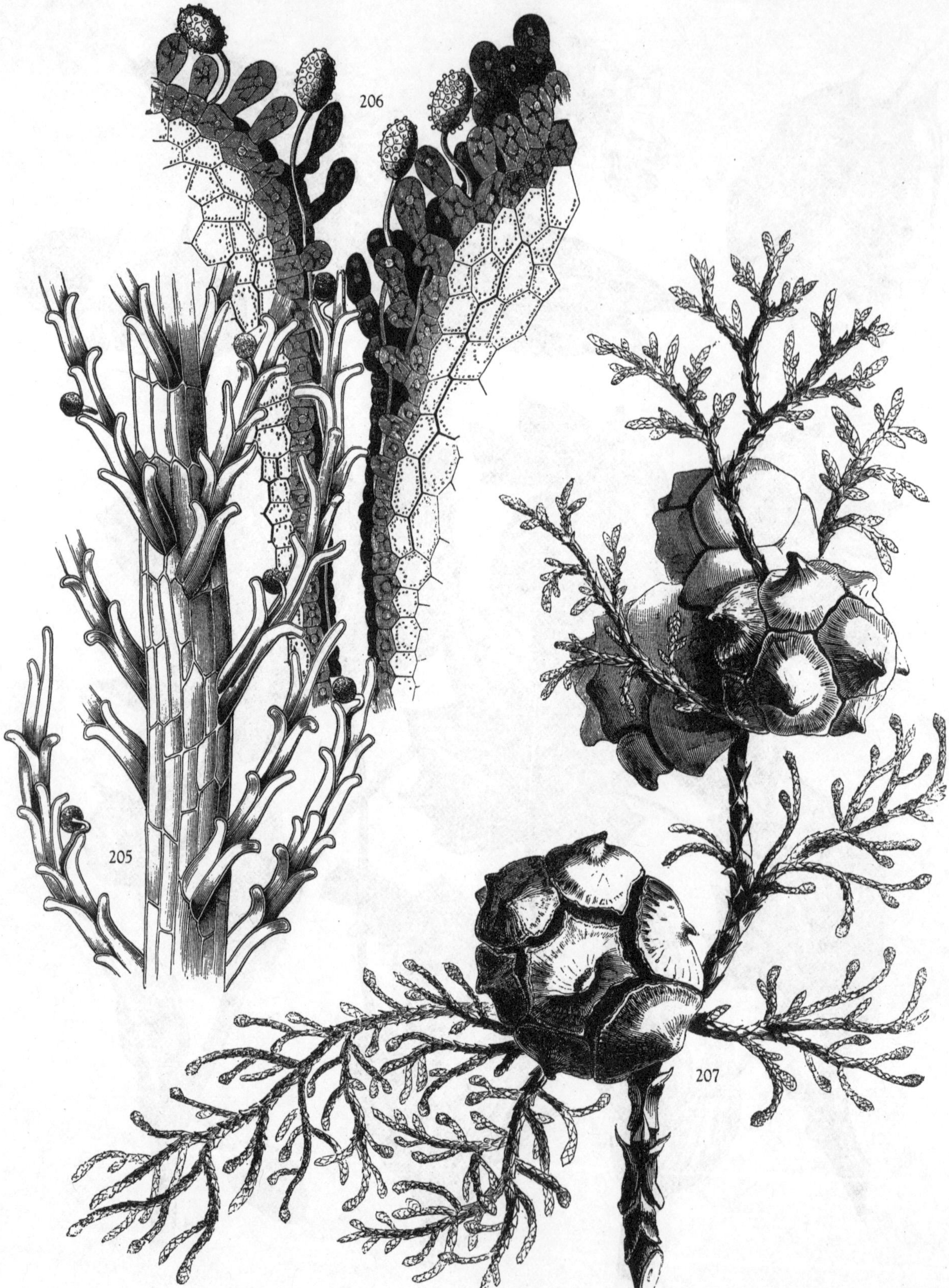

205. Portion of the feathery stigma of the tall oat grass *(Avena elatior)*. From the Mediterranean region. 206. Longitudinal section of the stigma and upper portion of the style of the martagon lily *(Lilium martagon)*. Orange-yellow flowers; from Europe and western Asia, east to Mongolia. 207. Bhutan cypress *(Cupressus torulosa)*. Glaucous leaves; from the Himalayas.

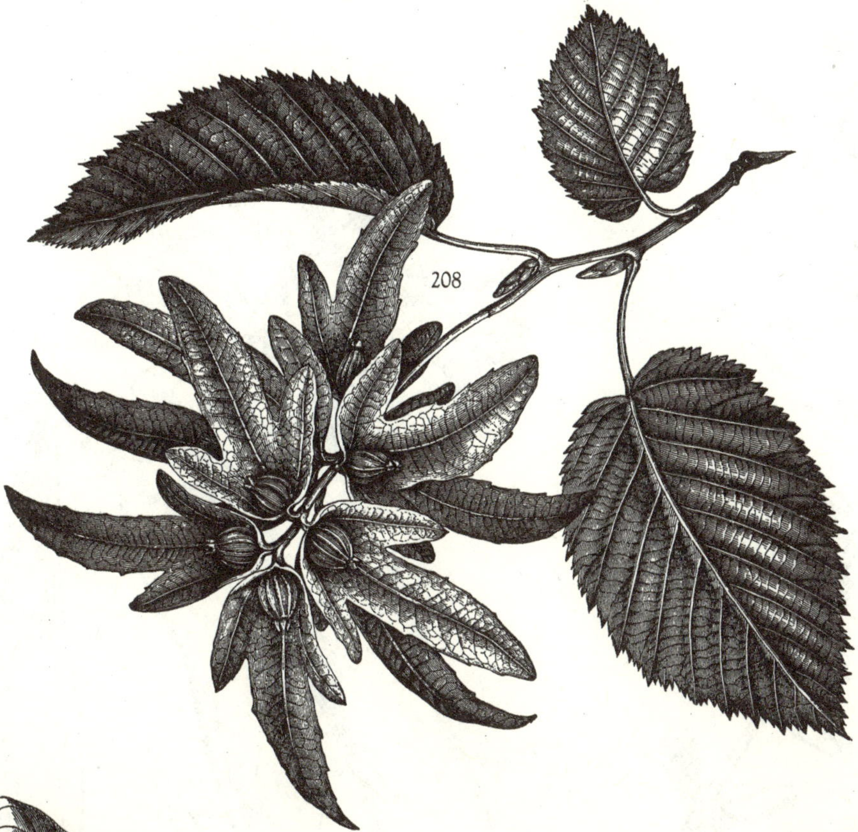

208

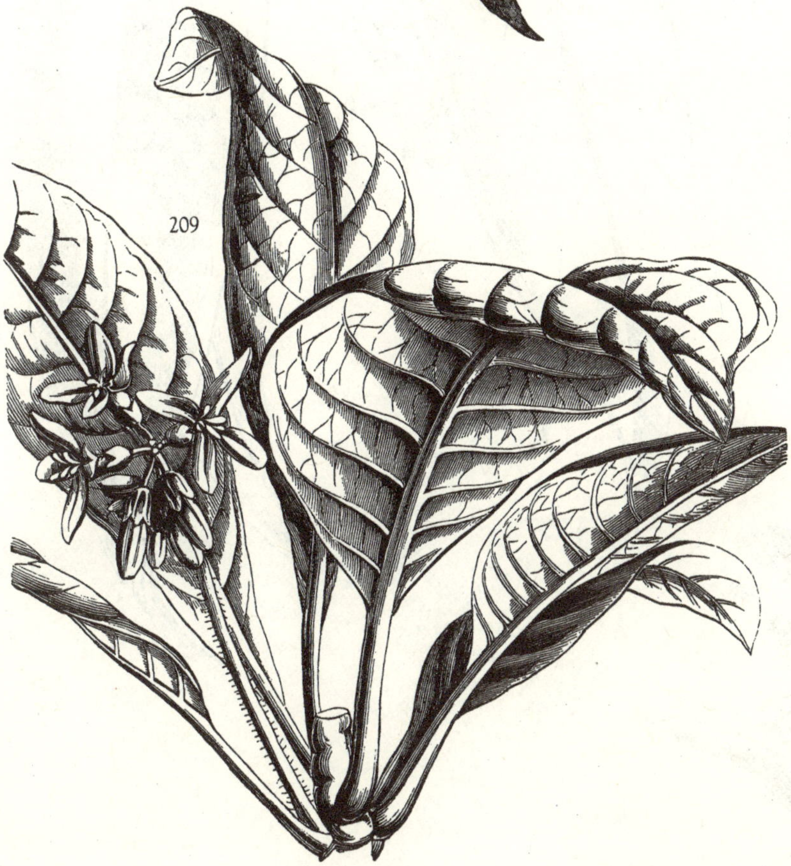

209

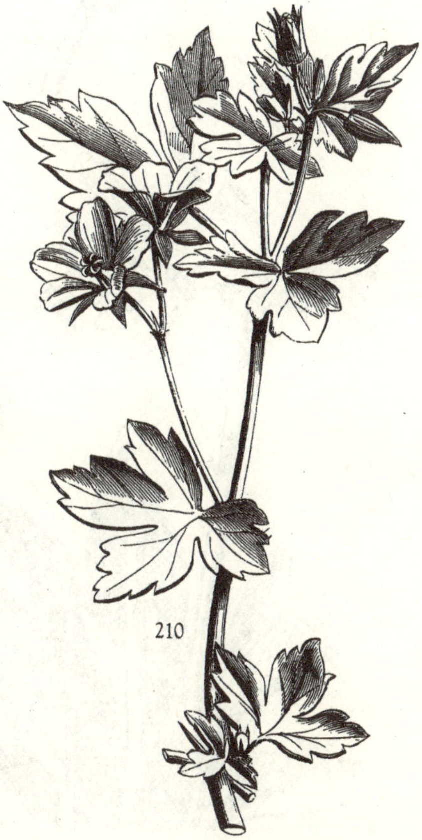

210

208. Common European hornbeam (*Carpinus betulus*). Fruiting catkins; from Europe. 209. *Campylobotrys discolor.* A dwarf half-shrubby plant, flowers rich red in clusters; from the Mexico-to-Argentina area. 210. *Geranium thunbergii.* A prostrate annual with small purple flowers; from Japan.

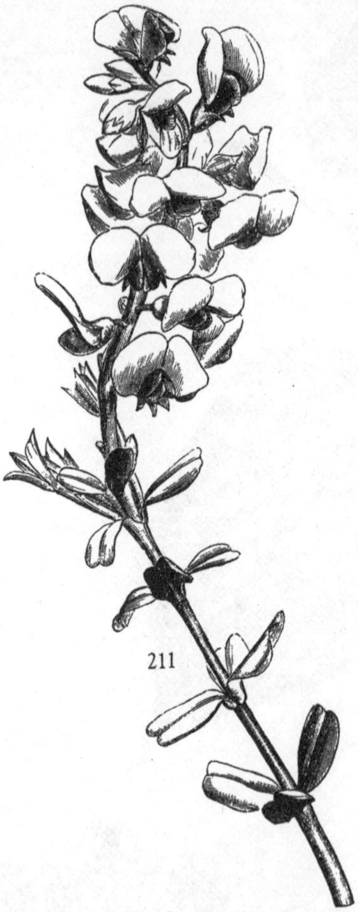
211

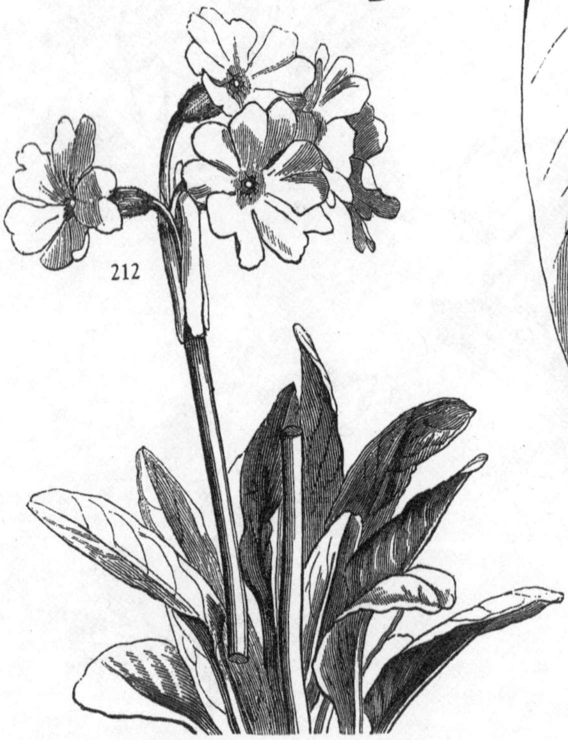
212

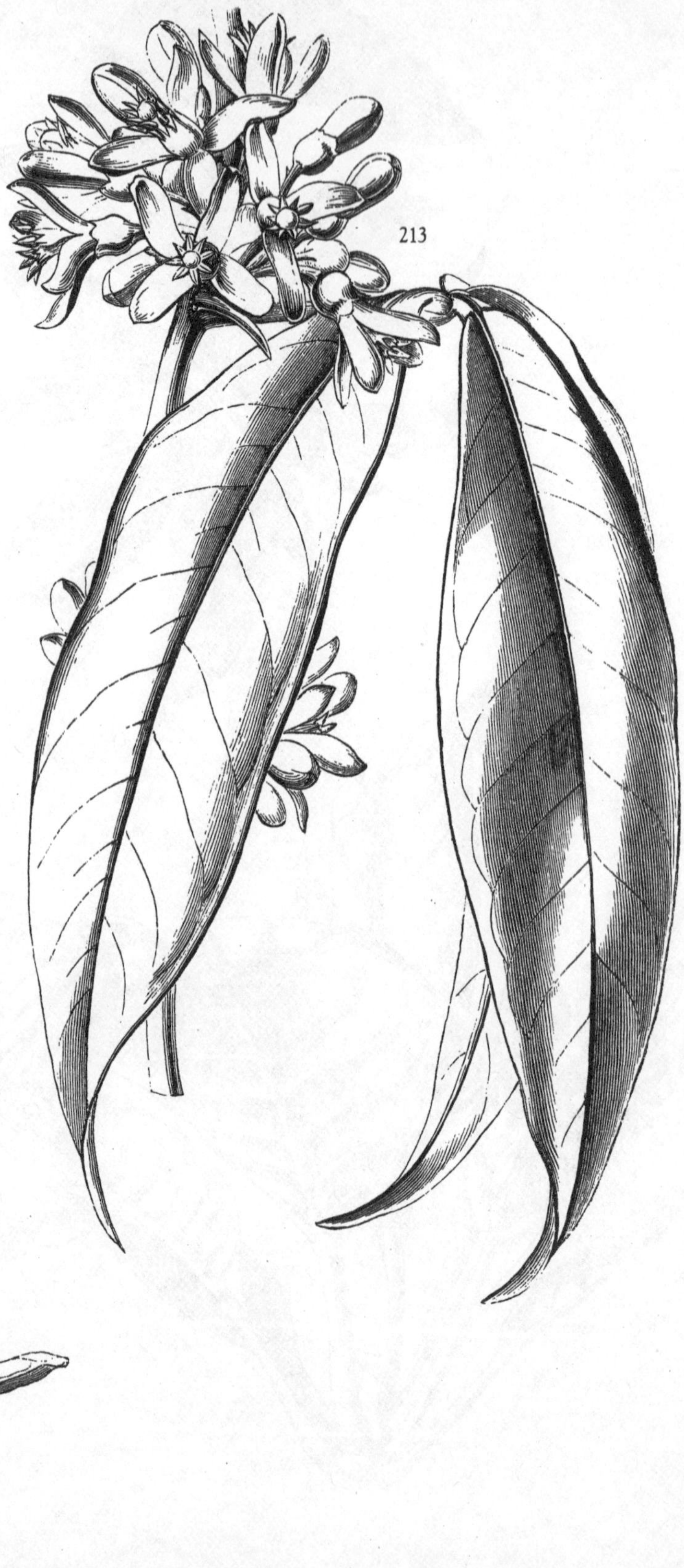
213

211. *Gastrolobium velutinum.* A shrub with rich orange flowers; from southwestern Australia. 212. *Primula involucrata.* A primrose, flowers white with a yellow eye; from the Himalayas. 213. *Luvunga scandens.* A plant with white flowers; from India.

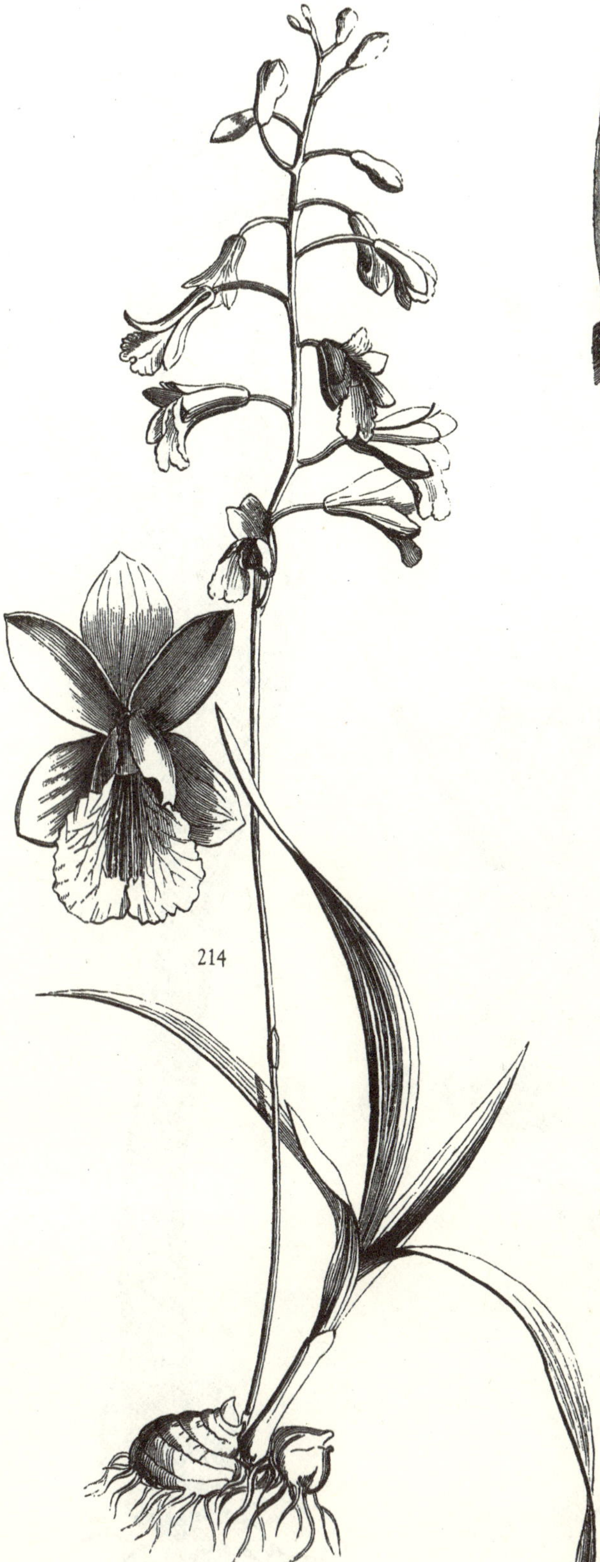

214

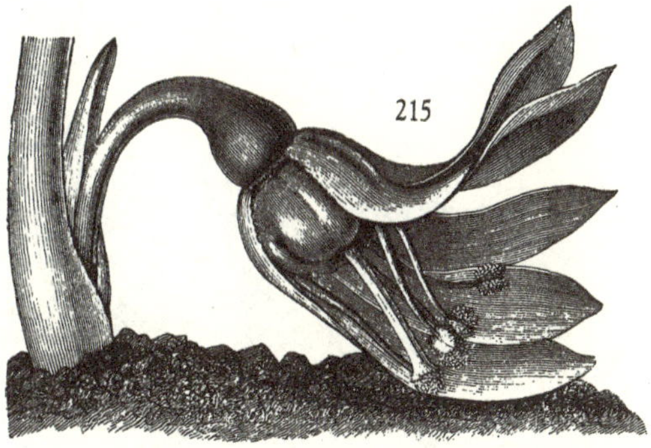

215

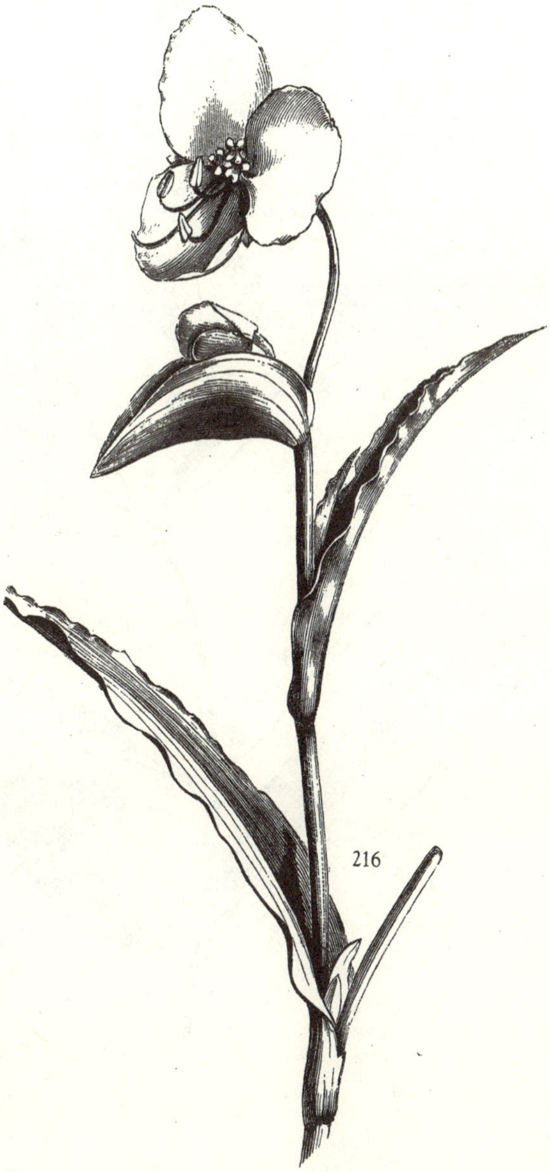

216

214. *Bletia patula.* A terrestrial tuberous orchid with rich purple flowers; from the West Indies. 215. *Allium chamaemoly.* See Fig. 24. 216. *Commelyna scabra.* A half-hardy perennial plant with glaucous waxy leaves and large dull purplish flowers; from Mexico.

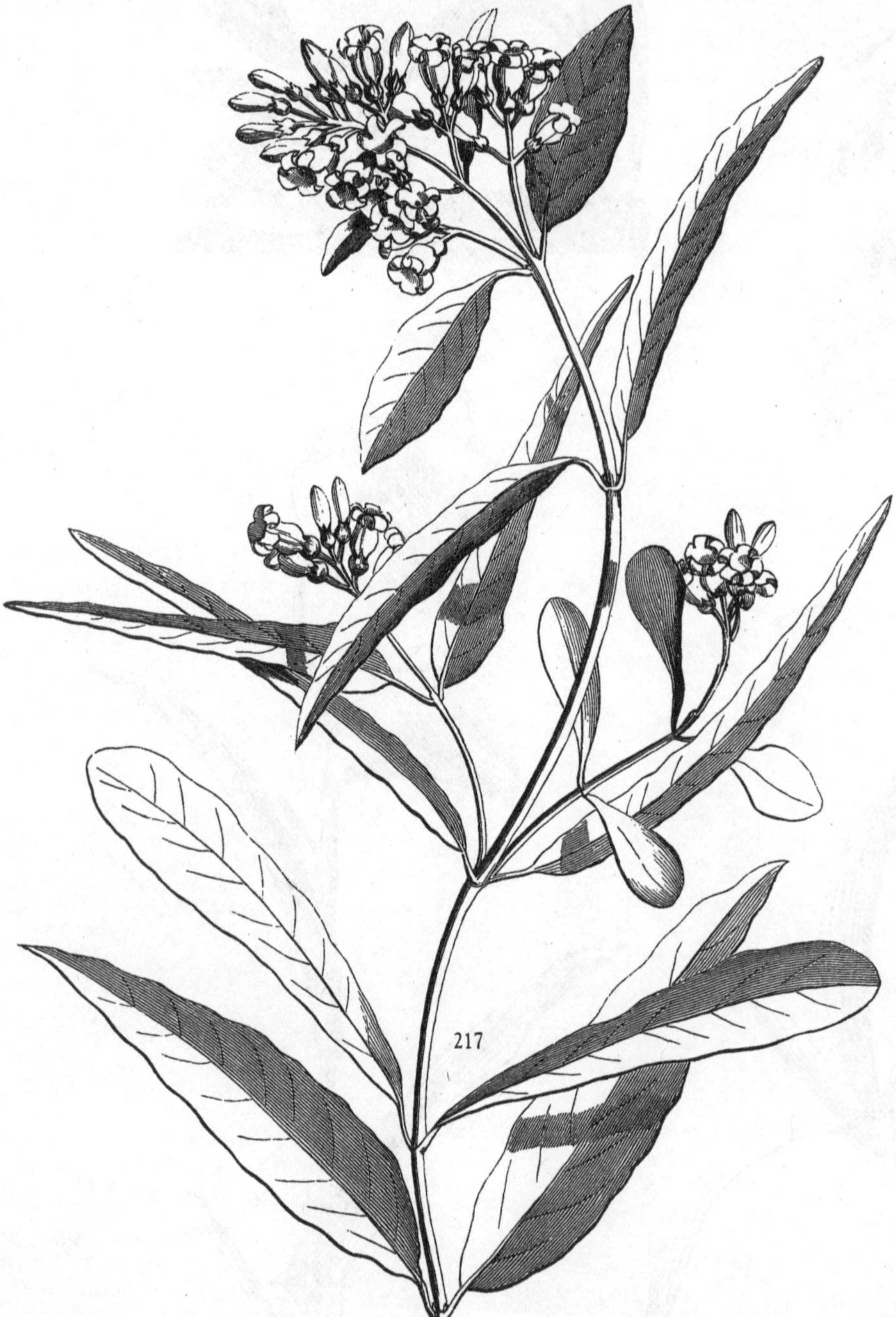
217

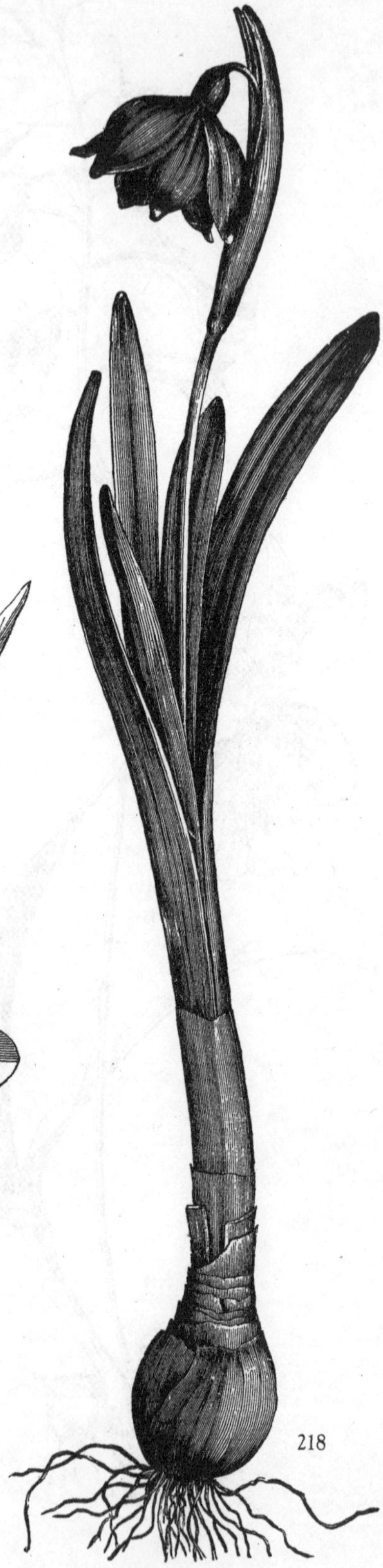
218

217. *Parsonsia heterophylla.* A twining evergreen shrub with white flowers; from New Zealand.
218. *Leucojum vernum.* A small herb with yellow flowers; from central Europe.

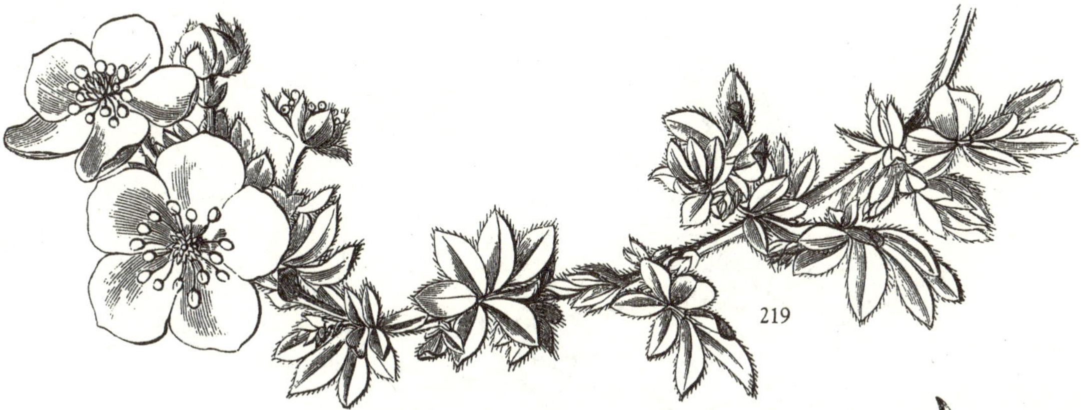
219

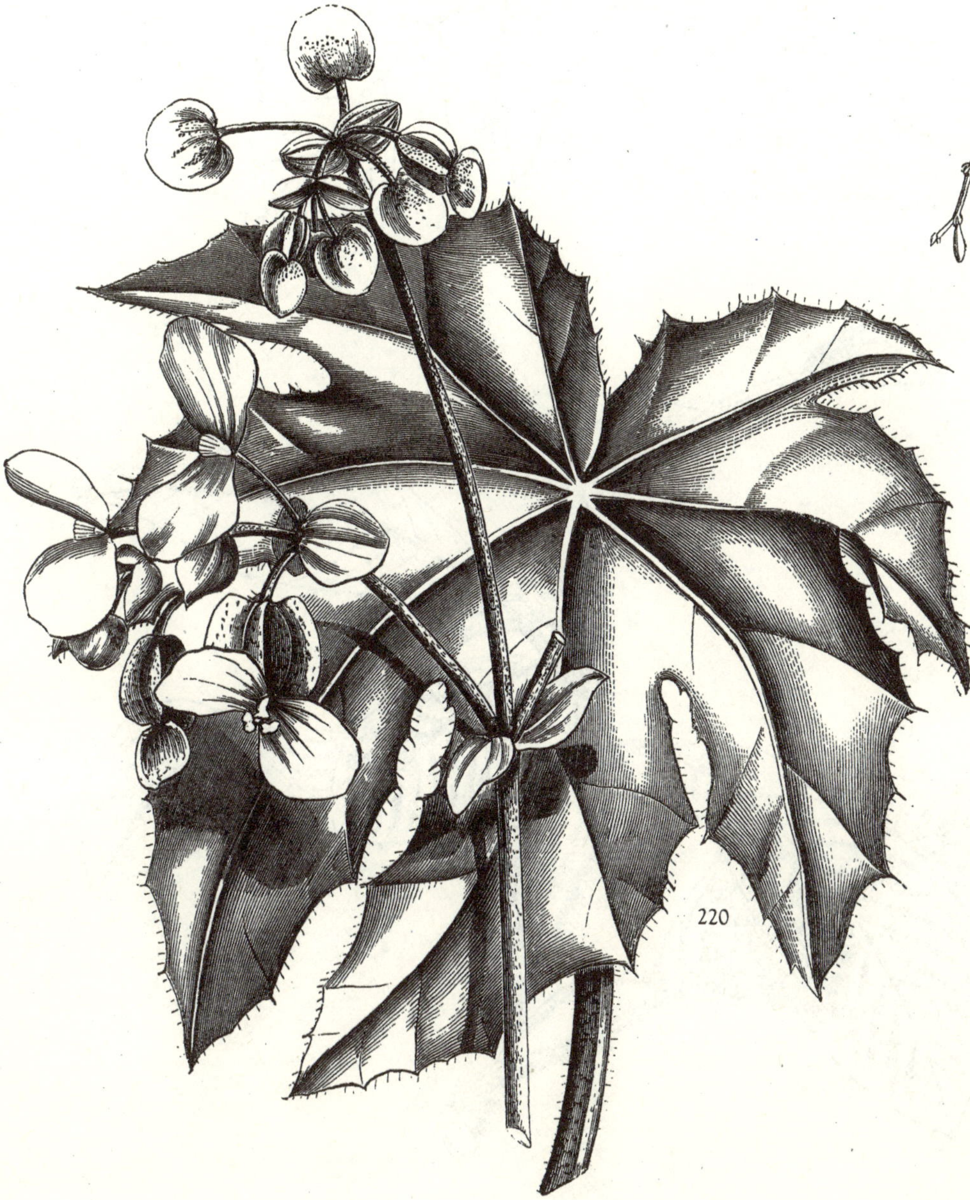
220

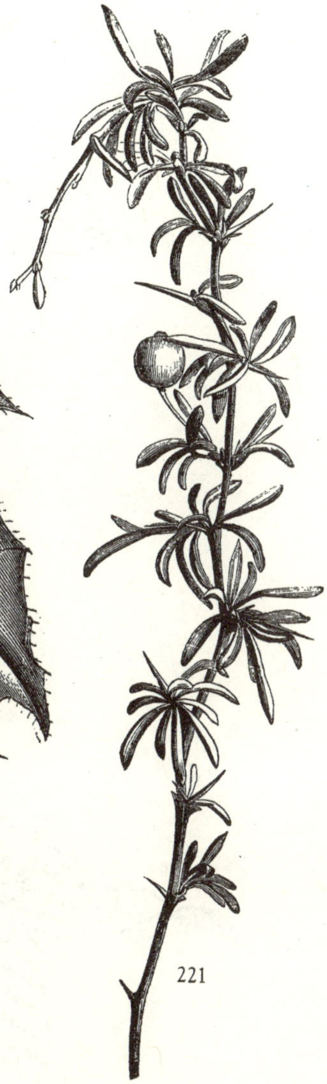
221

219. *Potentilla ochreata.* A hardy shrub with yellow flowers; from the Himalayas. 220. *Begonia punctata.* A perennial with pink flowers; from southern Mexico, Guatemala and Belize. 221. *Berberis empetrifolia.* A narrow-leaved dwarf evergreen bush with solitary deep yellow flowers; from Patagonia and southern Chile.

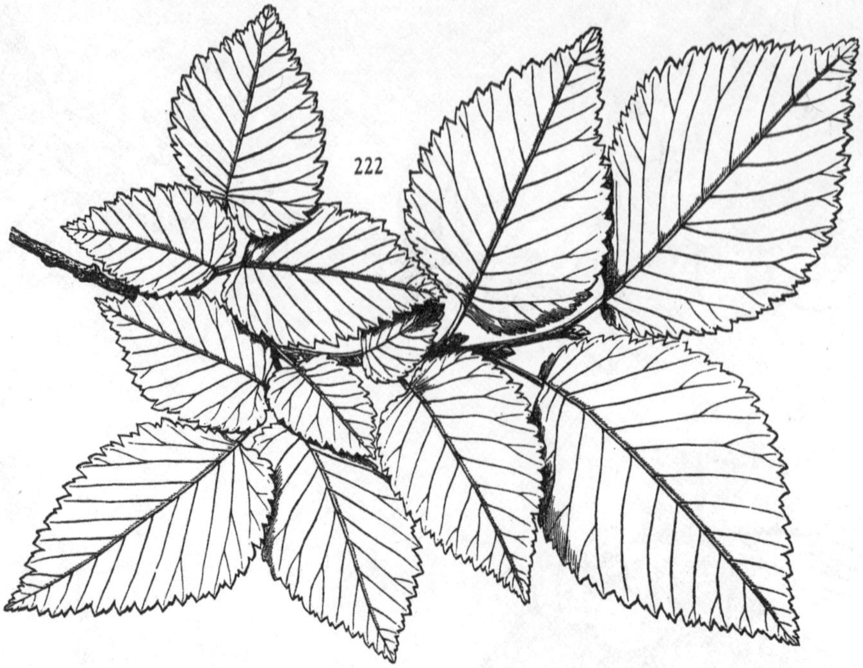

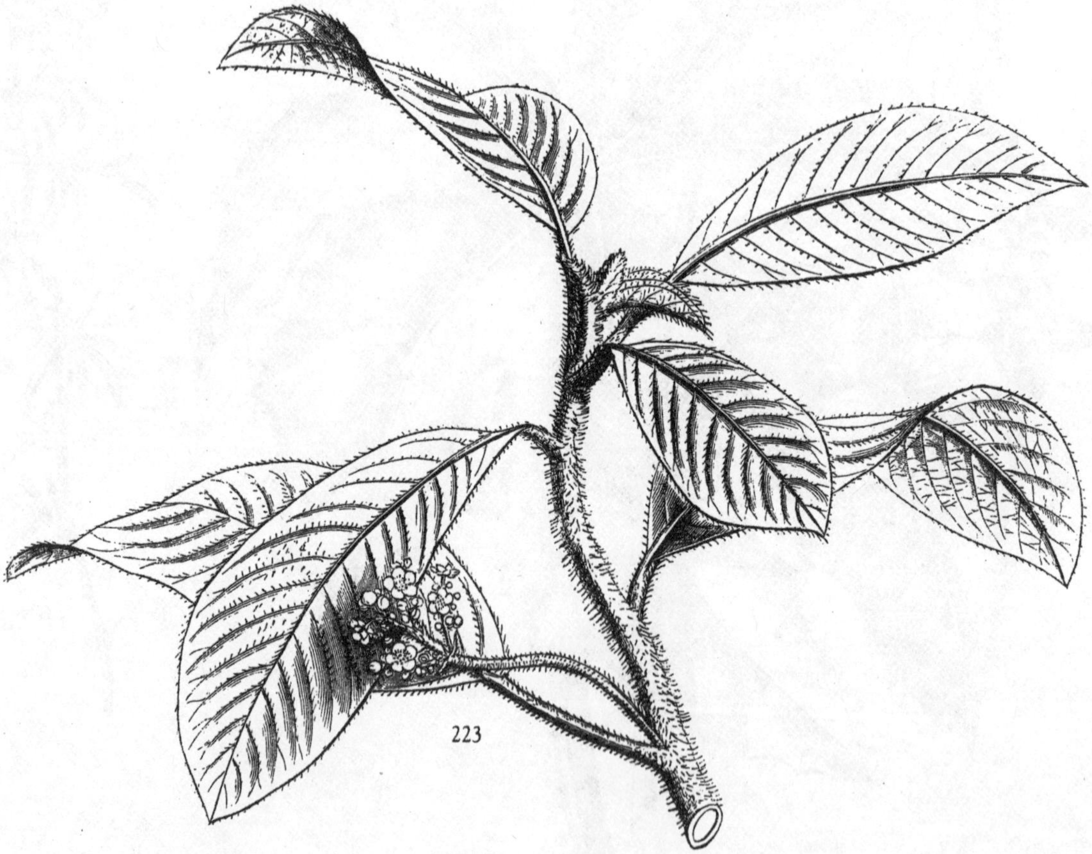

222. The leafy horizontal twig of an elm (*Ulmus*). 223. *Saurauja macrophylla.* See Fig. 47.

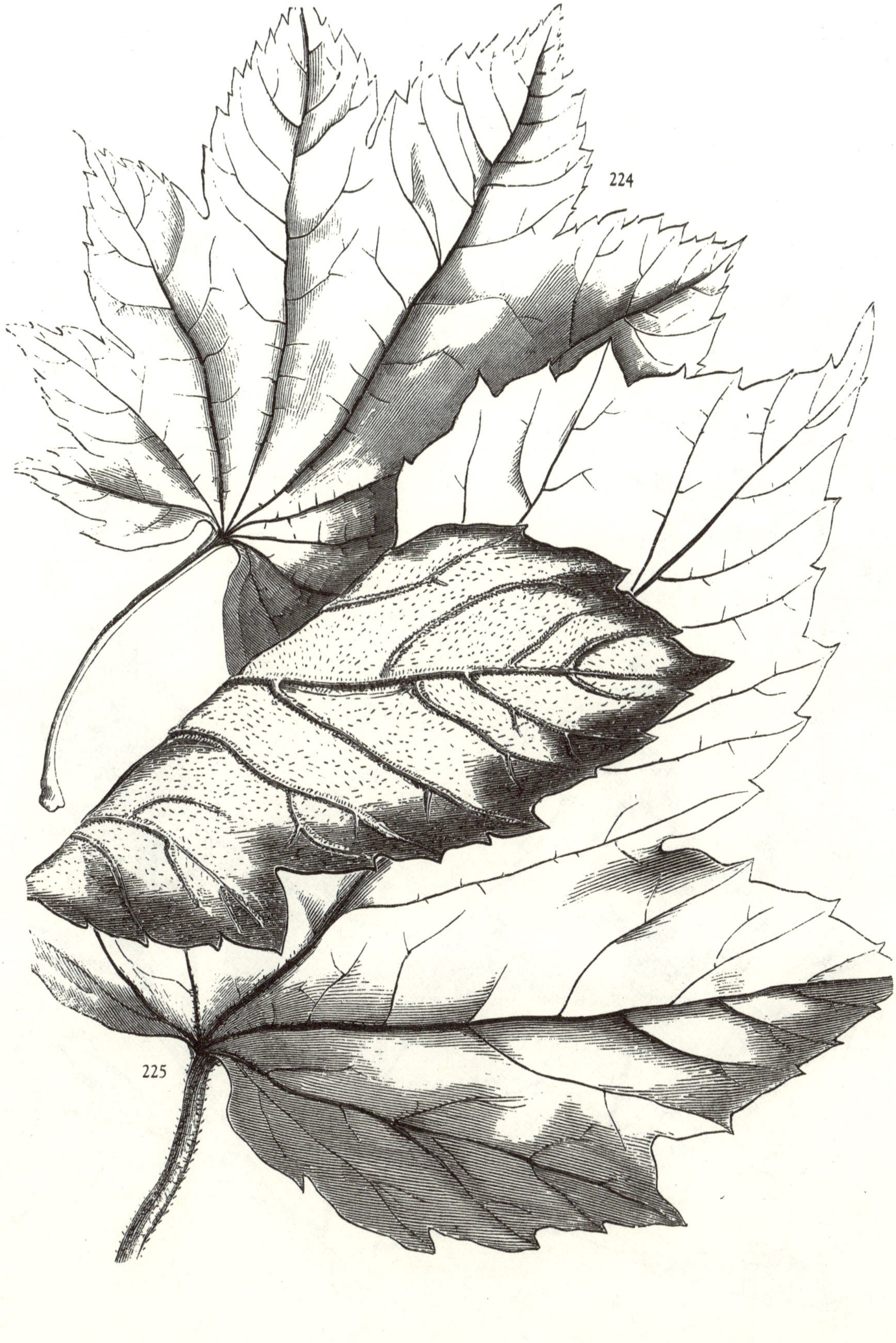

224. Vine maple *(Acer circinatum).* Purple and white flowers and leaves rich crimson in the autumn; from the area of British Columbia to northern California. 225. *Acer villosum.* A tree with the aspect of a sycamore; from the Himalayas.

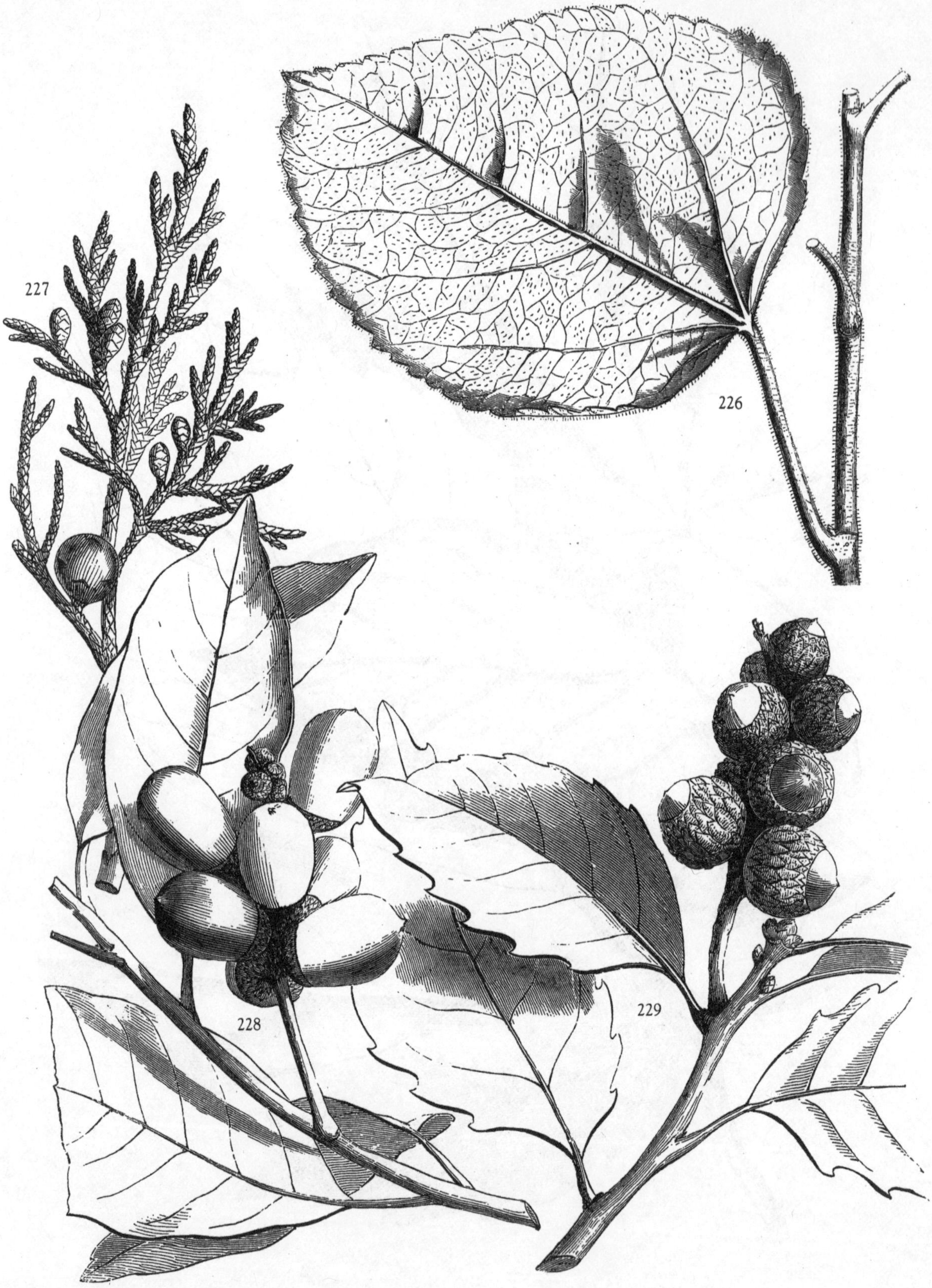

226. *Ficus virgata.* A fig with broad rough leaves; from the north of India. 227. *Juniperus sphaerica.* An evergreen tree; from the north of China. 228. *Quercus inversa.* An evergreen oak with deep green leaves; from the north of China. 229. *Quercus sclerophylla.* An evergreen oak; from the north of China.

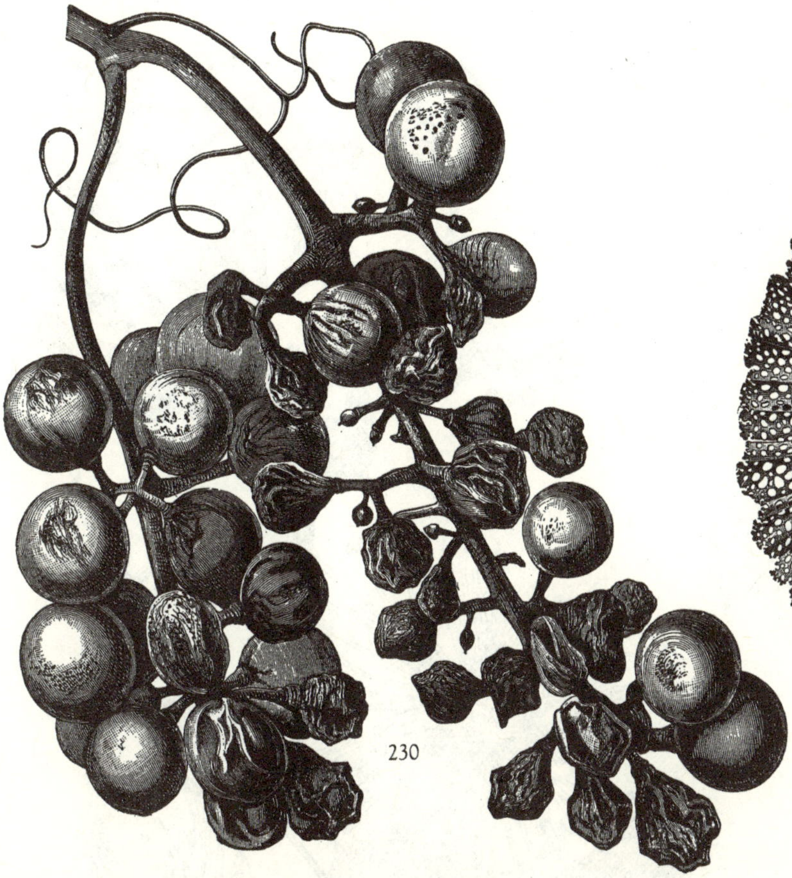

230

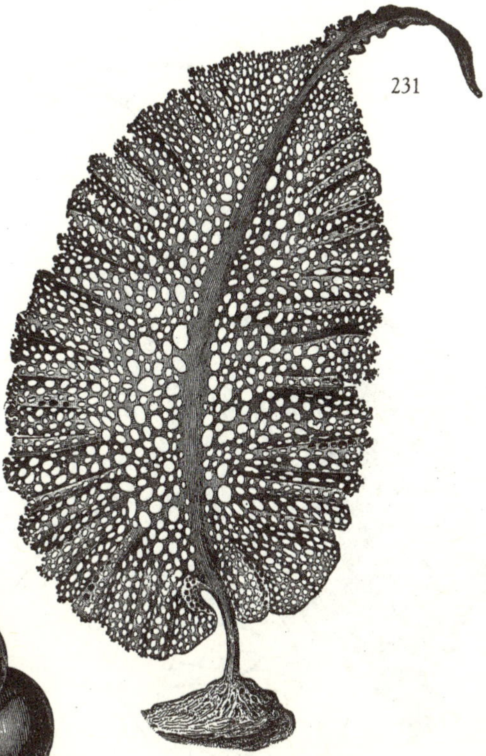

231

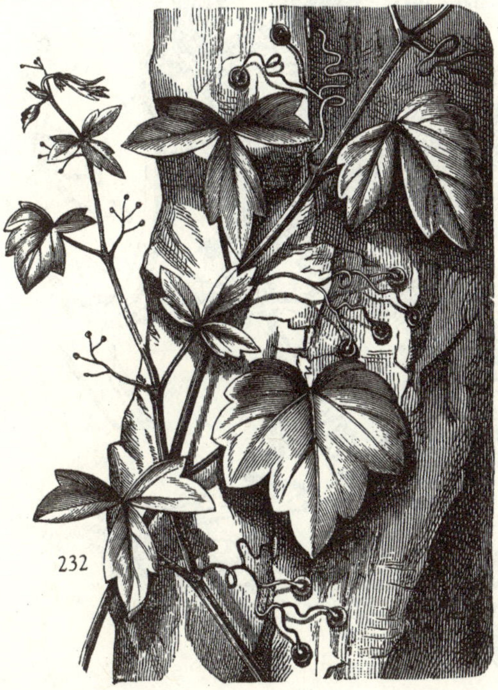

232

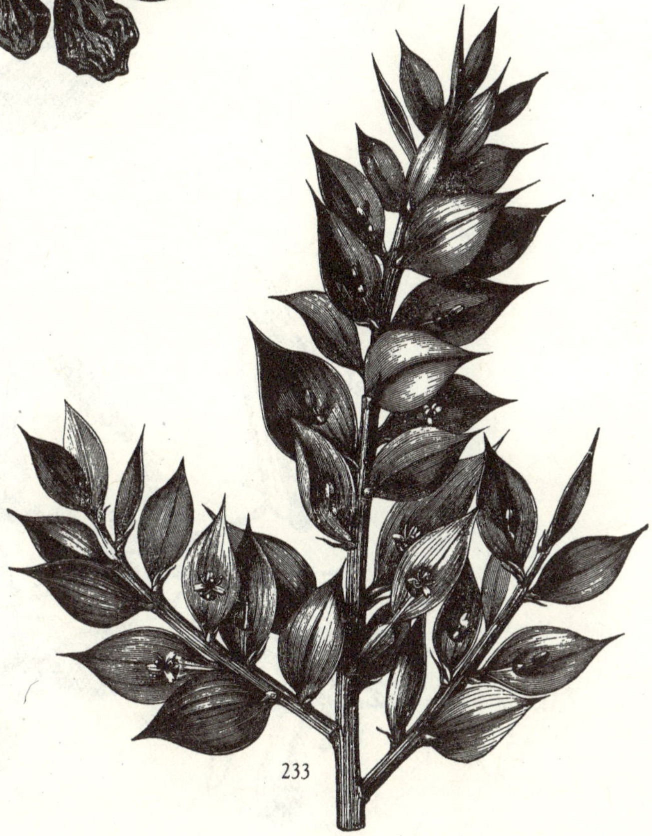

233

230. A bunch of grapes attacked by the false vine mildew (*Peronospora viticola*). 231. *Agarum gmelini.* A kelp frond; from the North Atlantic. 232. *Vitis (Ampelopsis) inserta.* A grape with light-avoiding tendrils. 233. A branch of butcher's broom (*Ruscus aculeatus*). See Fig. 22.

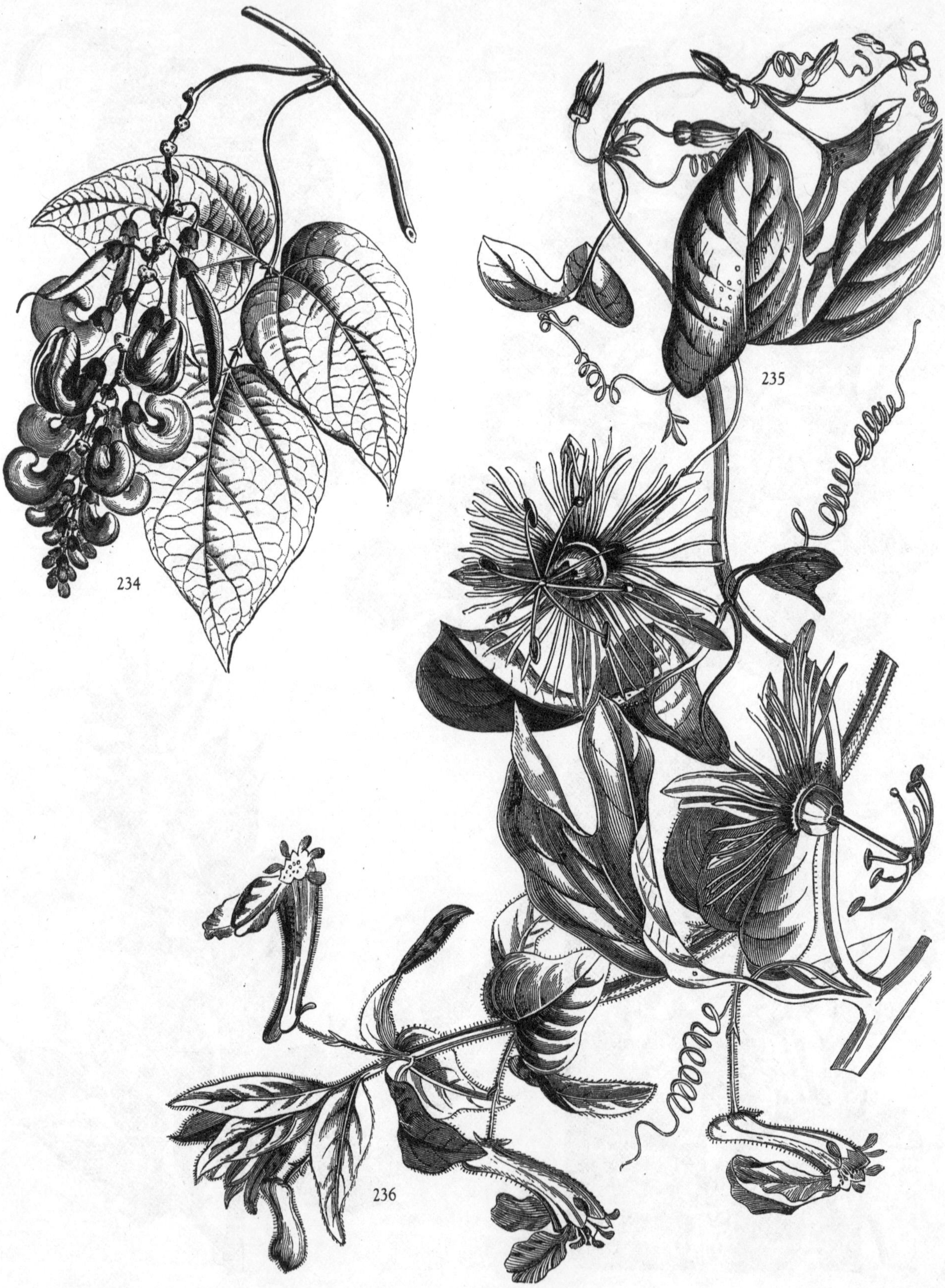

234. *Physostigma venenosum.* A woody vine yielding the calabar bean; from Africa. 235. *Passiflora medusaea.* A passionflower with red and yellow flowers; from tropical America. 236. *Cuphea cinnabarina.* A half-shrubby plant with crimson or deep purple flowers; from Guatemala.

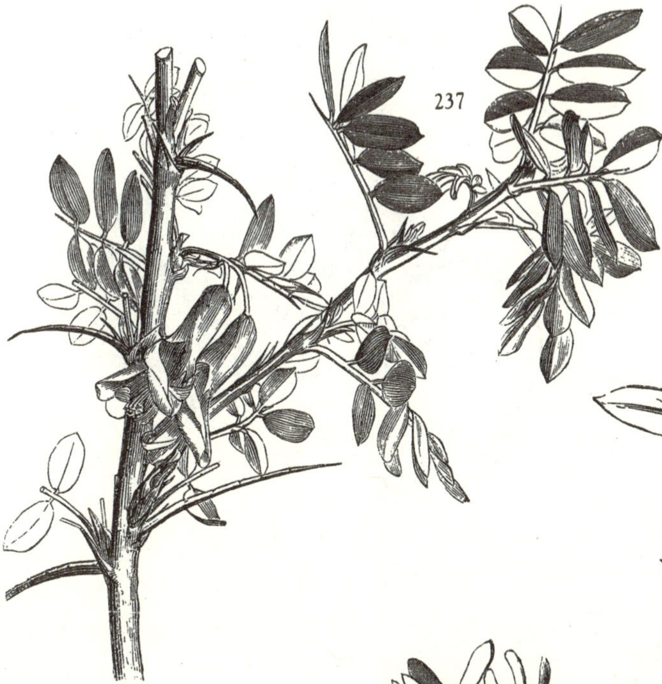

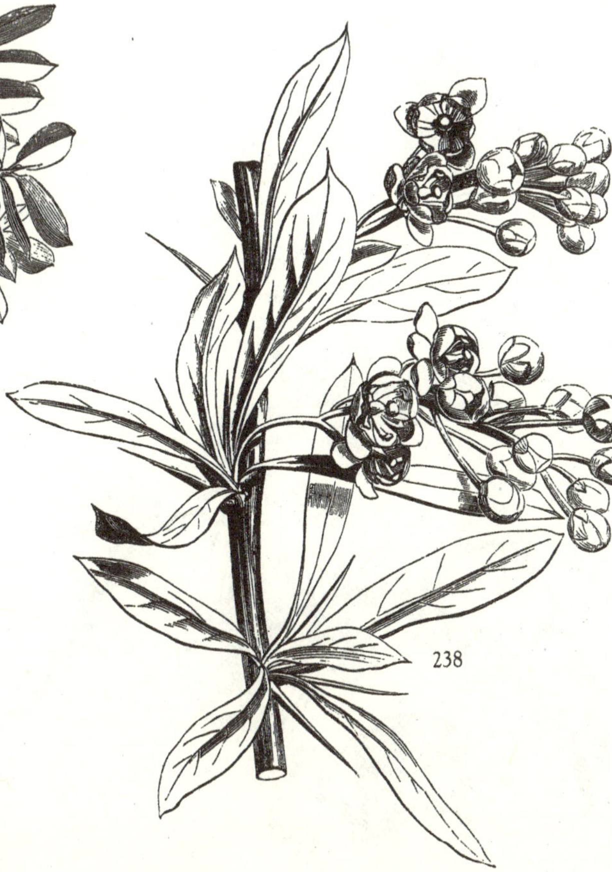

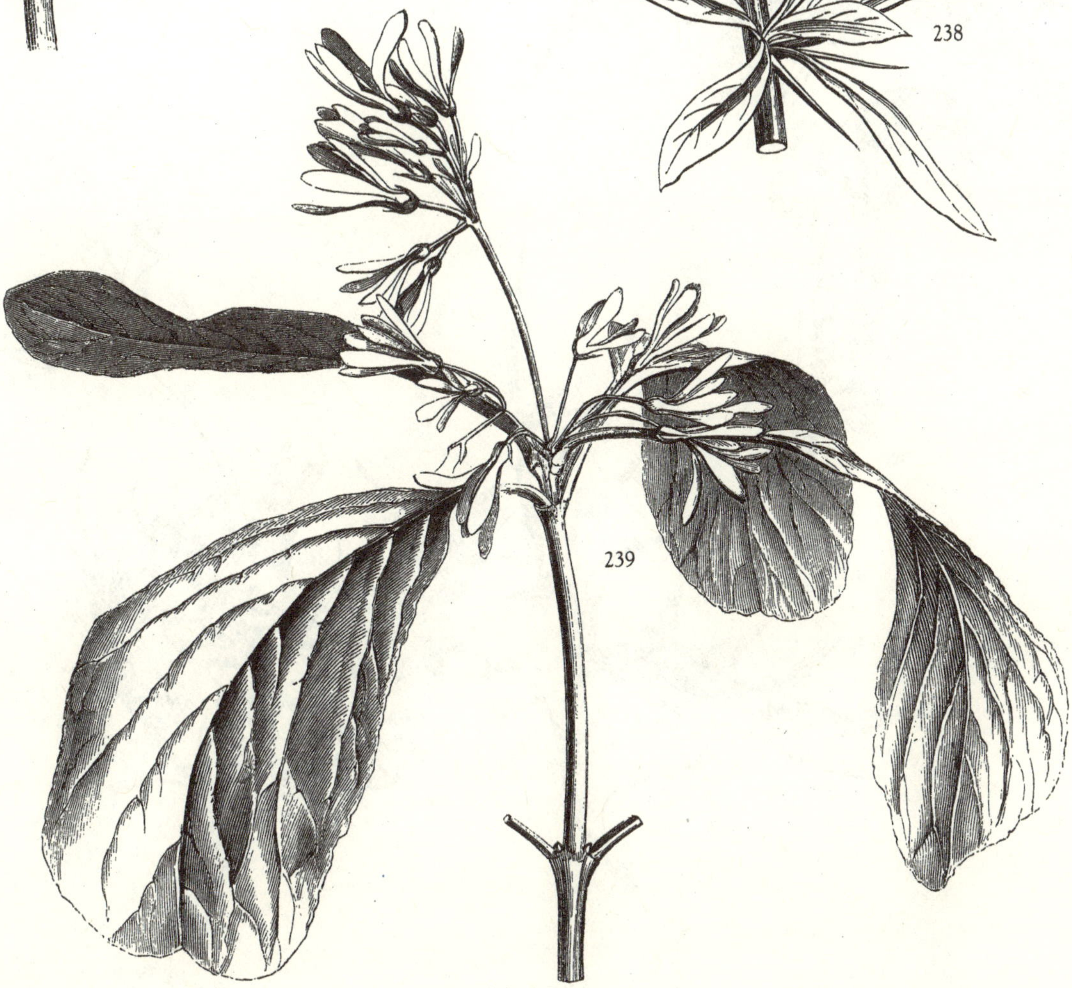

237. *Caragana triflora.* A hardy half-evergreen shrub with yellow flowers; from Nepal. 238. *Berberis umbellata.* A hardy evergreen bush with pale yellow flowers; from the Himalayas. 239. Fringe tree (*Chionanthus retusus*). White flowers; from China.

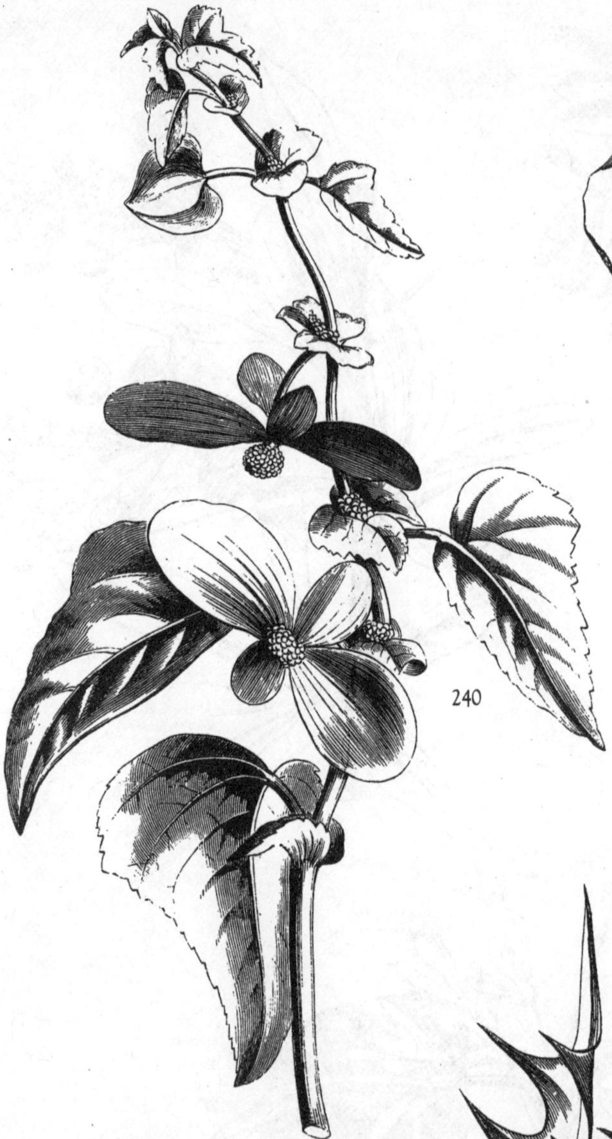

240

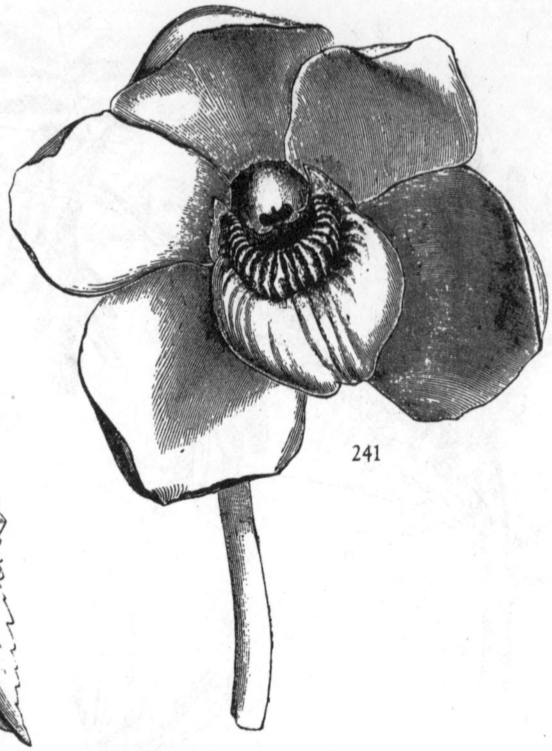

241

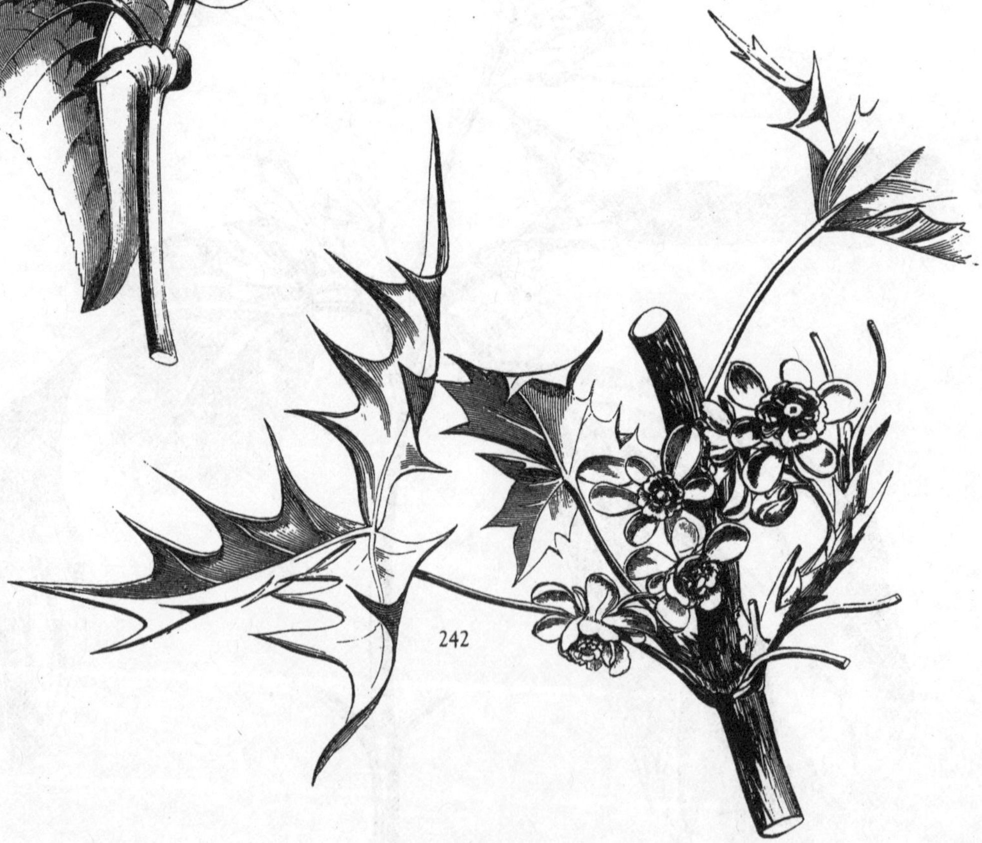

242

240. *Begonia bulbillifera.* See Fig. 72. 241. *Huntleya cerina.* An orchid with pale yellow flowers; from Central and South America. 242. *Berberis trifoliata.* A half-hardy evergreen shrub with small, pure yellow flowers; from Texas and Mexico.

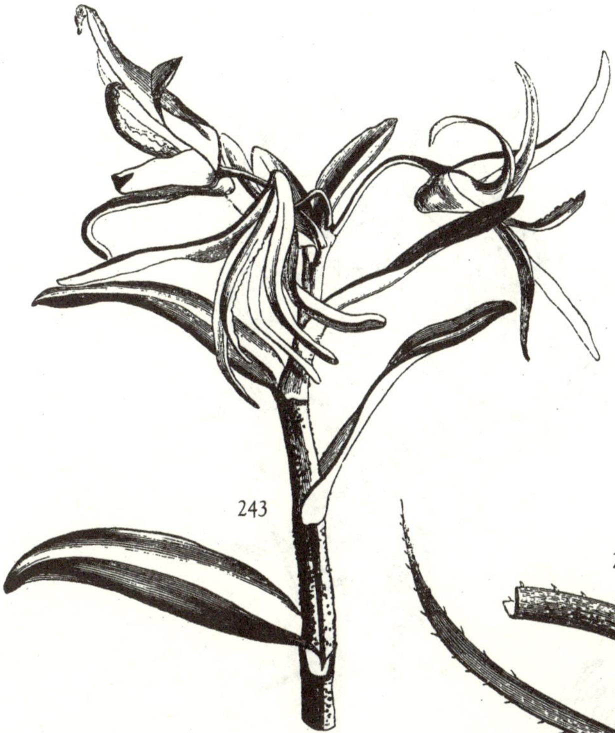

243

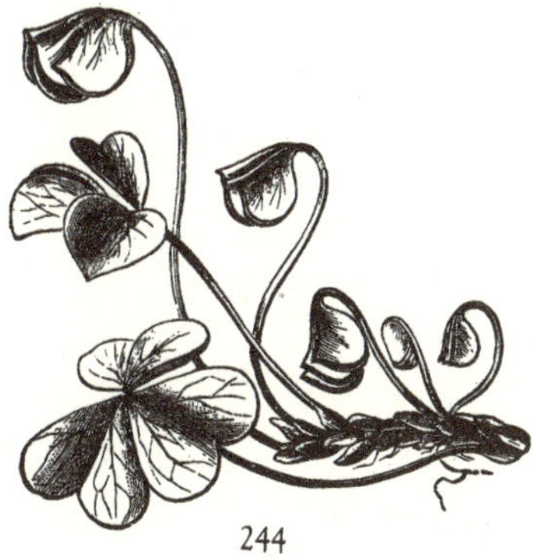

244

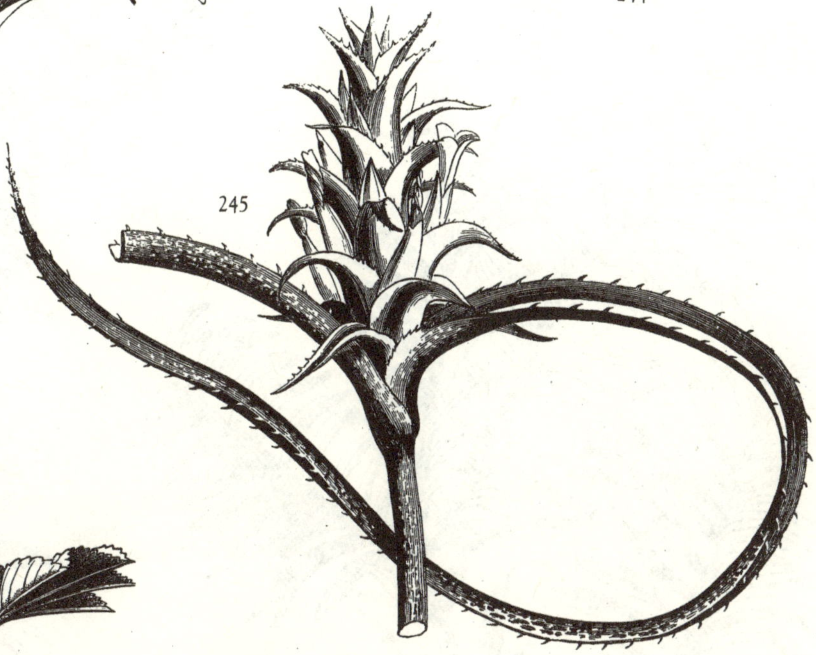

245

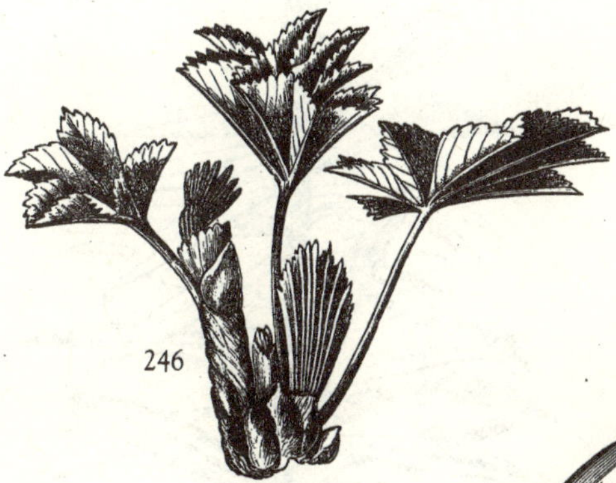

246

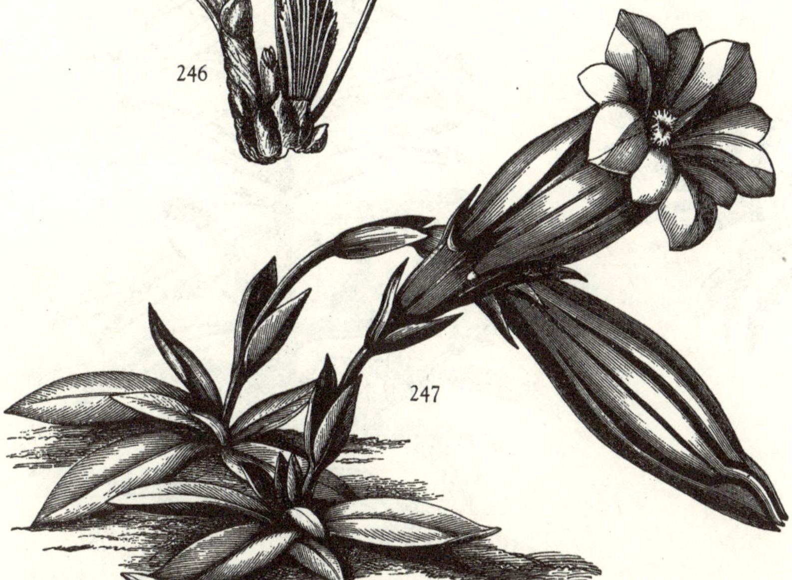

247

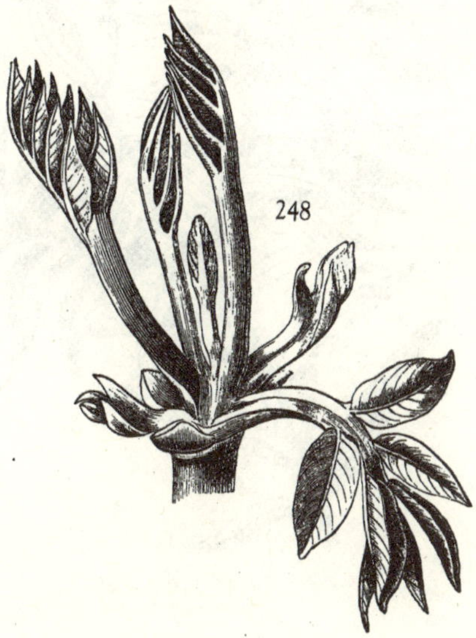

248

243. *Dendrobium villosulum.* An orchid with rich orange-colored flowers and rough stems; from India. 244. Wood sorrel *(Oxalis acetosella)* unfolding its leaves; from Europe, and north and central Asia to Japan. 245. *Acanthostachys strobilacea.* A perennial with very narrow spiny leaves and a short prickly cone of yellow flowers in orange-colored bracts; from Mexico. 246. Lady's mantle *(Alchemilla vulgaris).* An herb with greenish or yellowish flowers; from Europe. 247. *Gentiana clusii.* A perennial herb, in flower and furled; from the mountains of central and southern Europe. 248. *Juglans regia* unfolding its leaves. See Fig. 73.

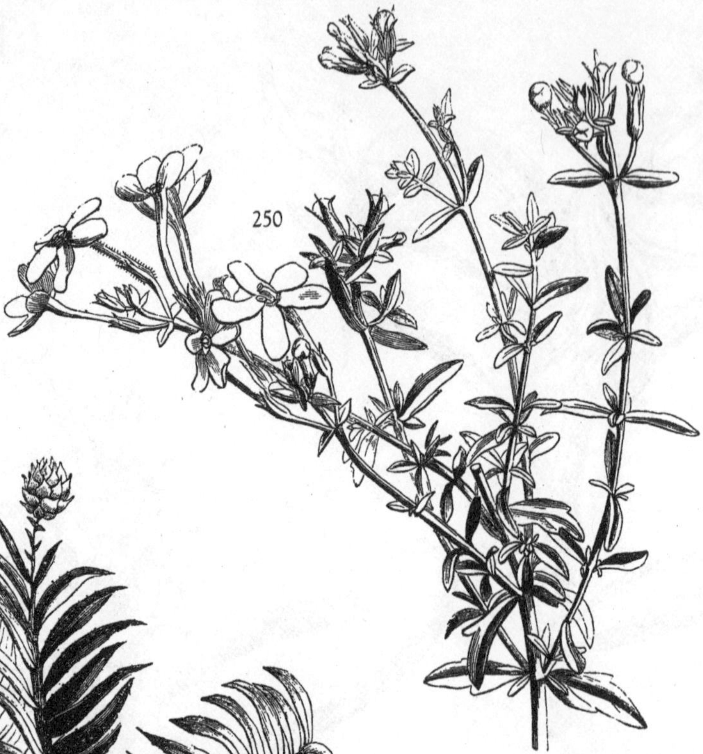

250

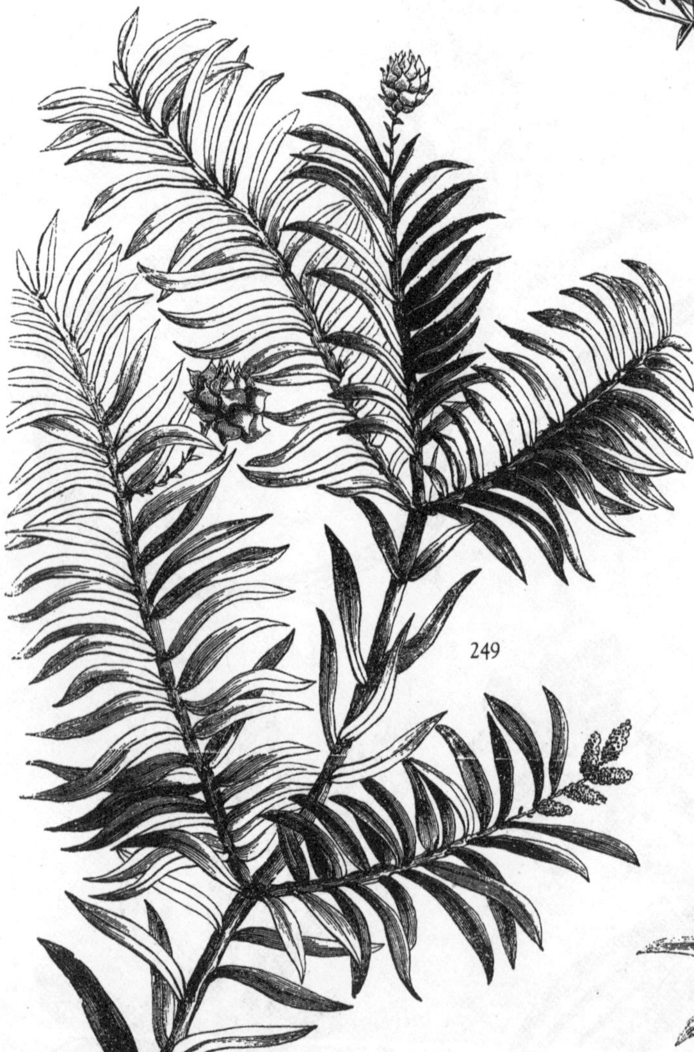

249

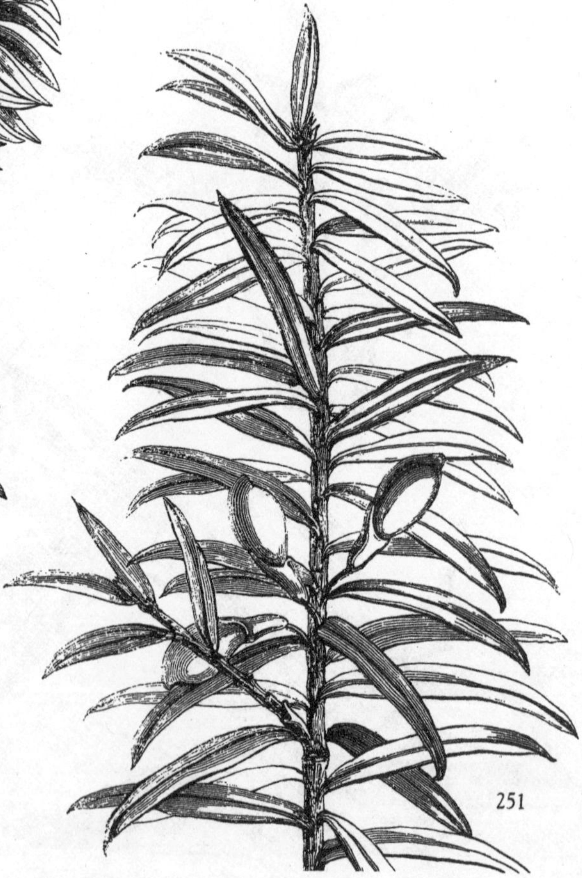

251

249. Prince Albert yew (*Saxe-Gothaea conspicua*). From northern Chile. 250. *Chaenostoma linifolium*. A little shrub with long white flowers having a yellow orifice; from South Africa. 251. *Podocarpus nubigena*. An evergreen bush or tree; from southern Chile.

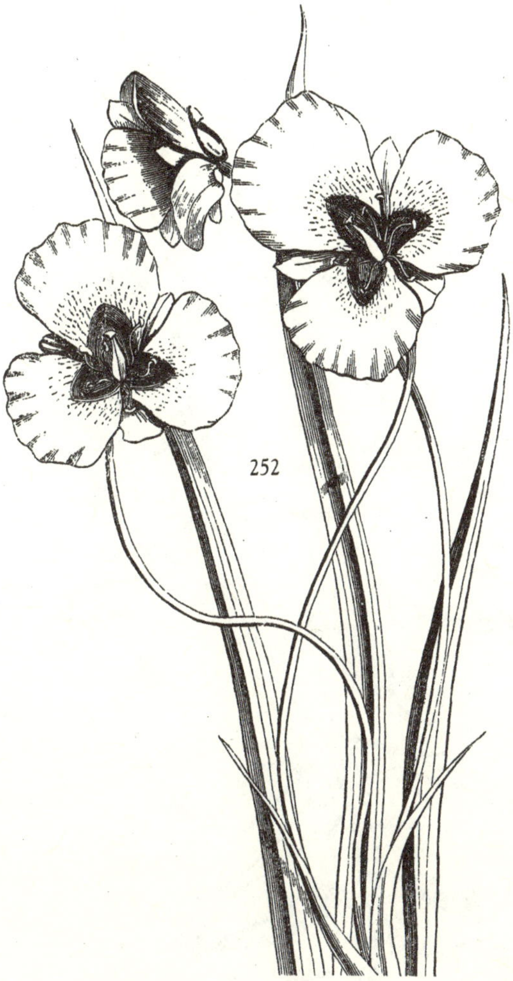

252

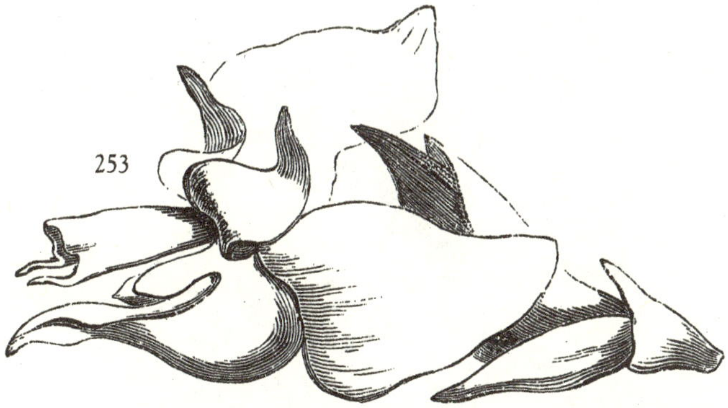

253

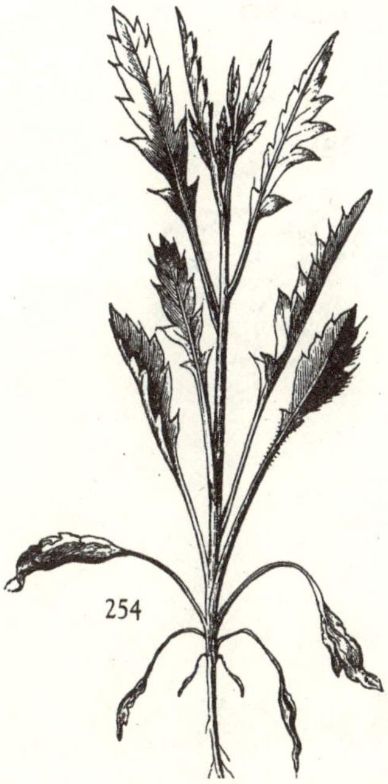

254

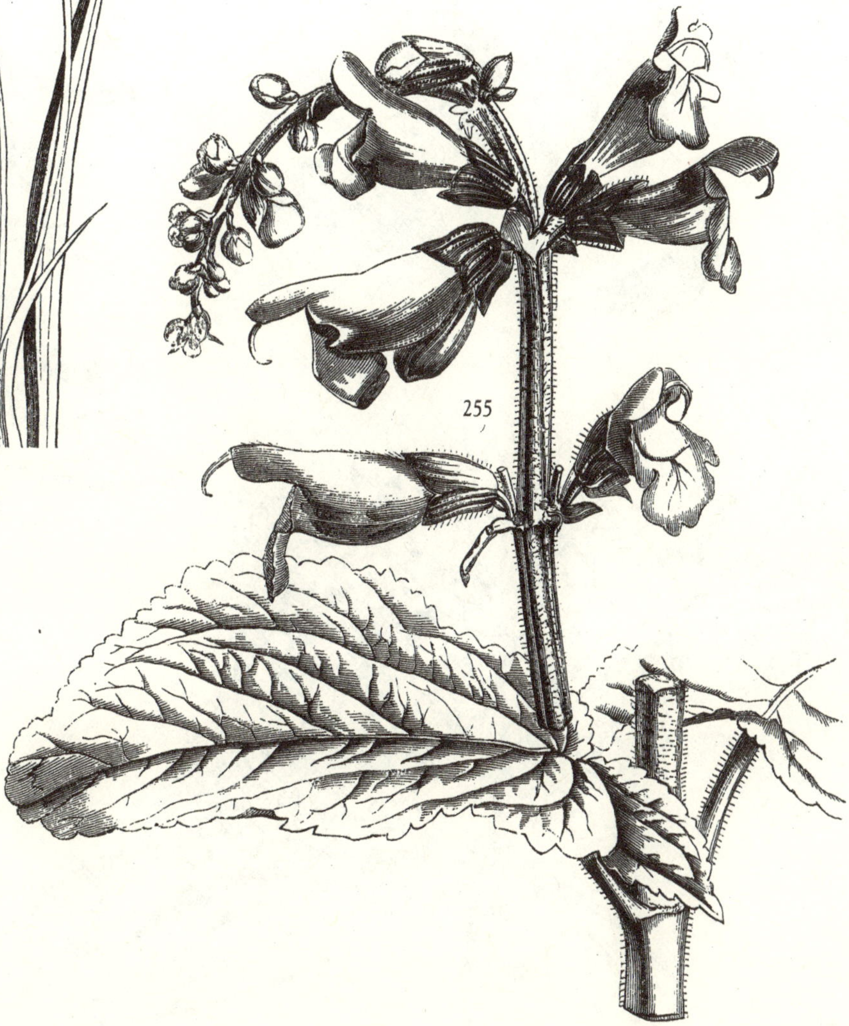

255

252. *Calochortus pallidus.* A tender bulbous plant, flowers dirty brown with a deep triangular spot at the base of each petal; from western North America. 253. *Stanhopea cirrhata.* An orchid; from tropical America. 254. *Papaver.* The metamorphoses of the leaves of the poppy. See Fig. 104. 255. *Salvia hians.* A hardy herbaceous plant with violet and white flowers; from Kashmir.

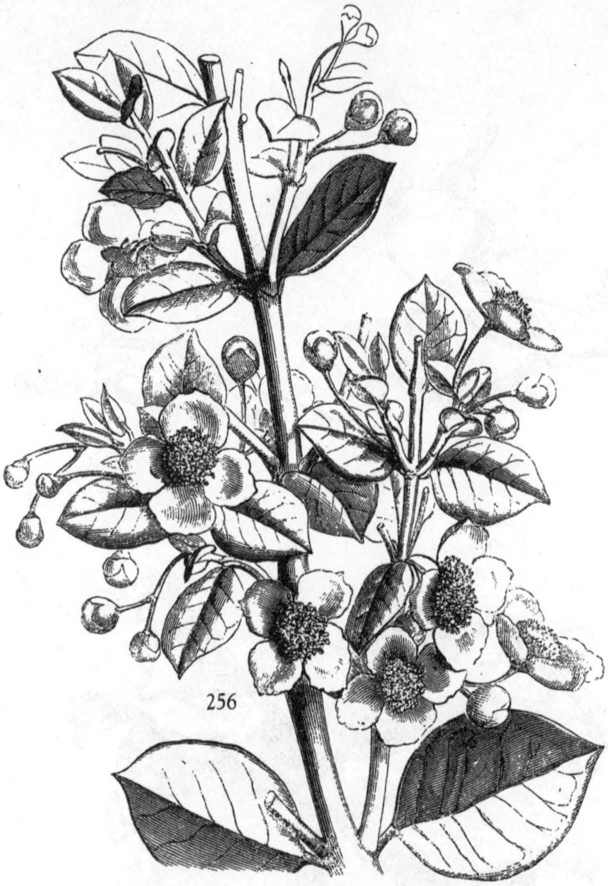

256

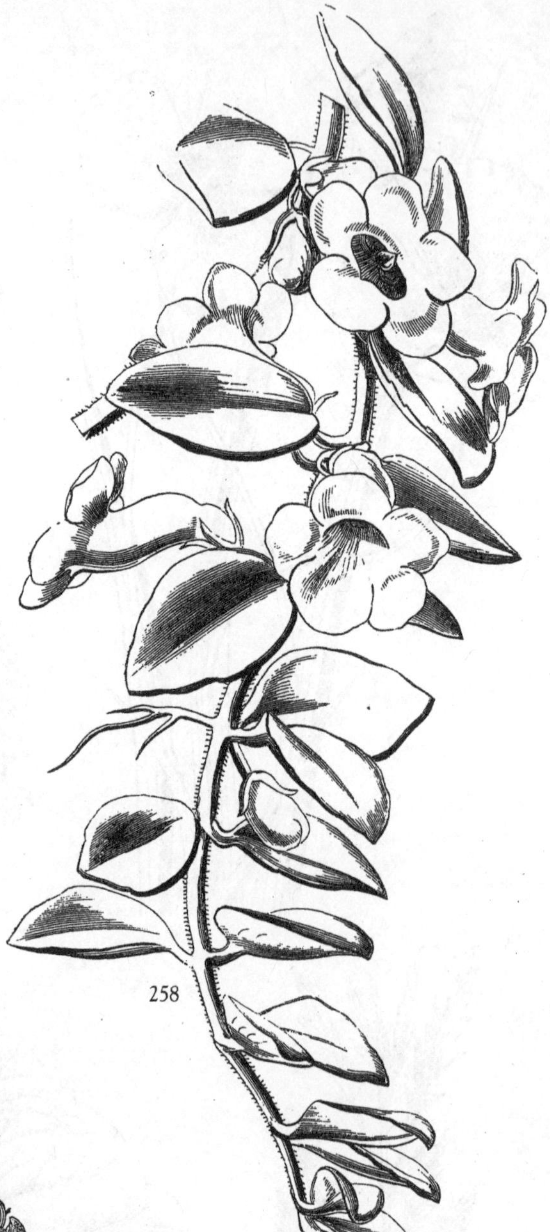

258

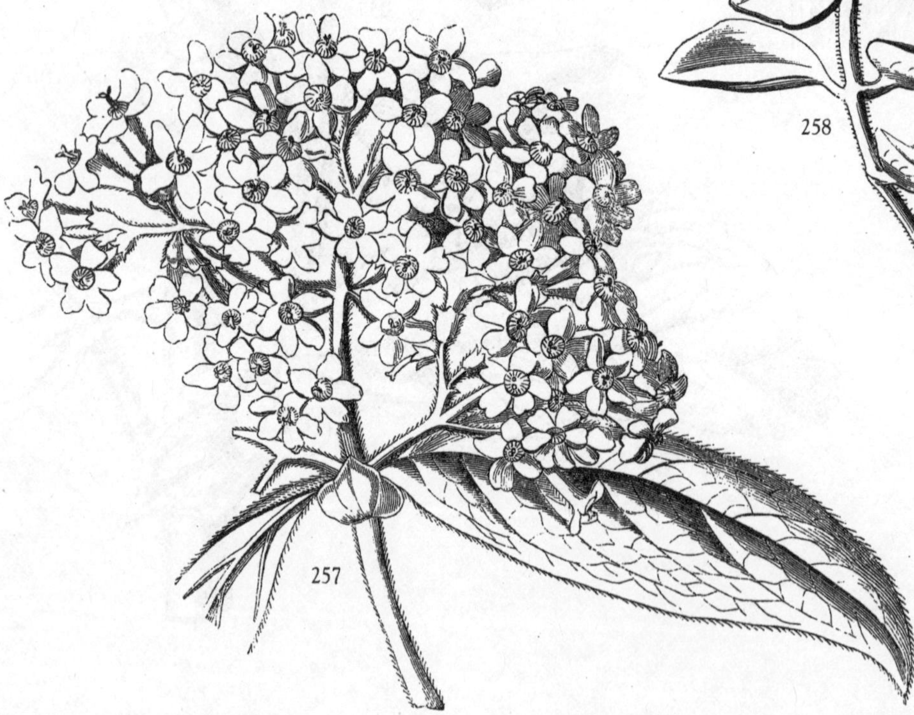

257

256. *Eugenia (?) apiculata.* An evergreen half-hardy shrub with white flowers and deep purple fruit; from Chile and adjacent Argentina. 257. *Rogiera amoena.* A shrub with clusters of rose-colored flowers; from Guatemala. 258. *Hypocyrta gracilis.* A creeping vine with warm-colored flowers; from Brazil.

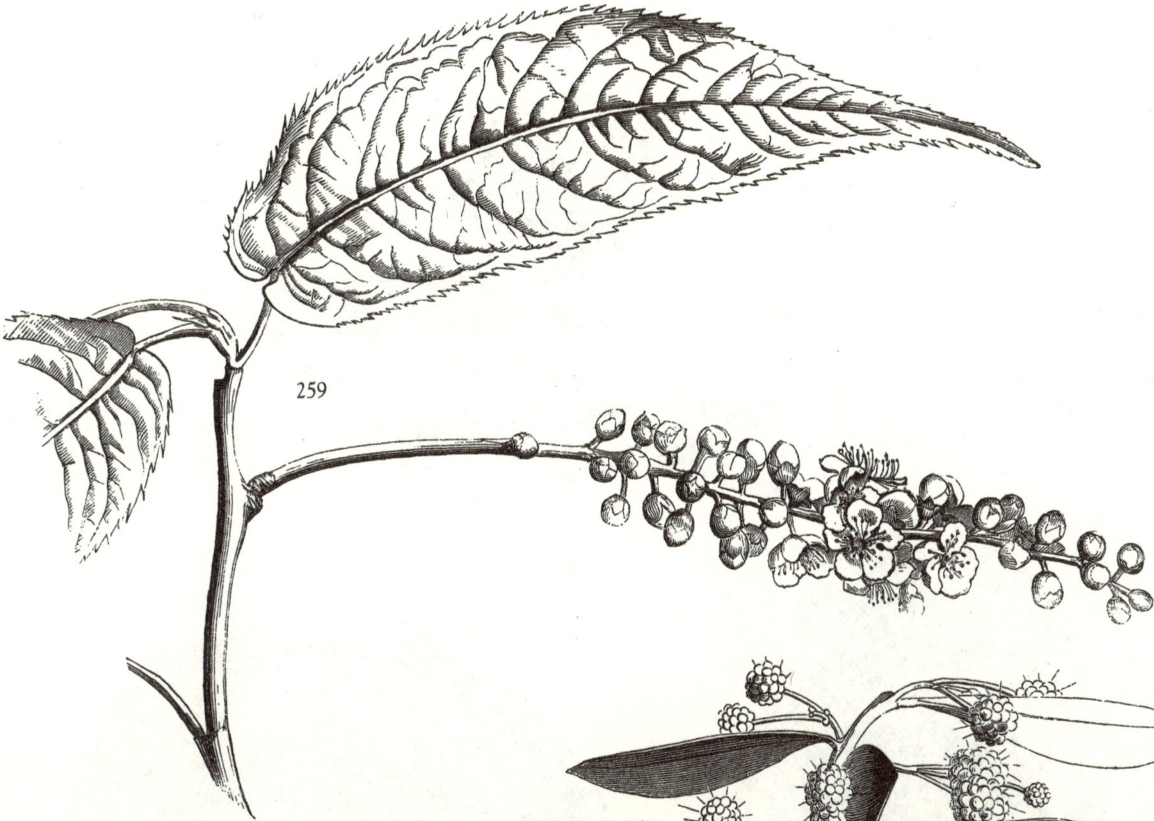

259

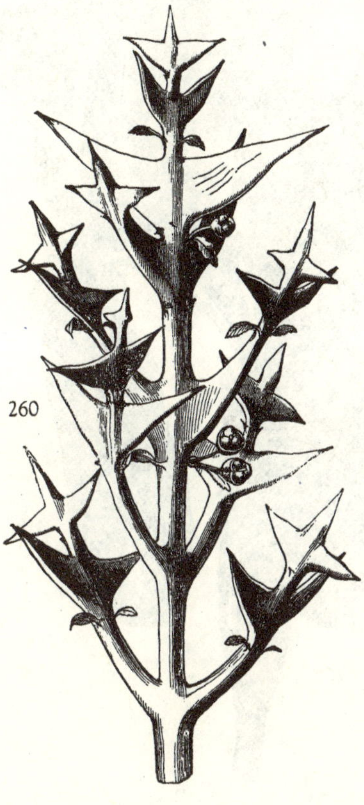

260

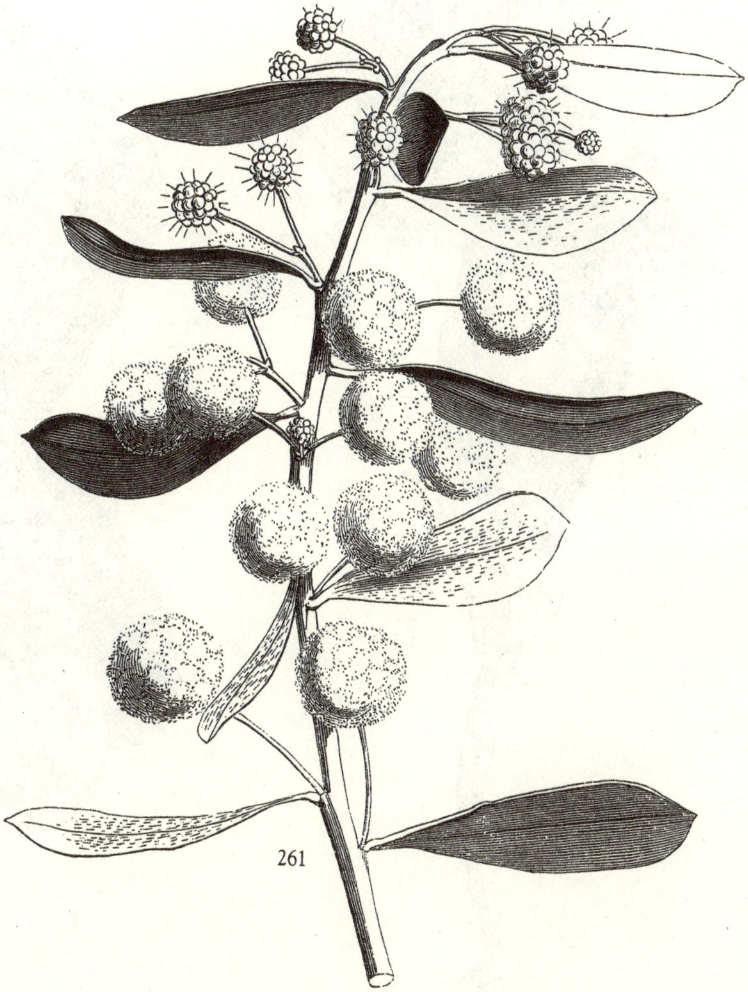

261

259. *Cerasus nepalensis.* A hardy deciduous tree with white flowers; from Nepal. 260. Anchor plant *(Colletia cruciata).* Yellowish-white flowers; from southern Brazil and Uruguay. 261. *Acacia bombycina.* A silky-leaved shrub with bright yellow flowers; from southwestern Australia.

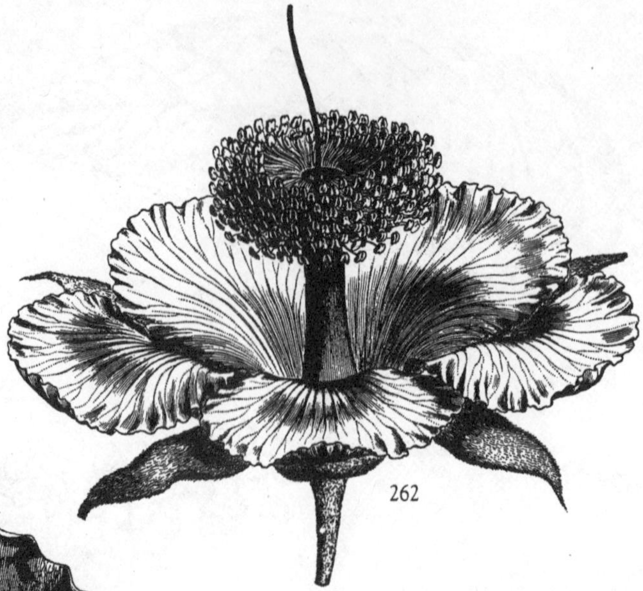

262

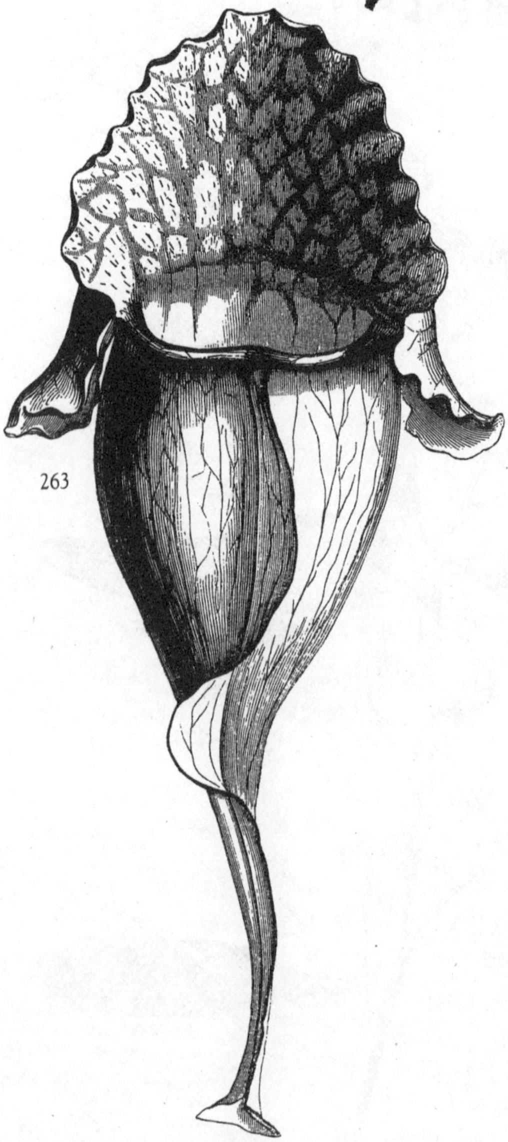

263

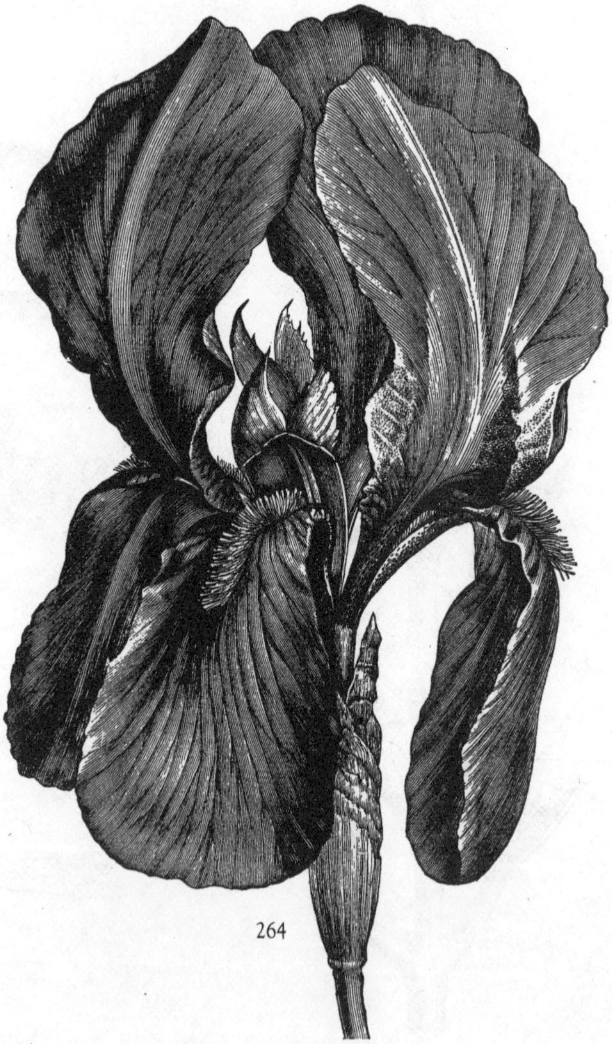

264

262. Baobab *(Adansonia)*. From Africa, Madagascar and Australia. 263. Common pitcher plant *(Sarracenia purpurea)*. Dull purple flowers; from eastern North America. 264. *Iris germanica.* An iris with violet flowers with strips of yellow hairs; from the Mediterranean region.

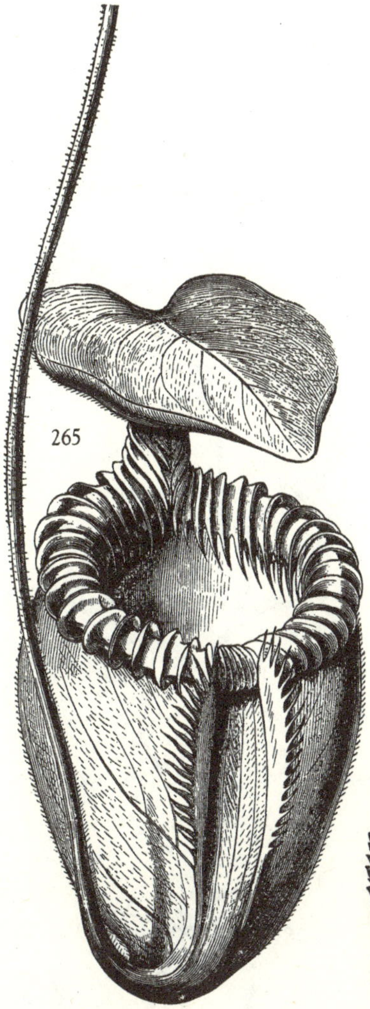

265

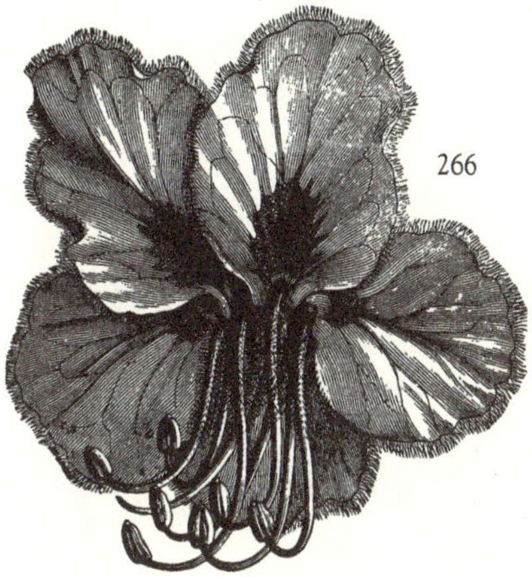

266

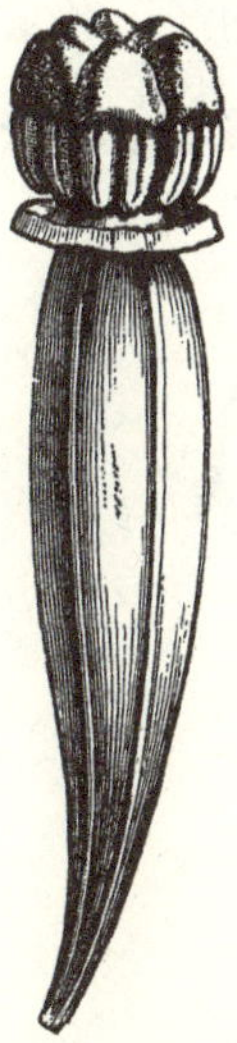

267

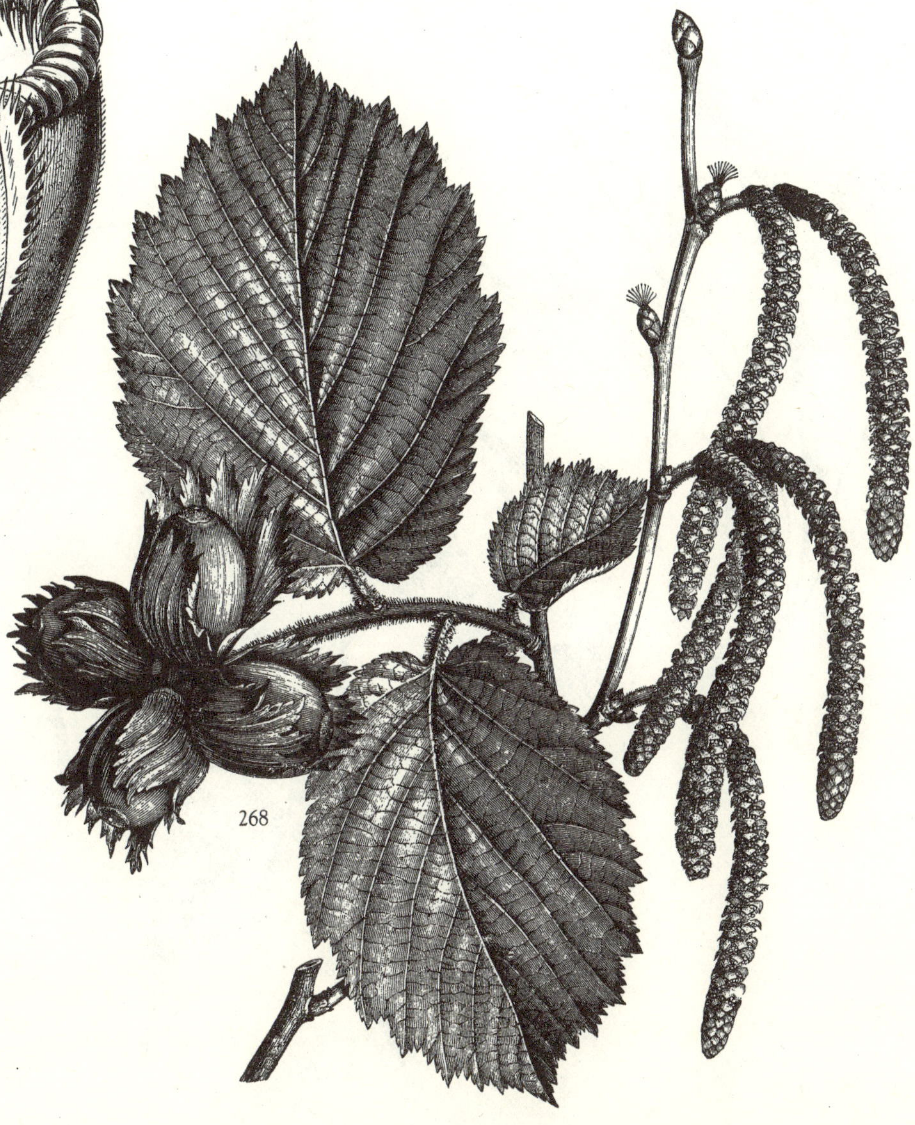

268

265. *Nepenthes villosa.* A pitcher plant; from Australia, Ceylon and Bengal. 266. European horse chestnut *(Aesculus hippocastanum).* White flowers; from the Balkan peninsula. 267. *Aristolochia clematitis.* A birthwort with perianth removed. 268. European hazel *(Corylus avellana).*

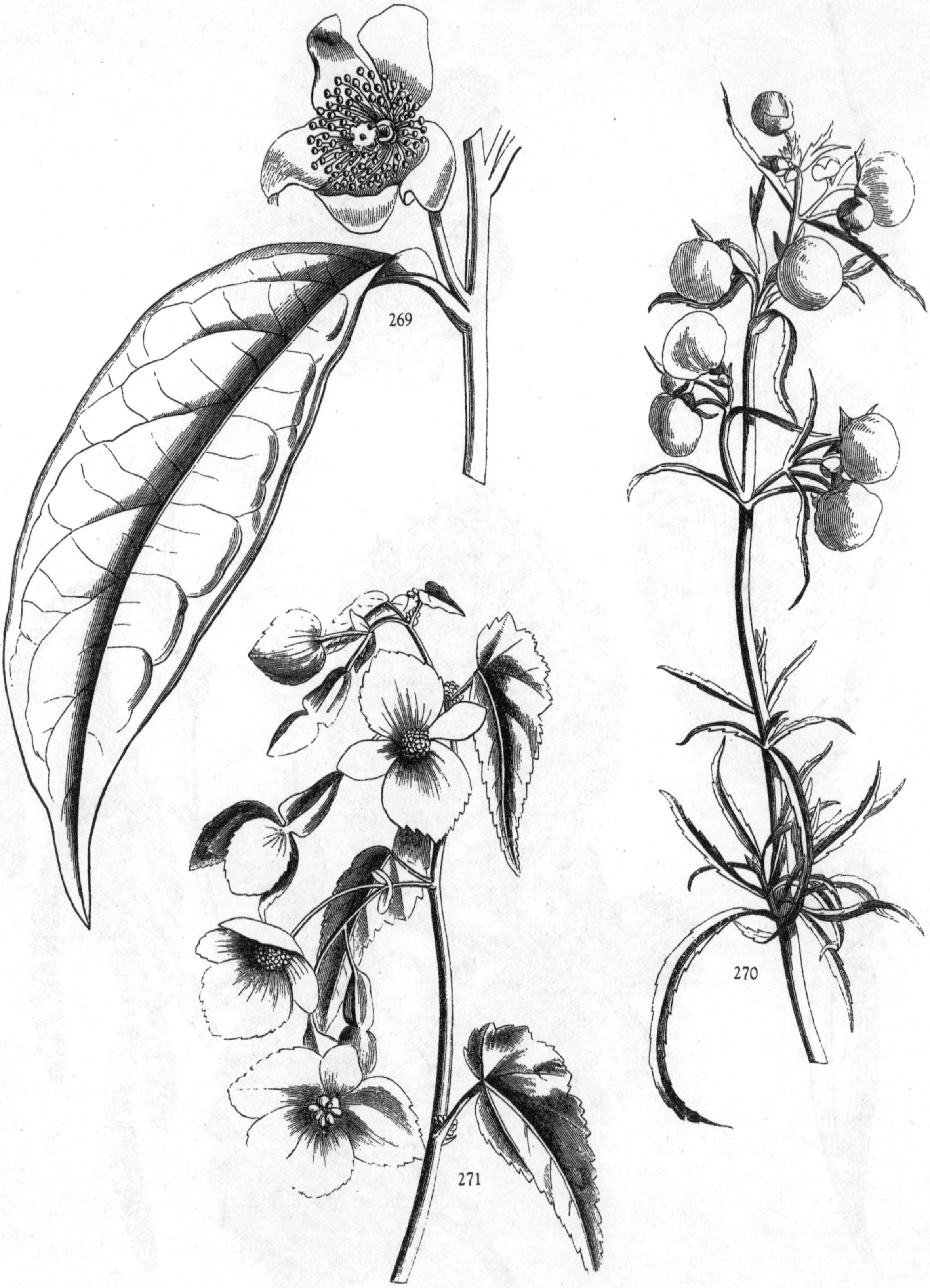

269. *Gordonia javanica.* A tea-like plant with white flowers; from Java. 270. *Calceolaria alba.* A shrubby white-flowered slender plant; from Chile. 271. *Begonia martiana.* A tuberous plant with rich rose-colored flowers; from Mexico.

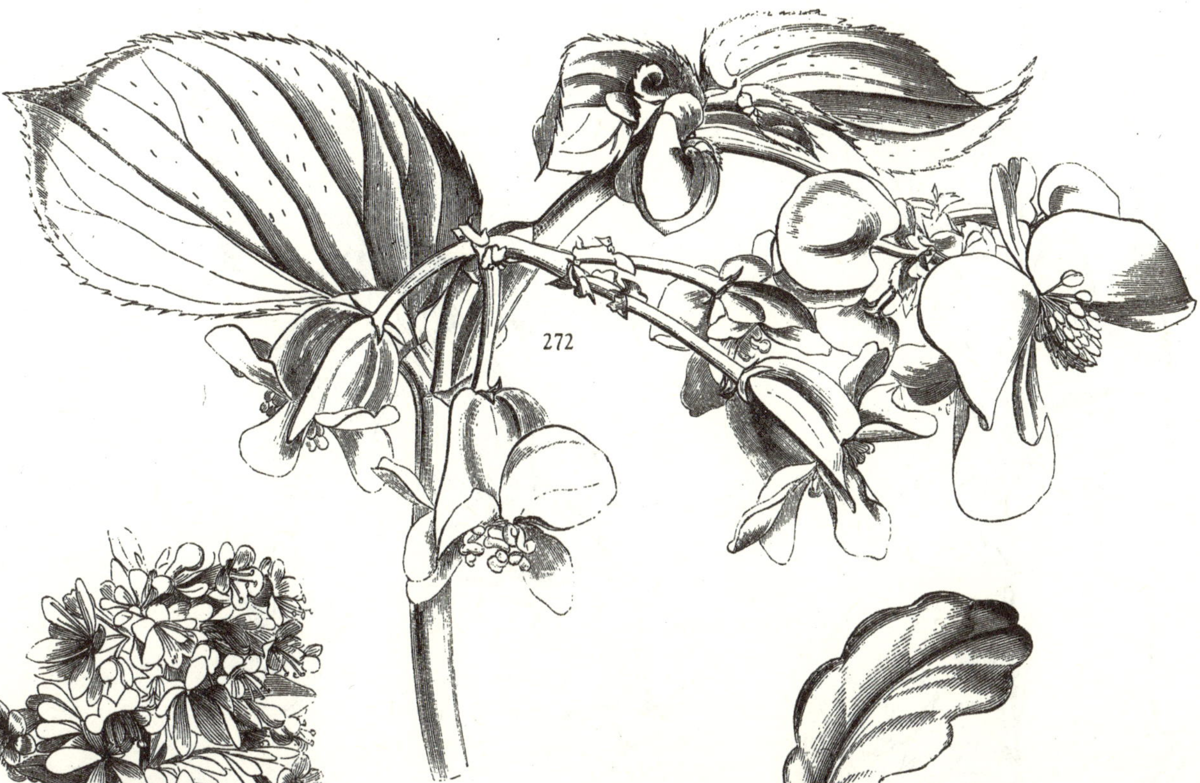

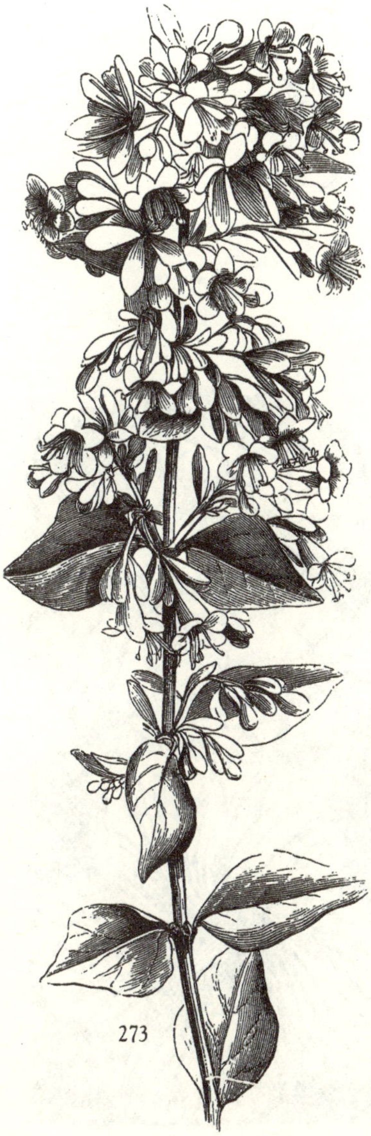

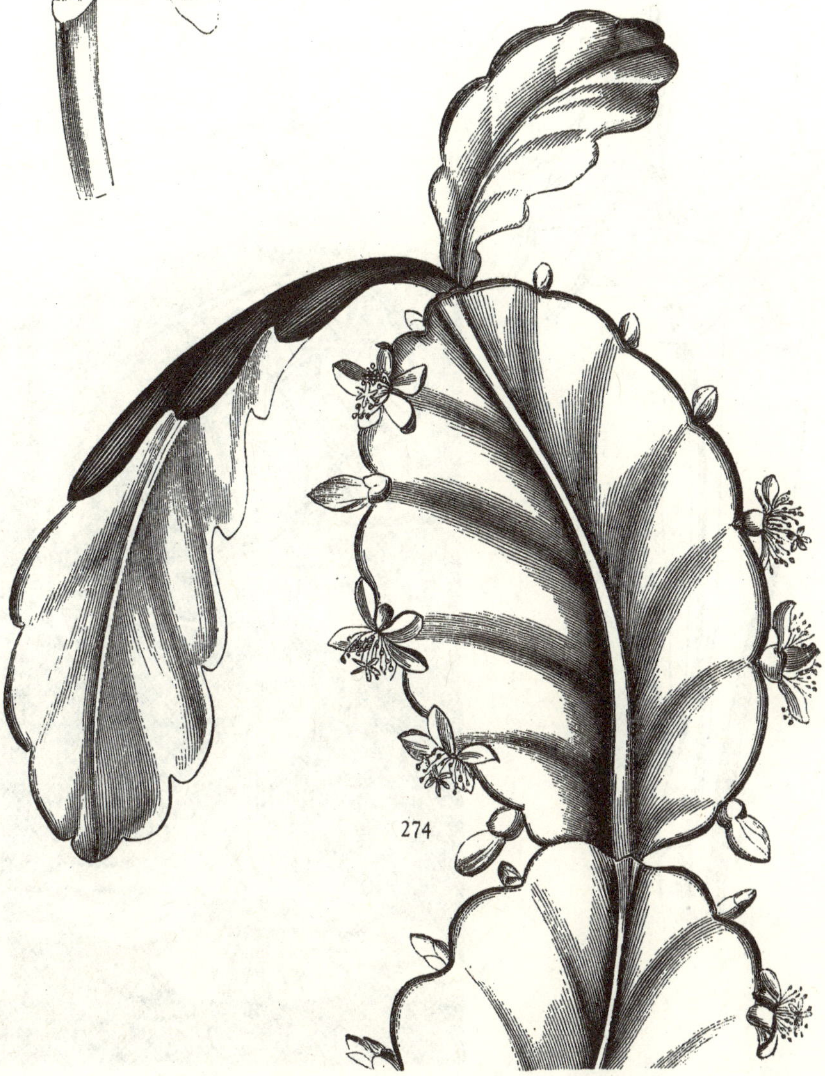

272. *Begonia (Diploclinium) semperflorens.* A succulent perennial with white flowers; from Brazil. 273. *Abelia rupestris.* A fine dwarf shrub with white flowers; from China. 274. *Rhipsalis pachyptera.* A trailing succulent shrub with leaf-like stems, small dirty-white flowers and red fruit; from Brazil.

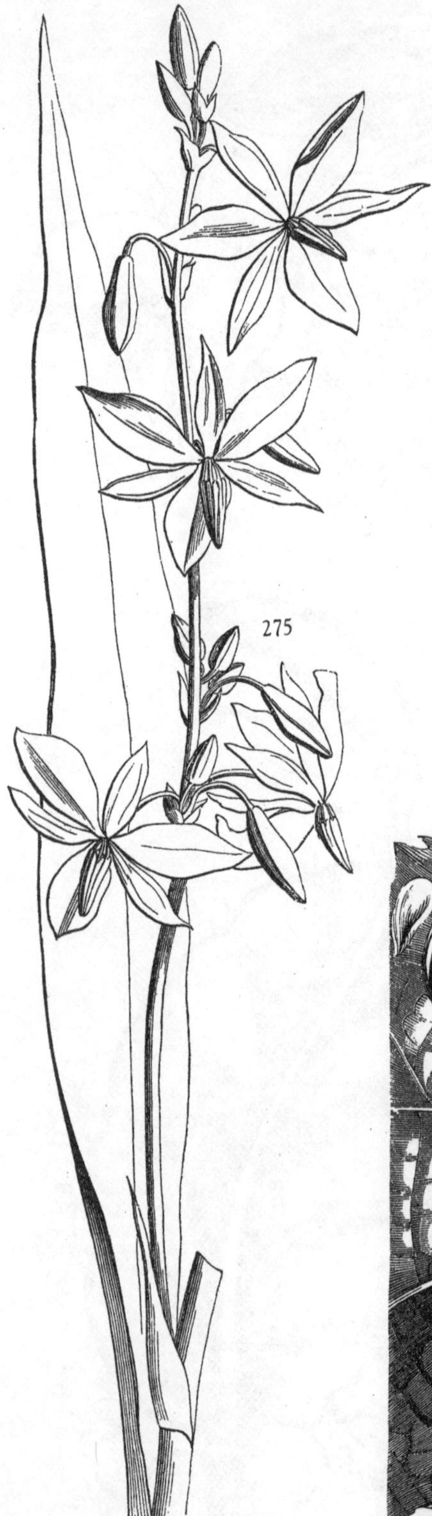

275

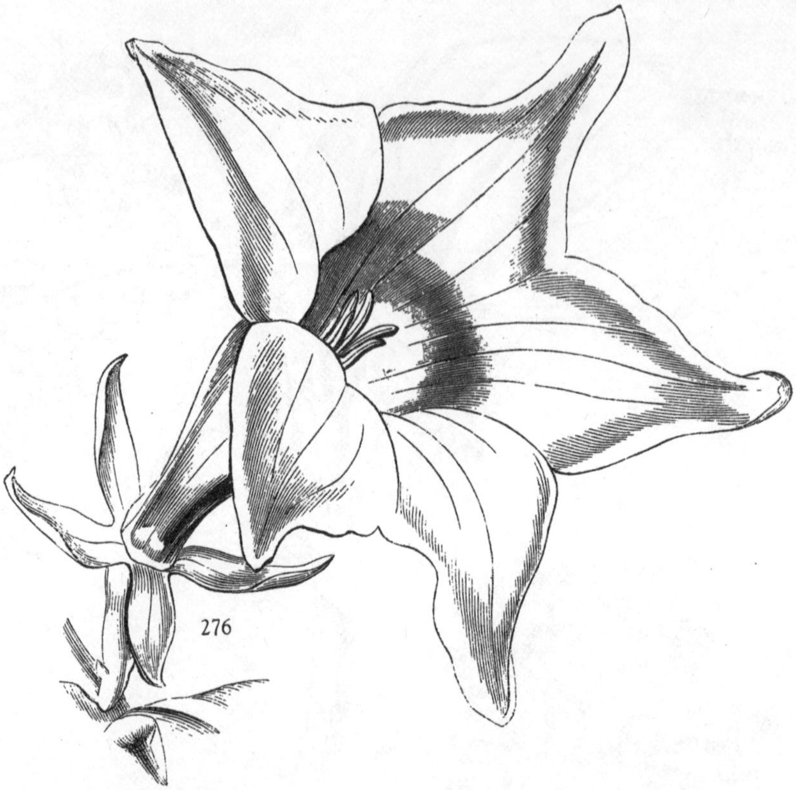

276

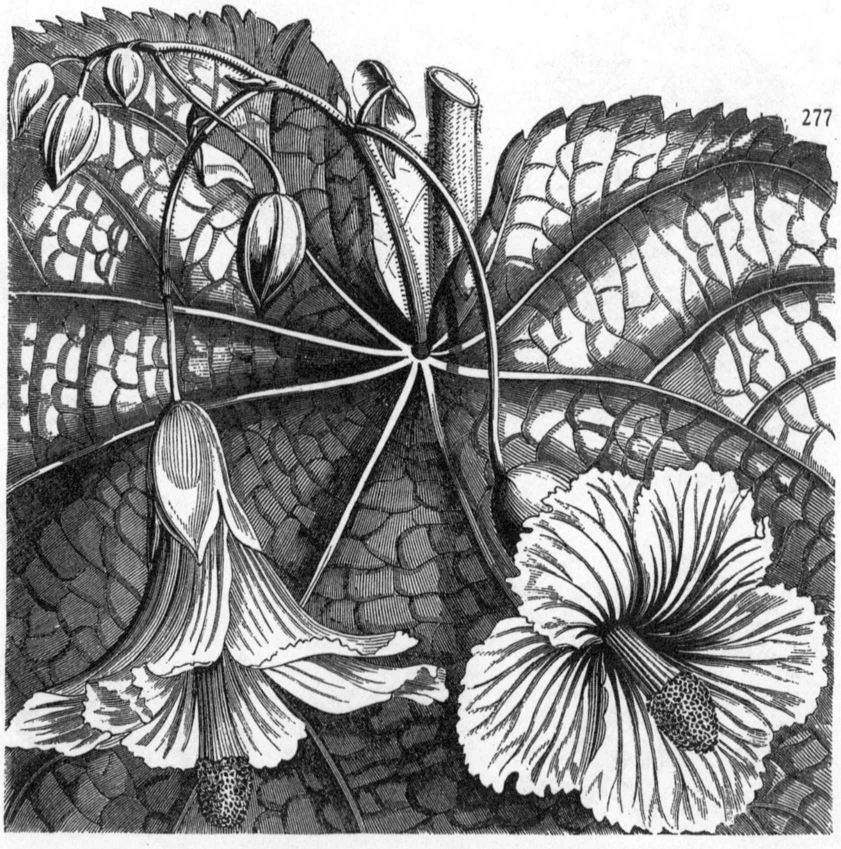

277

275. *Echeandia terniflora.* A half-hardy lilywort with yellow flowers; from Mexico. 276. *Portlandia platantha.* A white-flowered shrub; from Mexico, Central America and the West Indies. 277. *Abutilon insigne.* A shrub with large, heart-shaped leaves and pendulous flowers with broad, rich crimson veins; from Colombia and Venezuela.

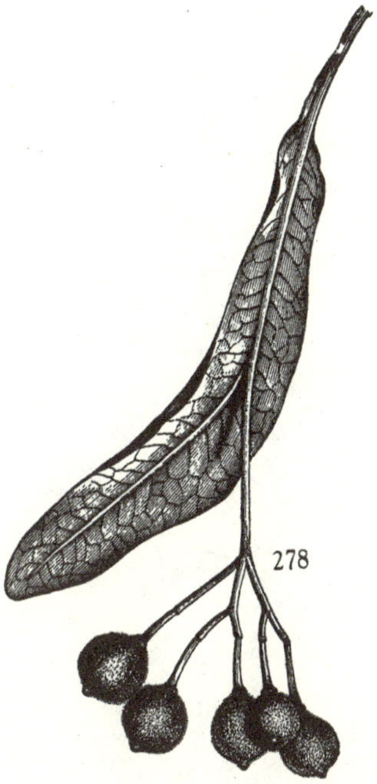

278

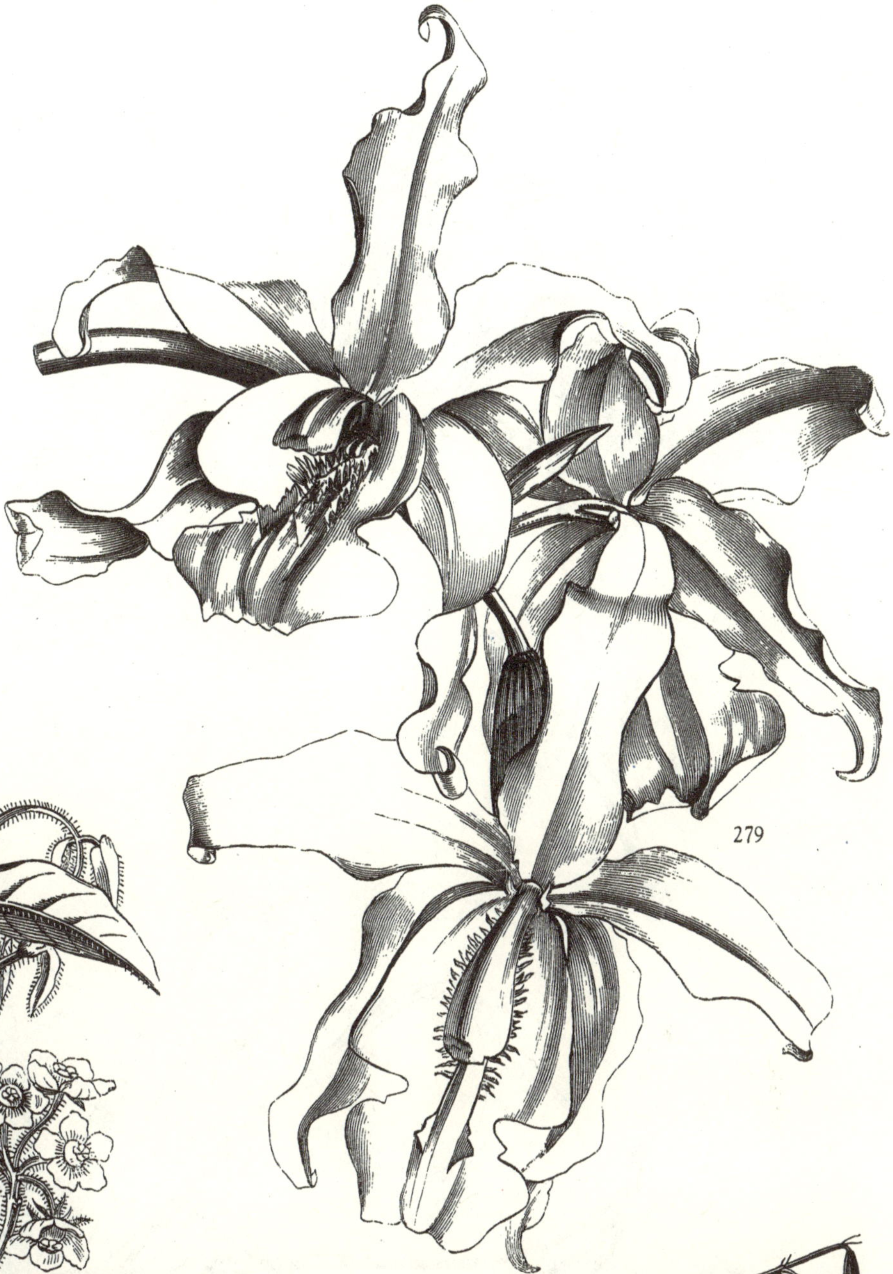

279

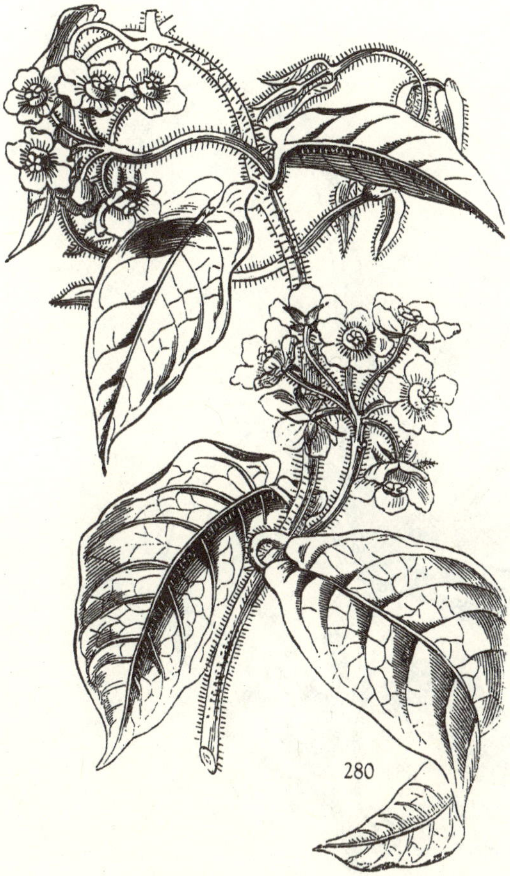

280

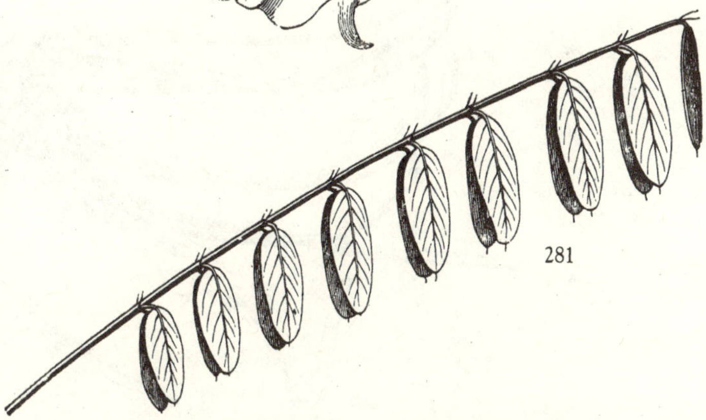

281

278. Fruiting branch of the lime tree *(Tilia)* with downy hairs investing the nut-like fruits; flowers are white or yellowish; from temperate regions of the Northern Hemisphere (see also Fig. 344). 279. *Coelogyne cristata.* An orchid, flowers large and pure white with numerous yellow fringes on the lip; from the Himalayas. 280. *Gonolobus martianus.* A twiner with many-flowered umbels of greenish-white flowers; from Brazil. 281. A leaf of false indigo *(Amorpha fruticosa)*, in night position. See Fig. 150.

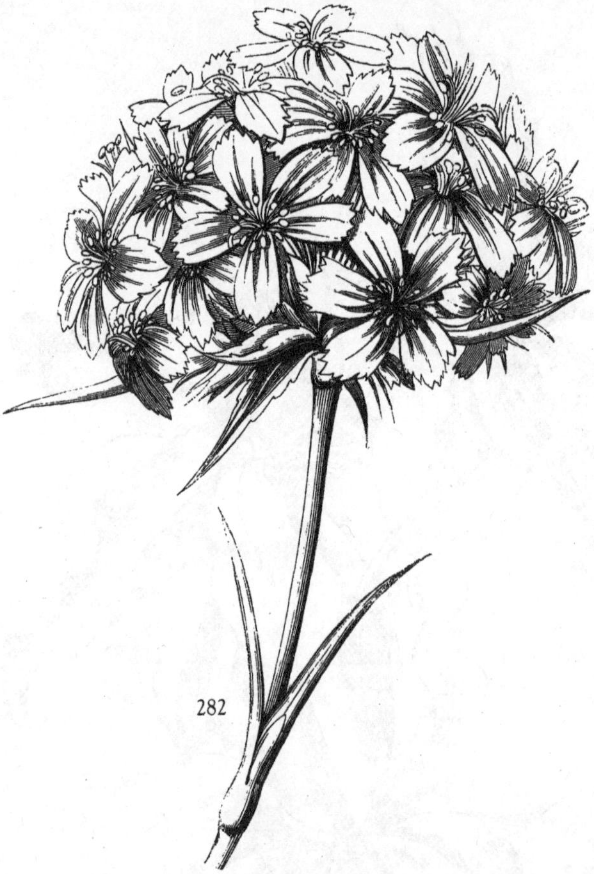

282

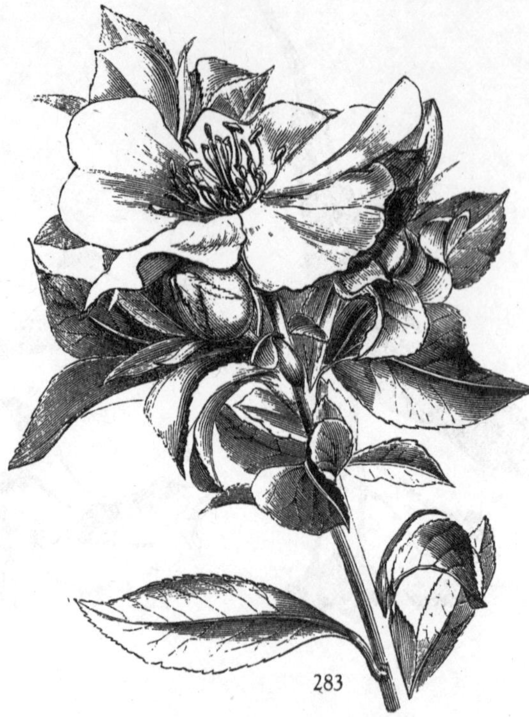

283

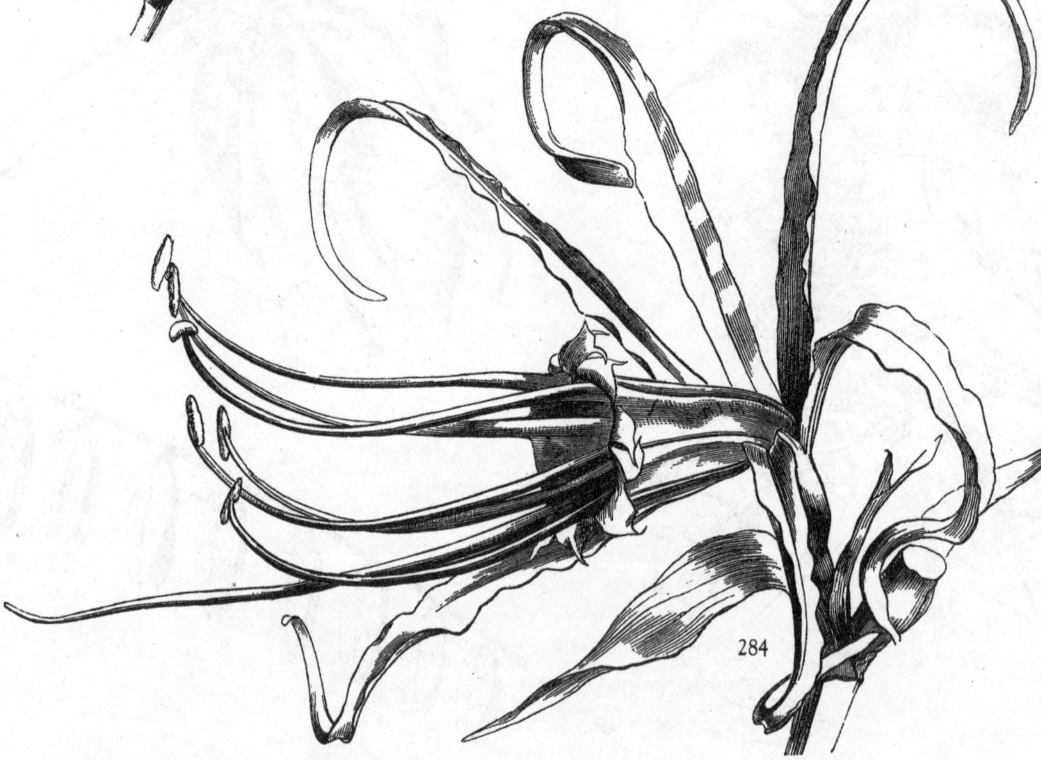

284

282. *Dianthus cruentus.* A hardy herbaceous plant with deep rose-colored flowers; from the Balkan Peninsula. 283. *Lindleya mespiloides.* An evergreen, half-hardy bush with white flowers; from Mexico. 284. Spider lily *(Elisena longipetala).* Flowers white tinged with green; from Peru.

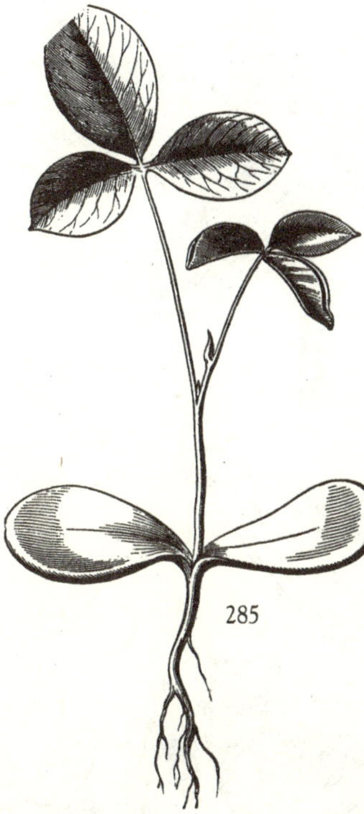

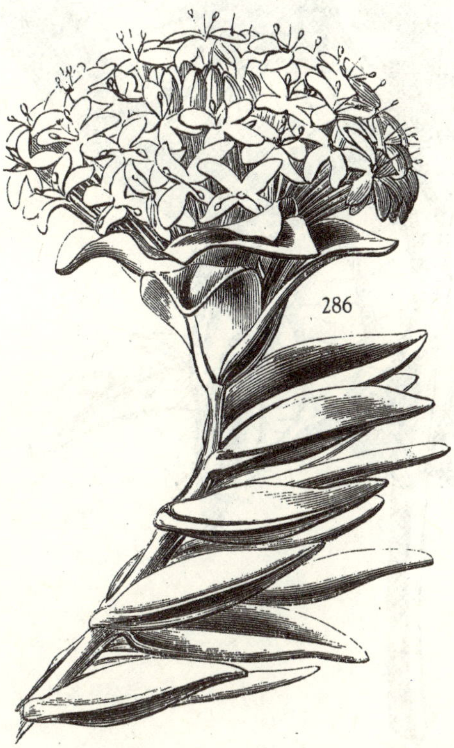

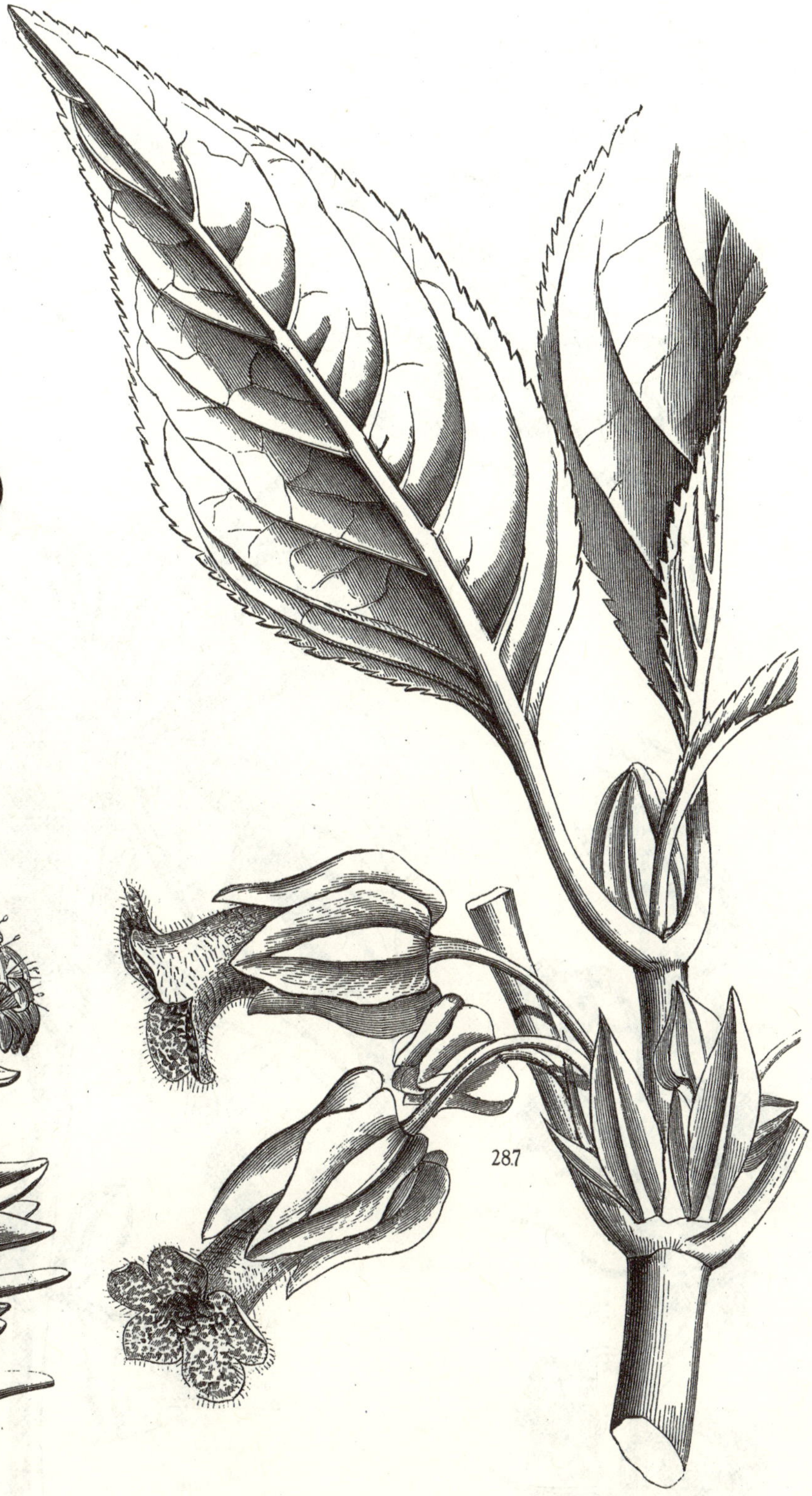

285. *Cytisus laburnum.* See Fig. 87. 286. *Pimelia macrocephala.* A stiff glaucous shrub with large nodding heads of cream-colored flowers; from southwestern Australia. 287. *Heintzia tigrina.* Flowers rose-color and white; from Venezuela.

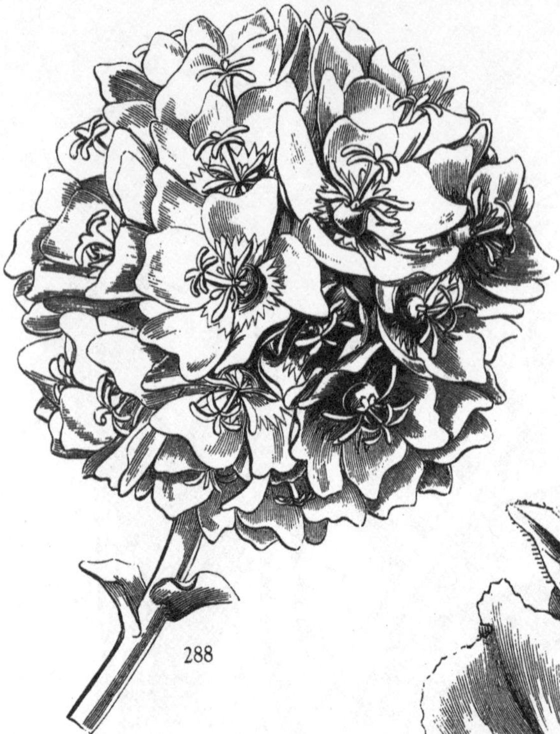

288

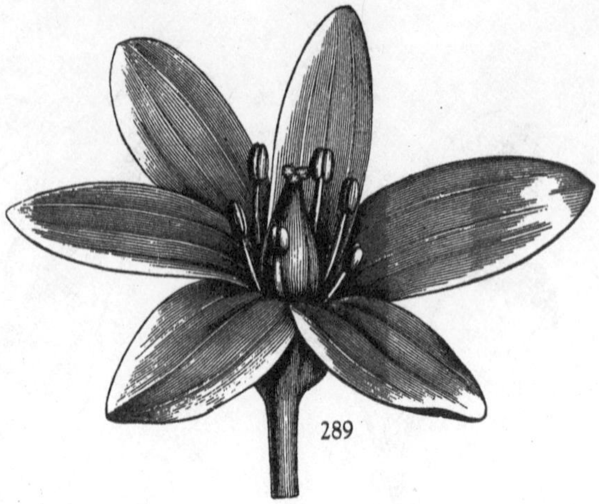

289

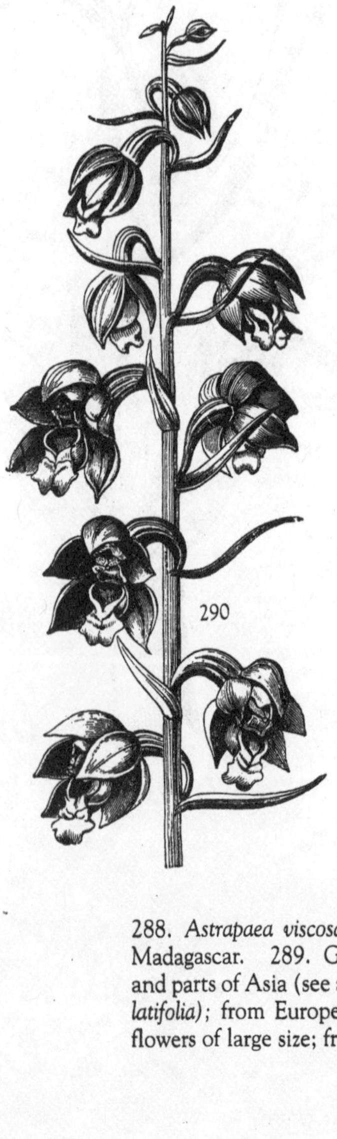

290

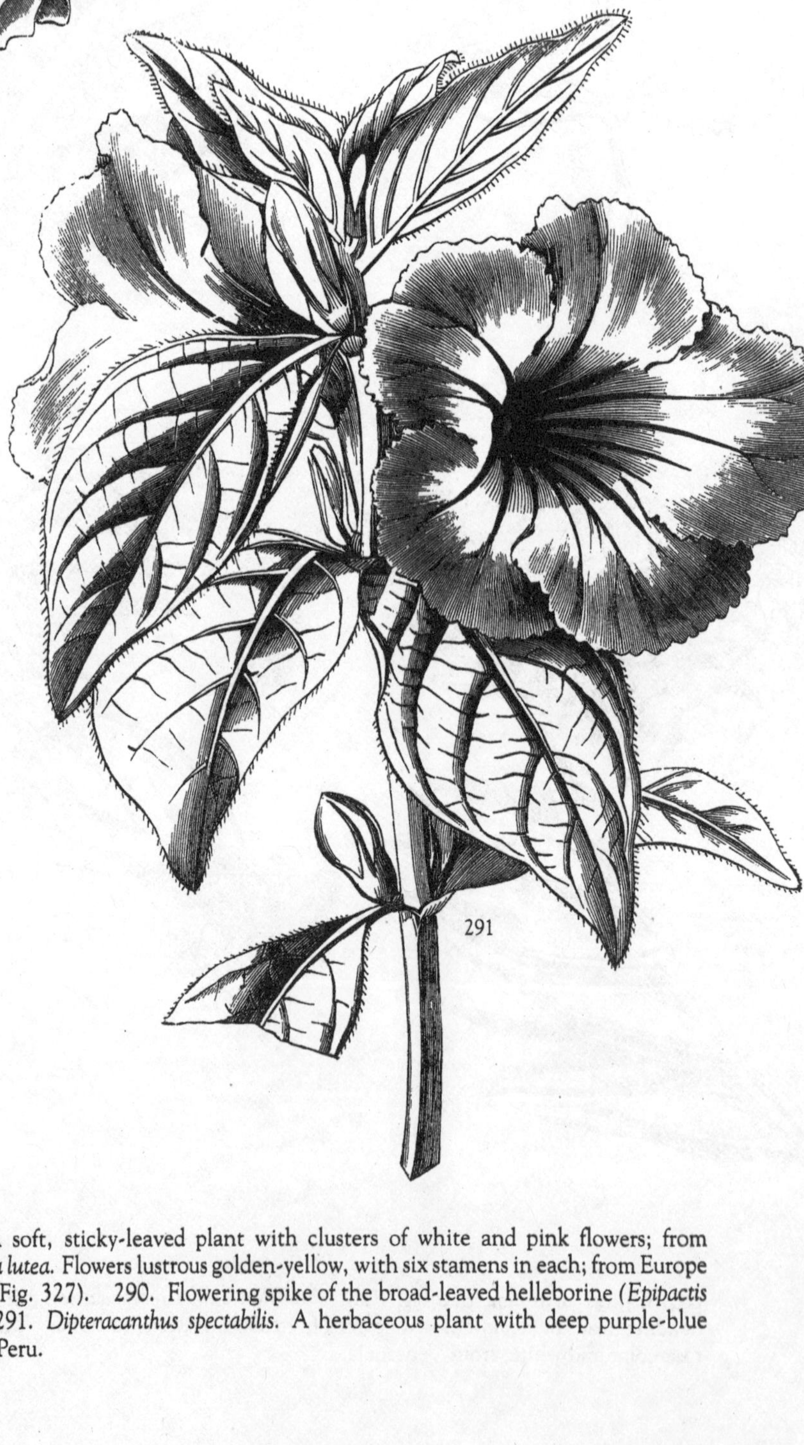

291

288. *Astrapaea viscosa.* A soft, sticky-leaved plant with clusters of white and pink flowers; from Madagascar. 289. *Gagea lutea.* Flowers lustrous golden-yellow, with six stamens in each; from Europe and parts of Asia (see also Fig. 327). 290. Flowering spike of the broad-leaved helleborine *(Epipactis latifolia)*; from Europe. 291. *Dipteracanthus spectabilis.* A herbaceous plant with deep purple-blue flowers of large size; from Peru.

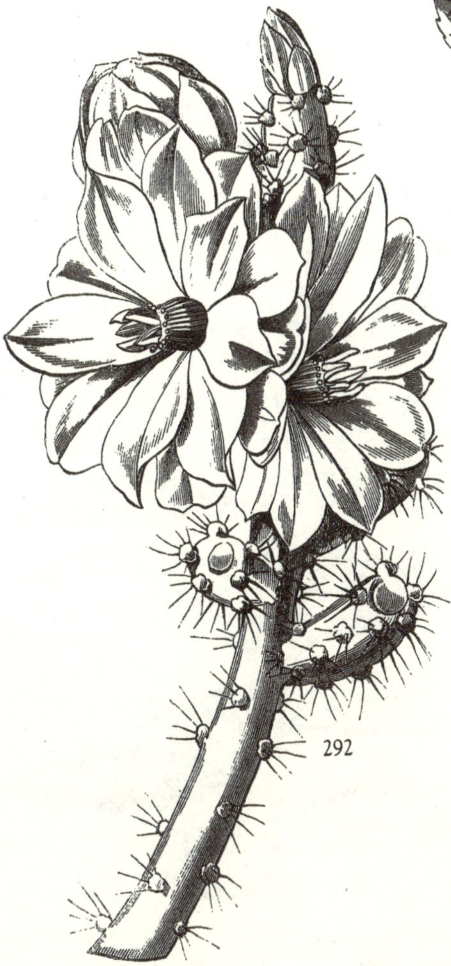

292

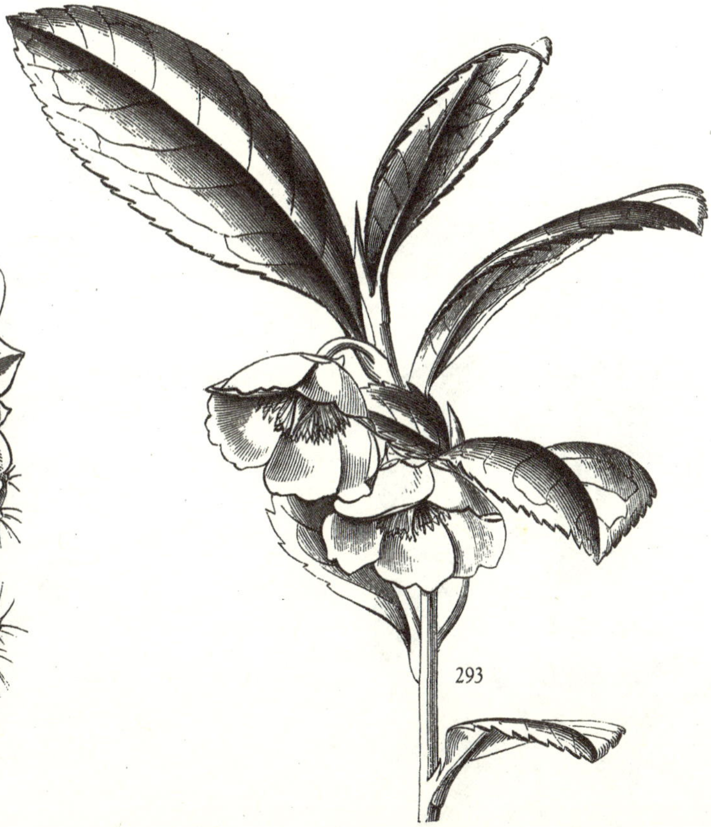

293

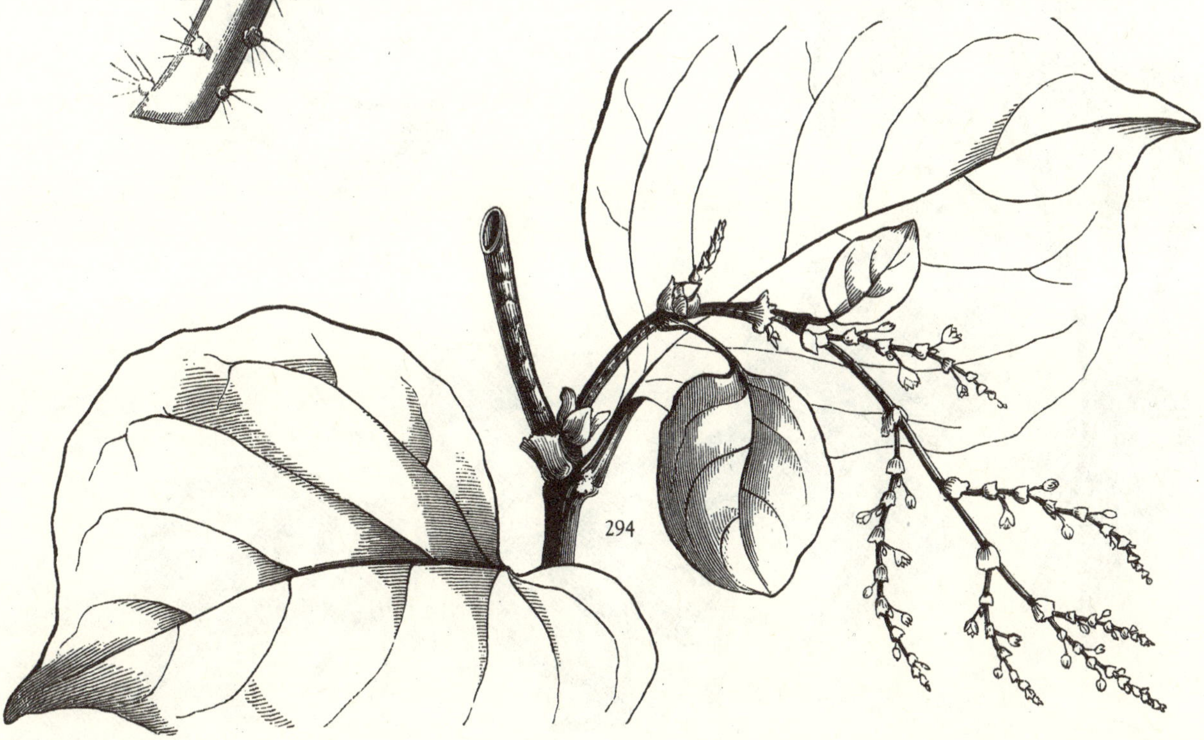

294

292. *Opuntia salmiana.* A succulent with pale yellow flowers; from Brazil. 293. *Freziera theoides.* A shrub with white flowers; from Jamaica. 294. *Polygonum cuspidatum.* A tall, hardy broad-leaved herbaceous plant, flowers greenish-white; from Japan.

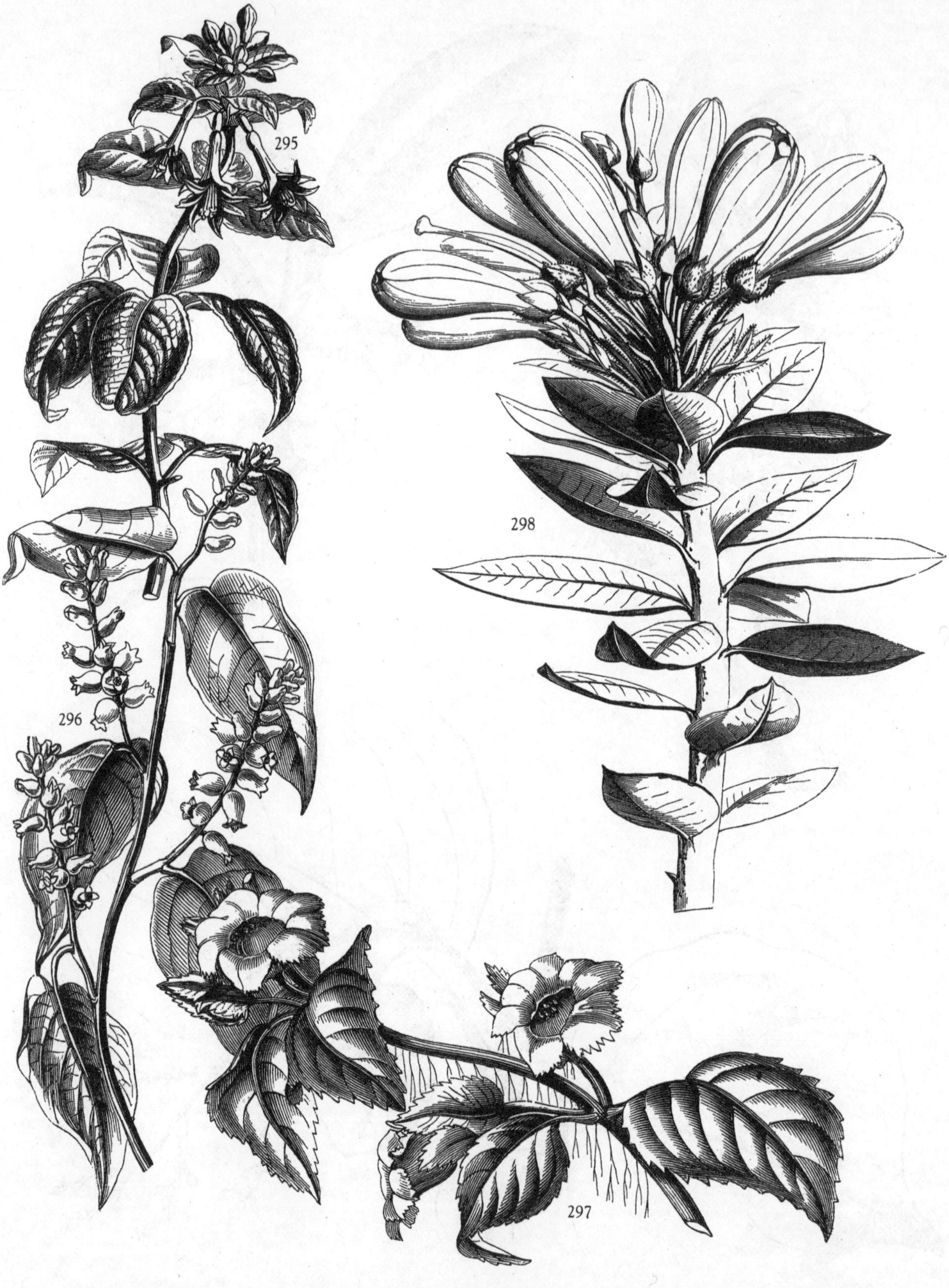

295. *Fuchsia nigricans.* A shrub with purple and rose-colored flowers; from the mountains of Central America. 296. *Lagetta lintearia.* A tree with oblong leaves and pitcher-shaped yellow flowers. 297. *Drymonia cristata.* A creeping, downy, fleshy-leaved vine with large lacerated green flowers; from Surinam. 298. *Bejaria lindeniana.* An evergreen bush with pink flowers and shiny leaves; from Venezuela.

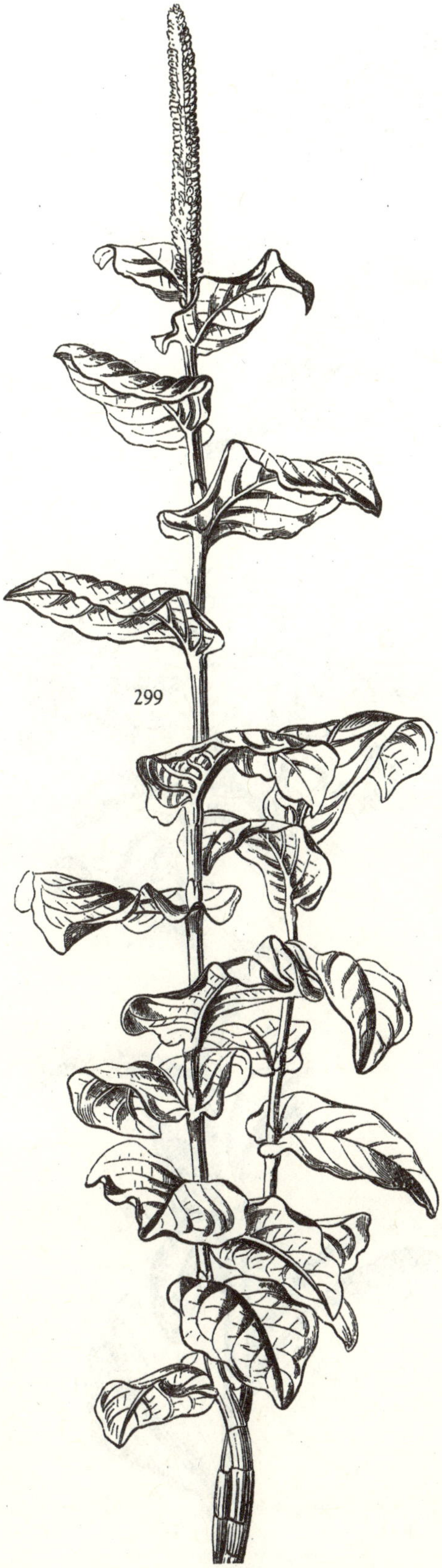

299

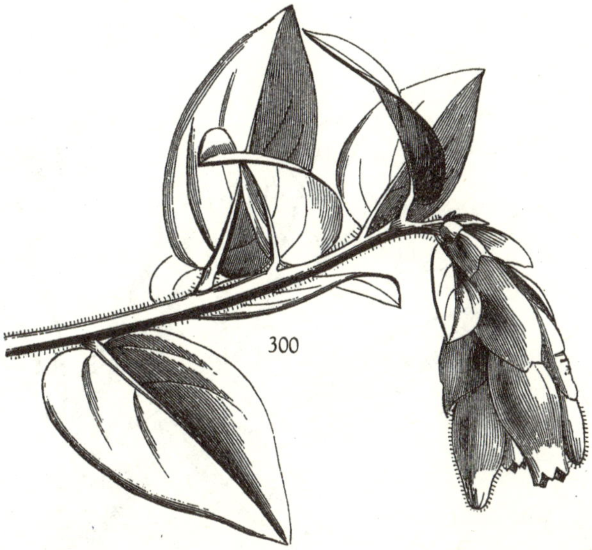

300

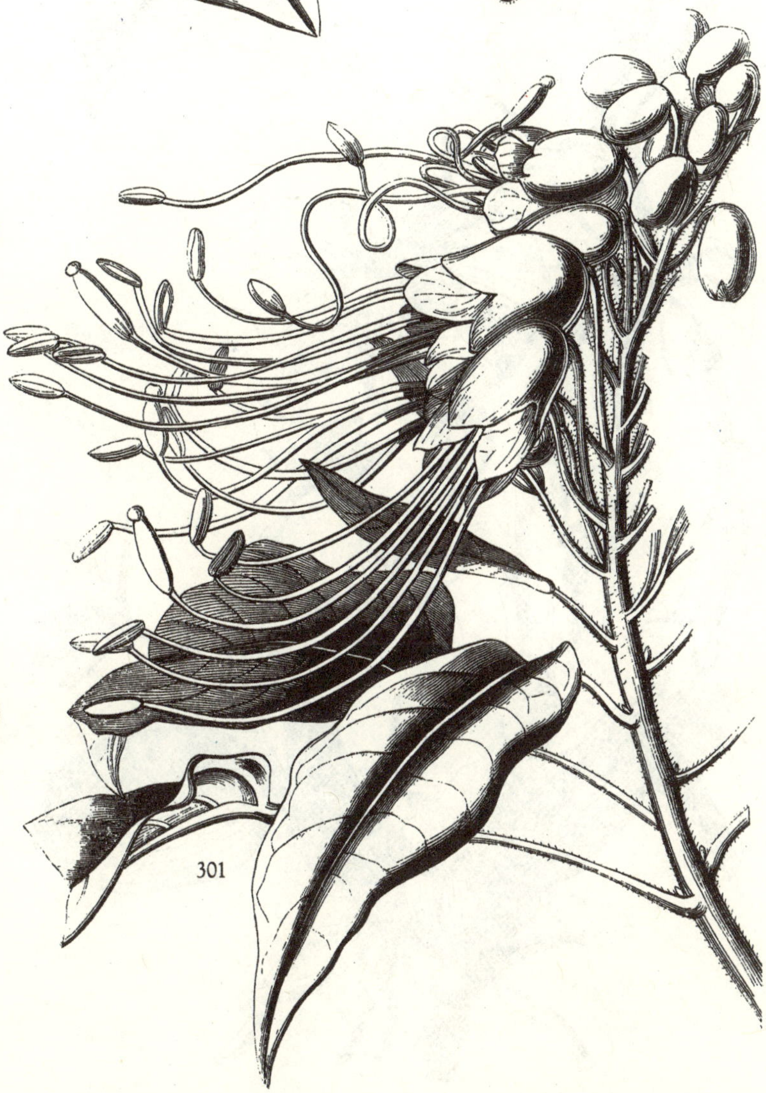

301

299. *Coccoloba macrophylla.* A simple-stemmed erect tree with large leathery leaves and straight spikes of crimson flowers; from tropical and subtropical America. 300. *Thiebaudia scabriuscula.* An evergreen bush belonging to the order of cranberries; from Colombia and Panama. 301. *Steriphoma paradoxum.* A small shrub with bright yellow flowers; from Venezuela.

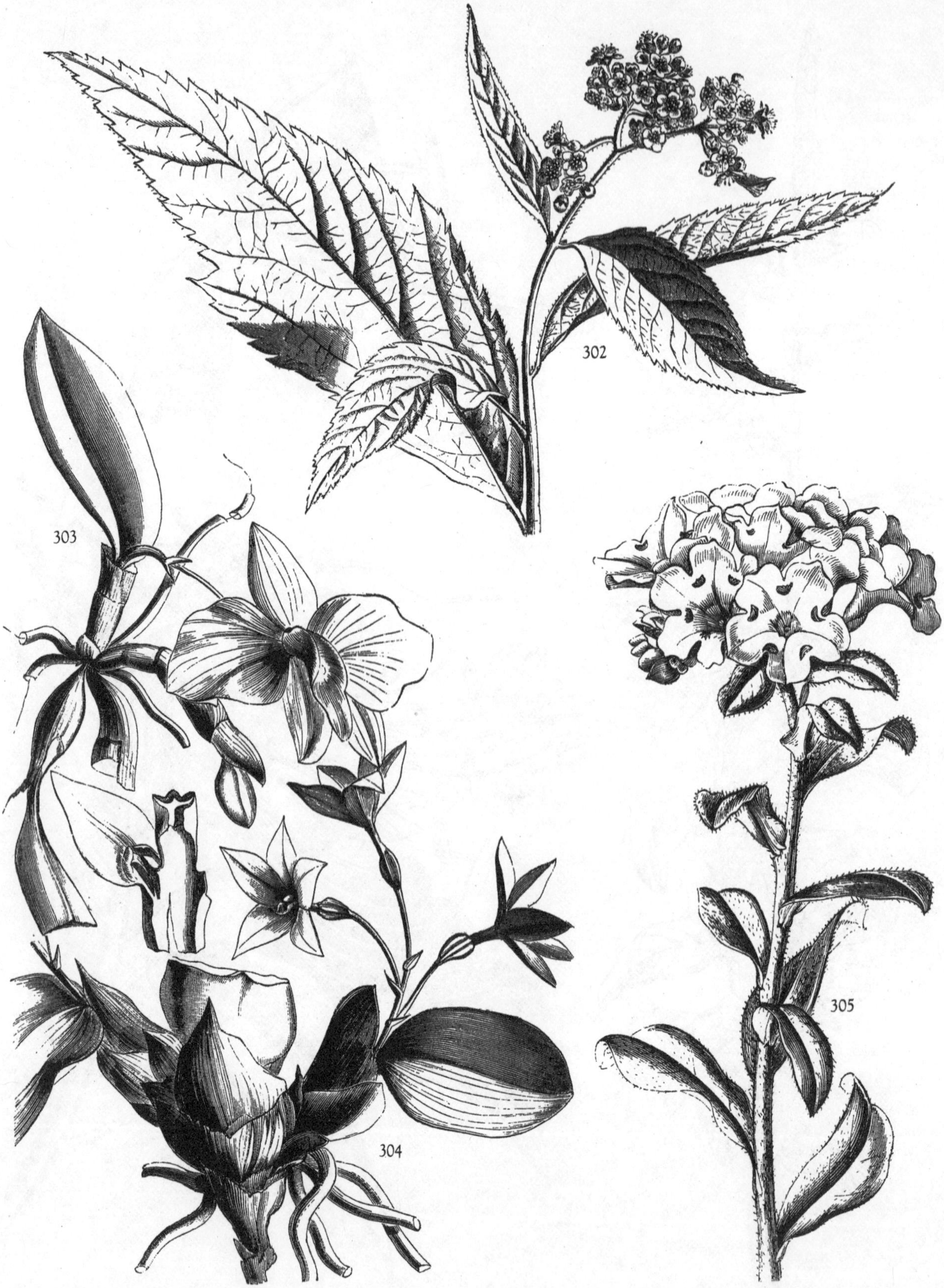

302. *Spiraea callosa.* A hardy deciduous shrub with brilliant rose-colored flowers; from the north of China and Japan. 303. *Sophronitis grandiflora.* Flowers bright scarlet or cinnabar, lip yellow; from Brazil. 304. *Sophronitis pterocarpa.* Rosy purple flowers; from Brazil. 305. *Arnebia echioides.* A hardy herbaceous plant with showy yellow flowers; from Armenia, the Caucasus and northern Iran.

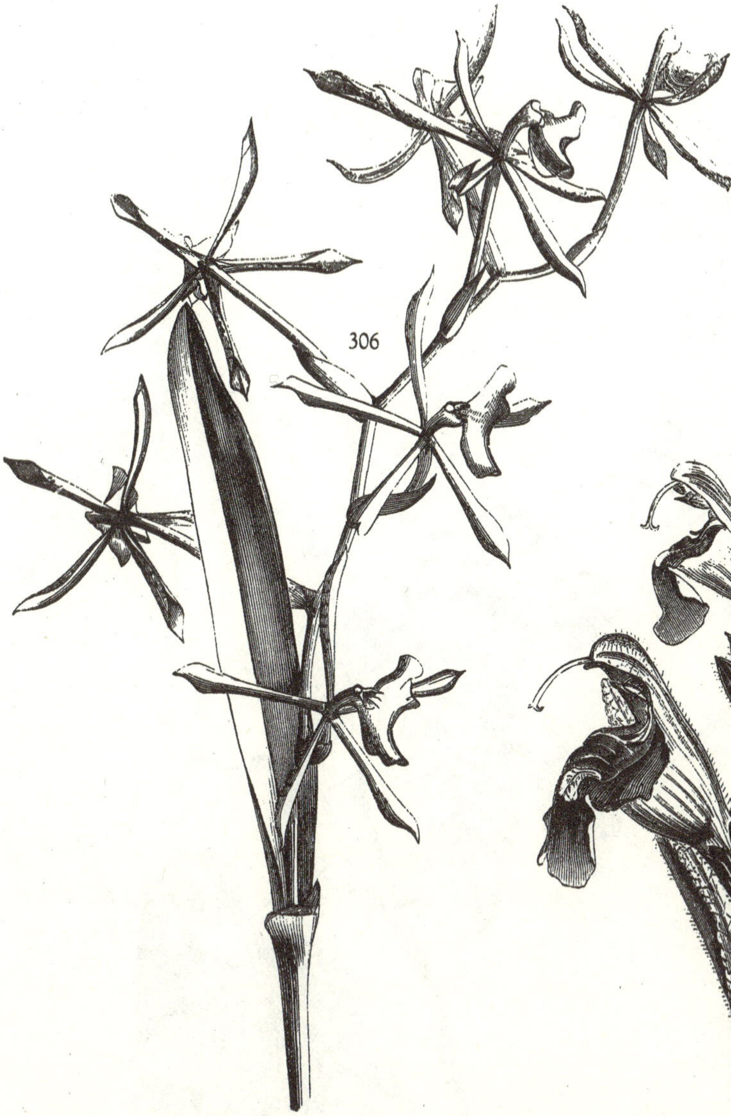

306

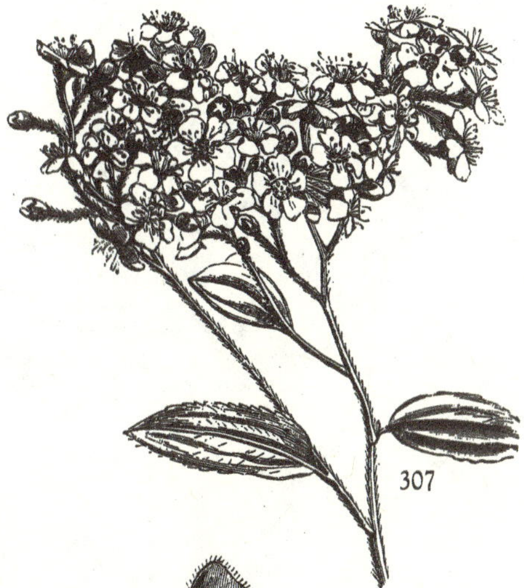

307

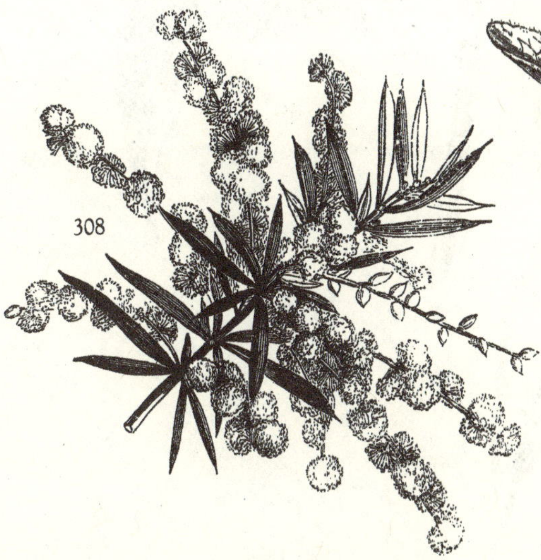

308

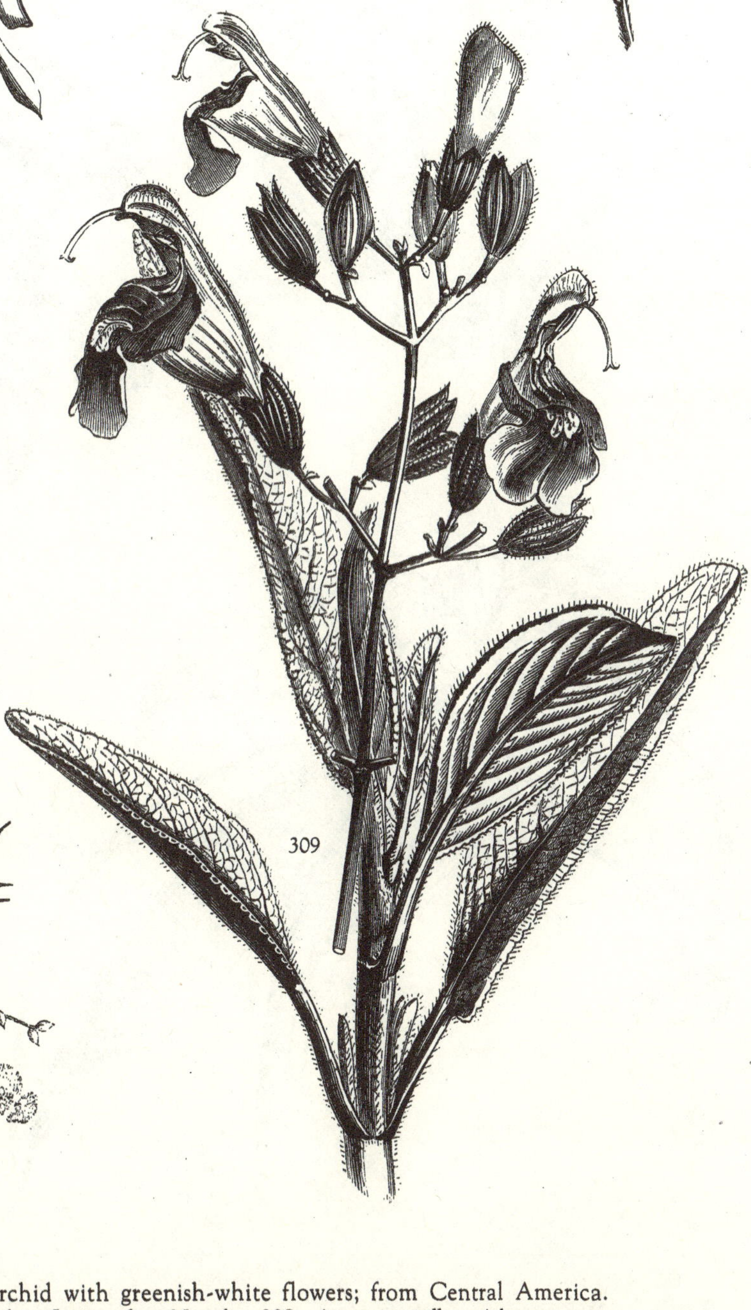

309

306. *Epidendrum volutum.* An orchid with greenish-white flowers; from Central America. 307. *Spiraea laxiflora.* A shrub with white flowers; from Nepal. 308. *Acacia verticillata.* A loose, straggling, prickly shrub with light yellow flowers; from southeast Australia. 309. *Salvia candelabrum.* A sage with large leafless panicles of violet and yellow flowers; from the south of Spain.

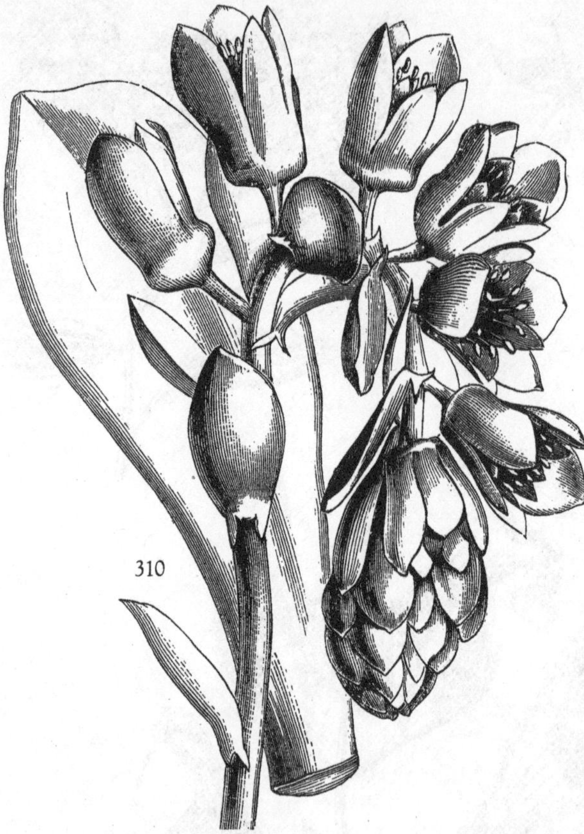

310

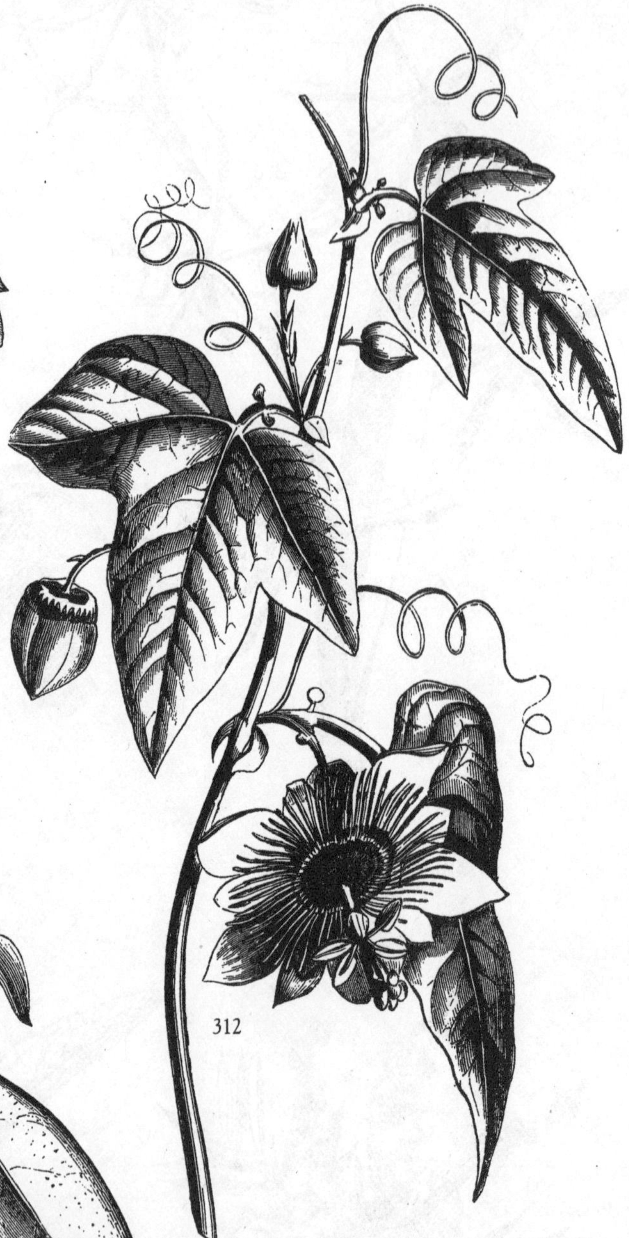

312

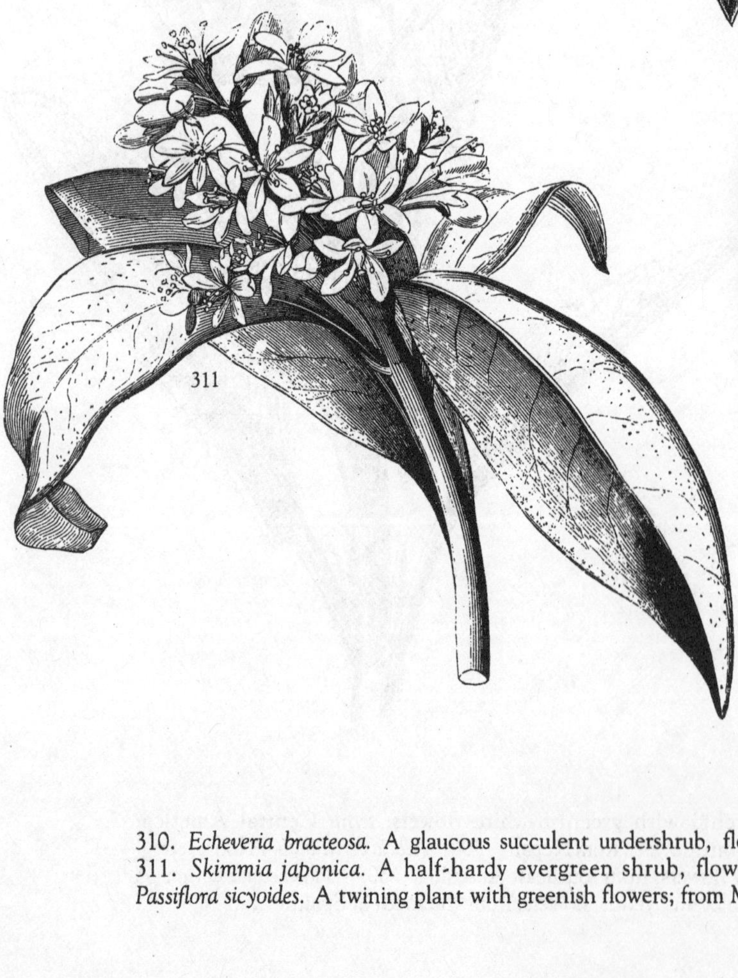

311

310. *Echeveria bracteosa.* A glaucous succulent undershrub, flowers green and red; from Mexico. 311. *Skimmia japonica.* A half-hardy evergreen shrub, flowers pale green; from Japan. 312. *Passiflora sicyoides.* A twining plant with greenish flowers; from Mexico.

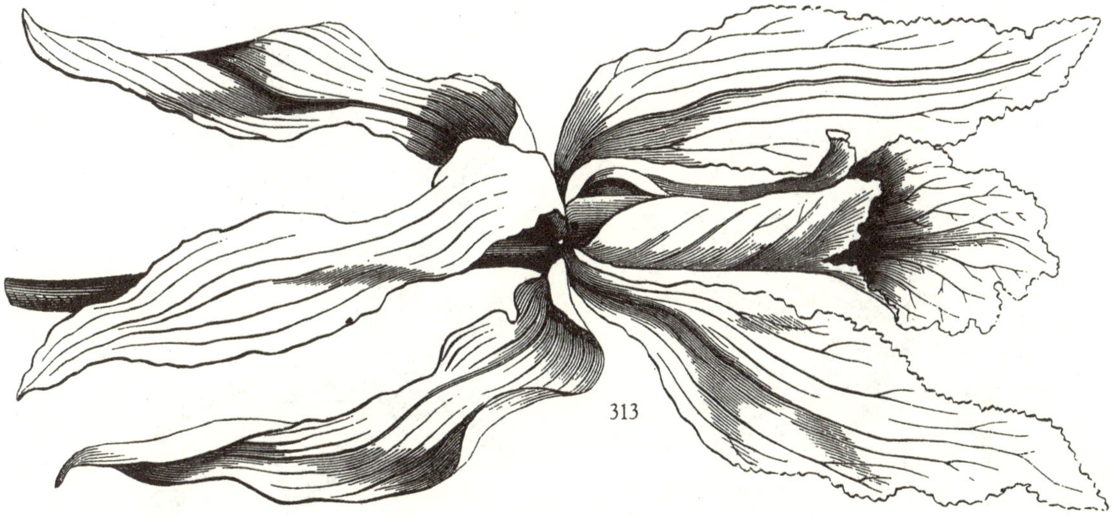
313

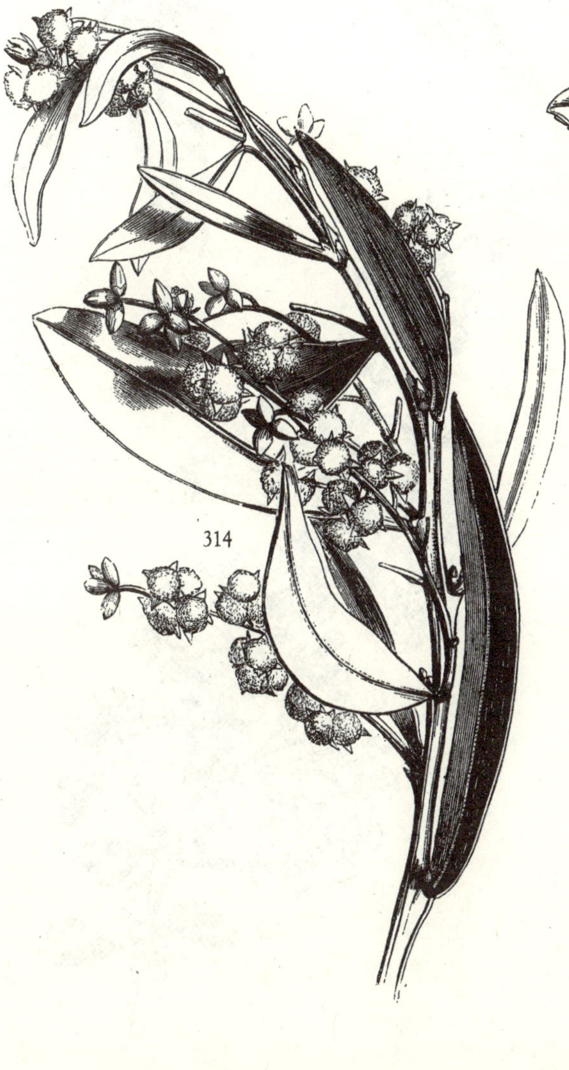
314

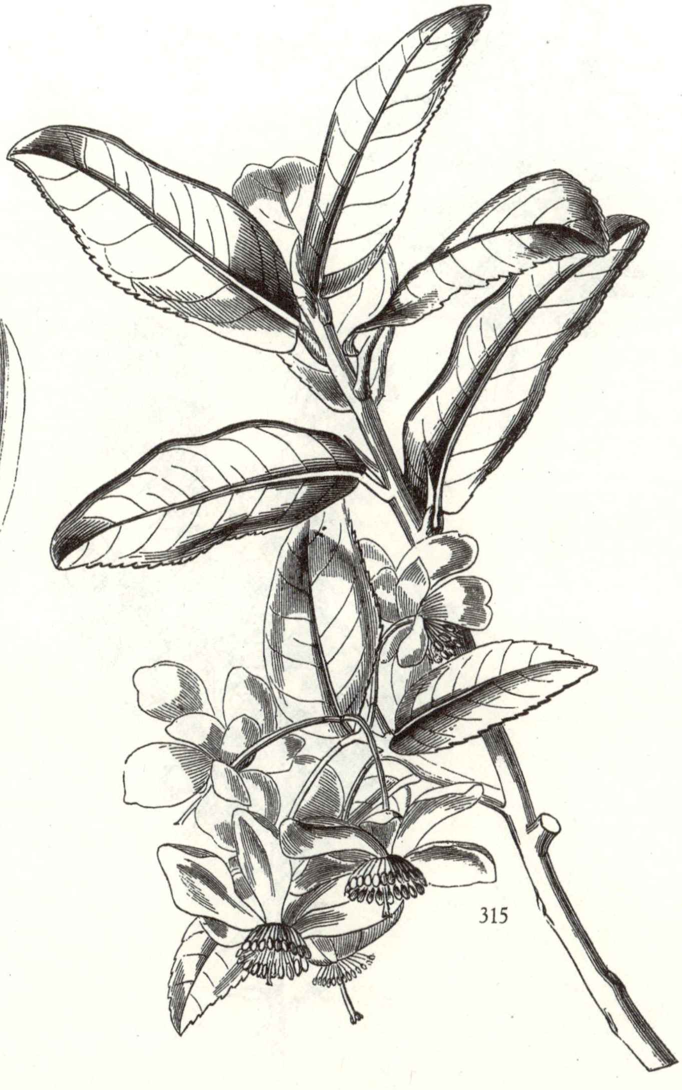
315

313. *Laelia grandis.* An orchid with very large nankeen-colored flowers; from Brazil. 314. *Acacia marginata.* A shrub with dark green leaves and bright yellow blossoms; from Australia. 315. *Ochna atropurpurea.* A shrub with deep purple flowers; from southern Africa.

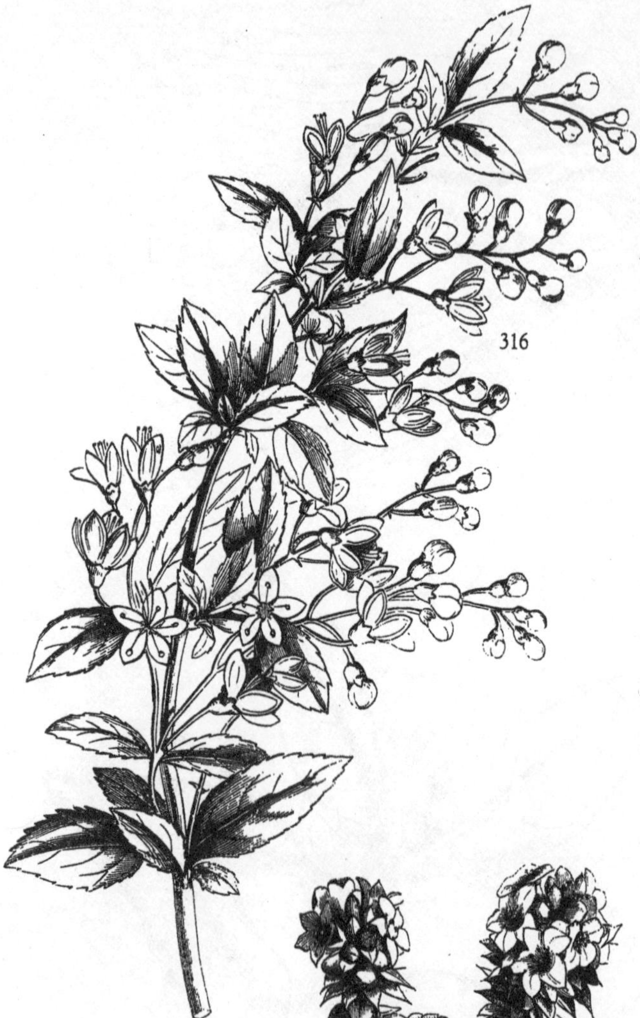

316

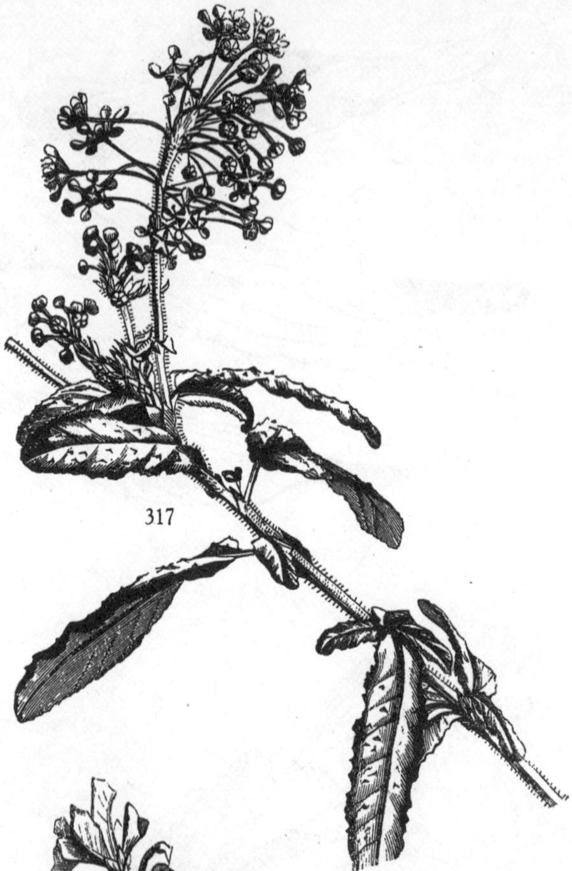

317

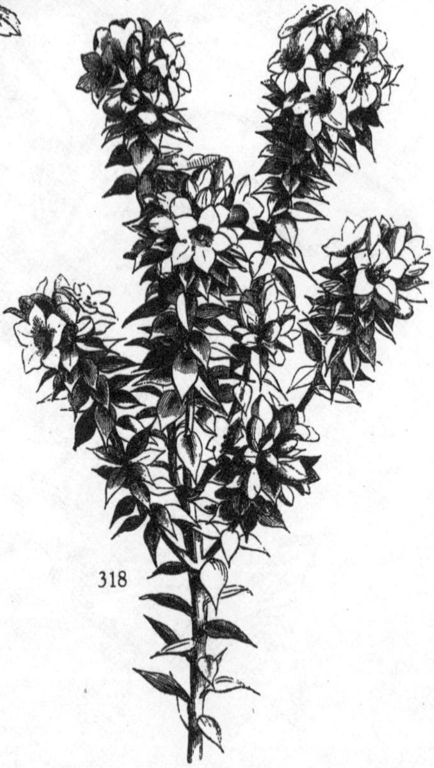

318

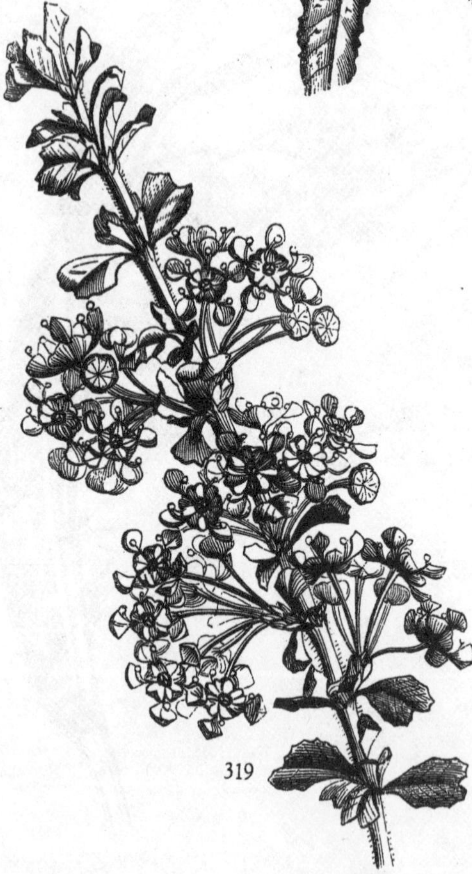

319

316. *Deutzia gracilis.* A hardy deciduous shrub with weeping branches profusely covered with small white flowers; from Japan. 317. *Ceanothus papillosus.* A bush with bright blue flowers; from California. 318. *Epacris nivalis.* A half-hardy evergreen bush, flowers pure white; from Australia. 319. *Ceanothus rigidus.* A hardy evergreen purple-flowered bush; from California.

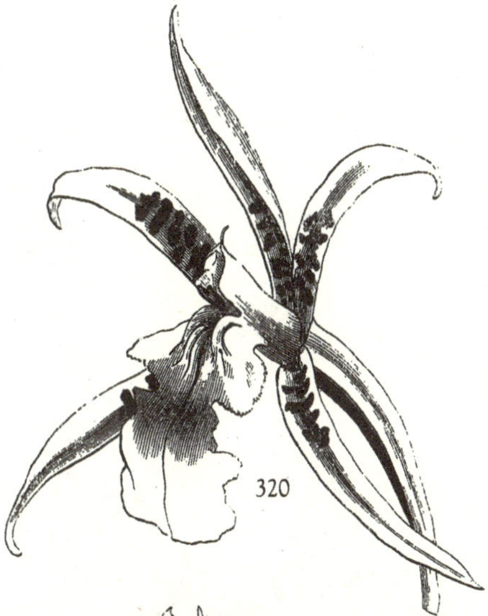

320

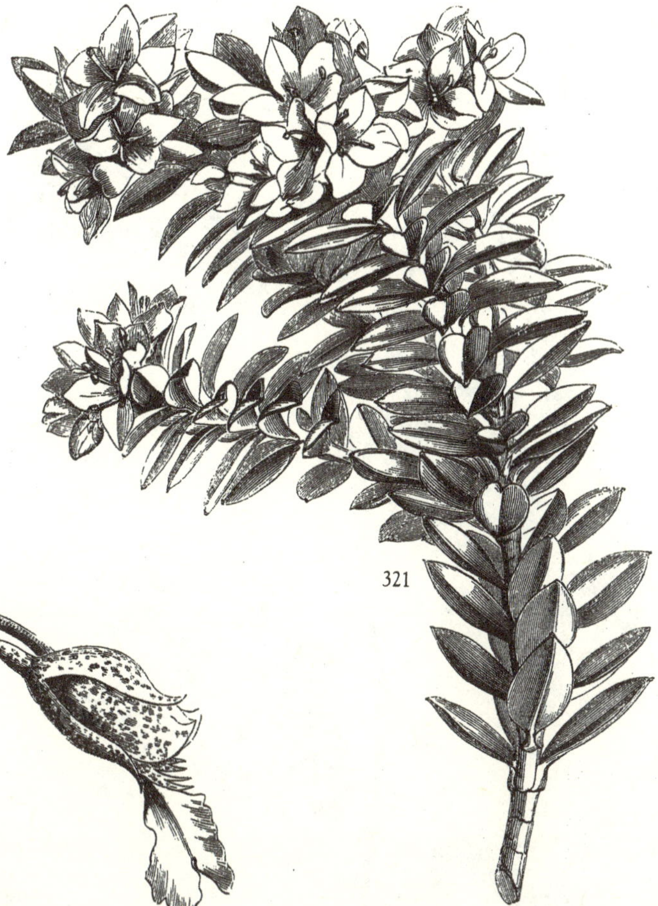

321

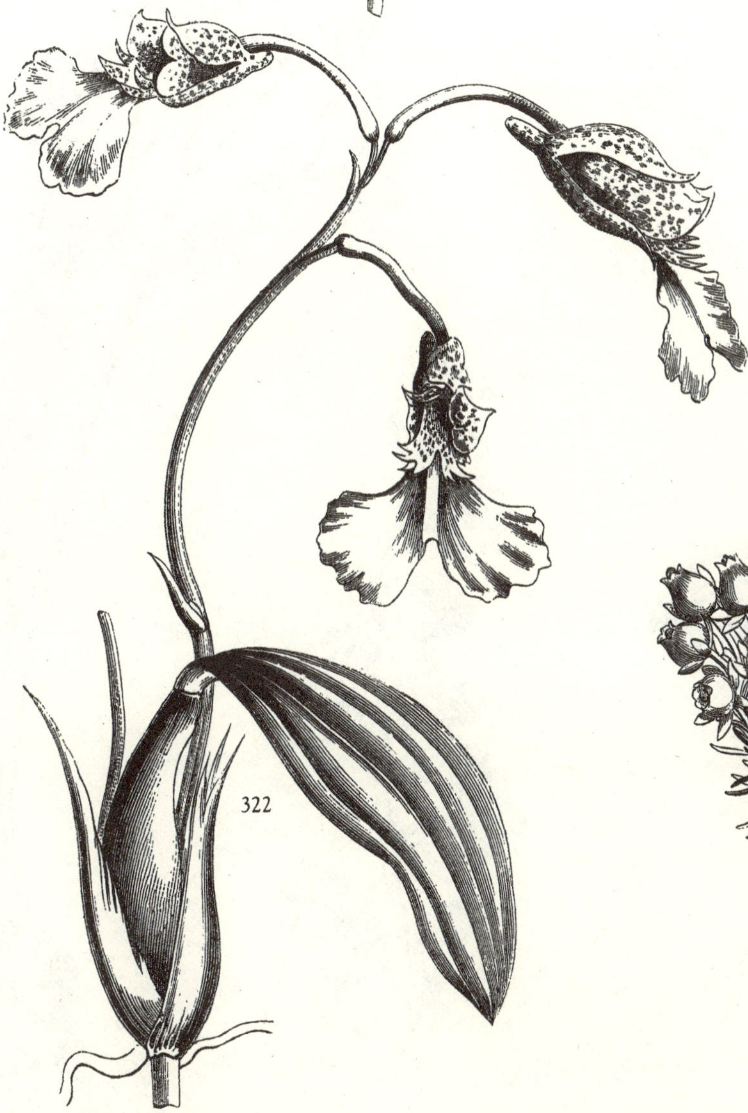

322

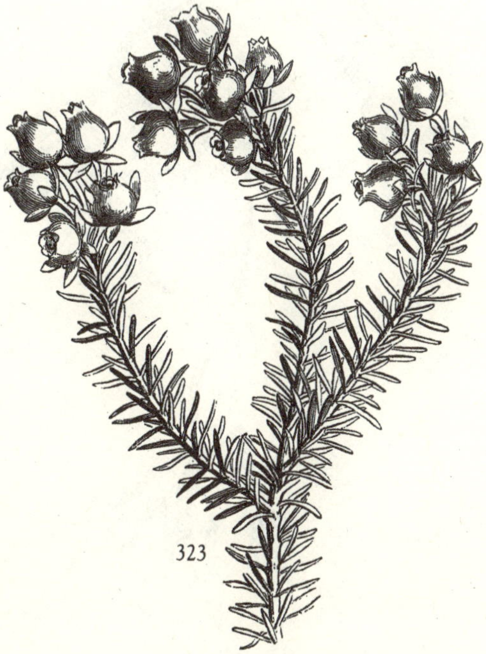

323

320. *Aspasia lunata.* An orchid with pale green speckled flowers; from Brazil. 321. *Veronica elliptica.* An evergreen bush with deep green leaves and white flowers; from New Zealand, the Falkland Islands and southern Chile. 322. *Burlingtonia decora.* An orchid, flowers rose-colored spotted with red, and a white lip; from Brazil. 323. *Pentapera sicula.* A half-hardy evergreen shrub with globular pale pink flowers; from Sicily.

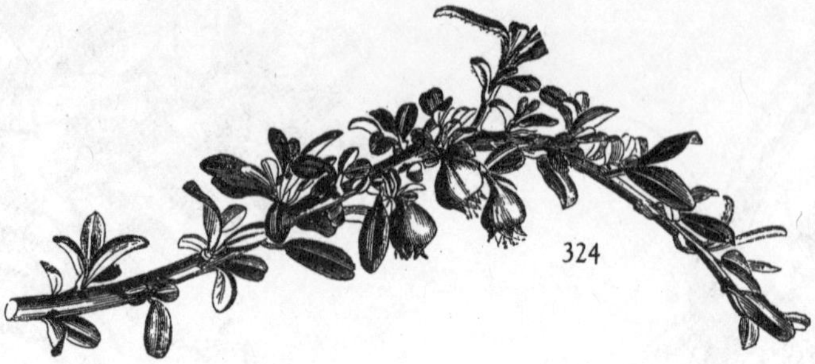
324

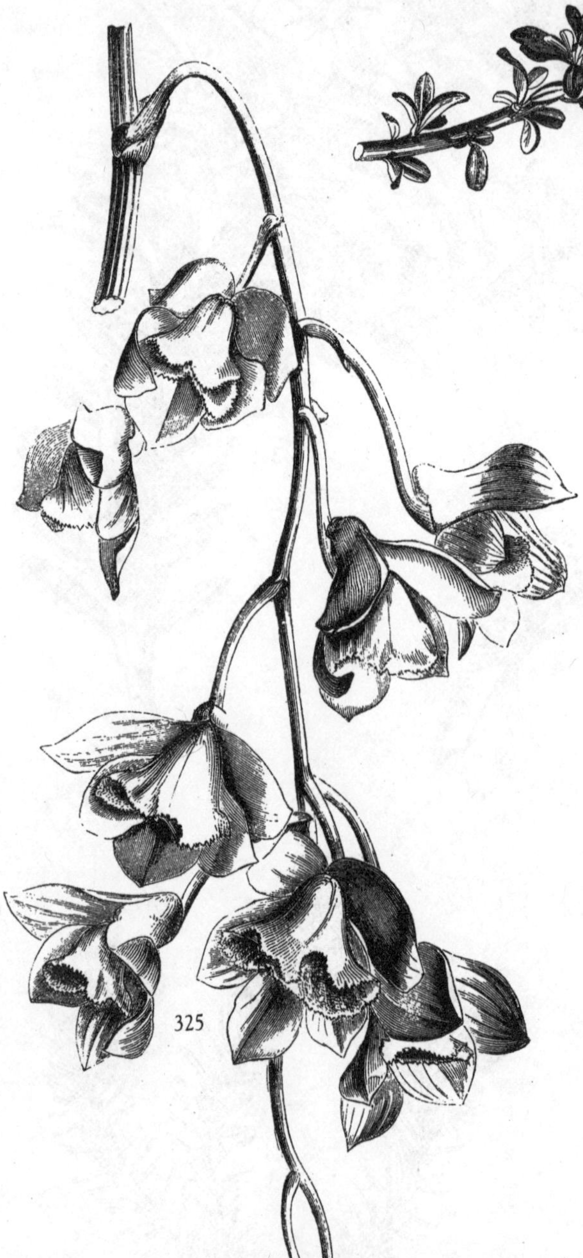
325

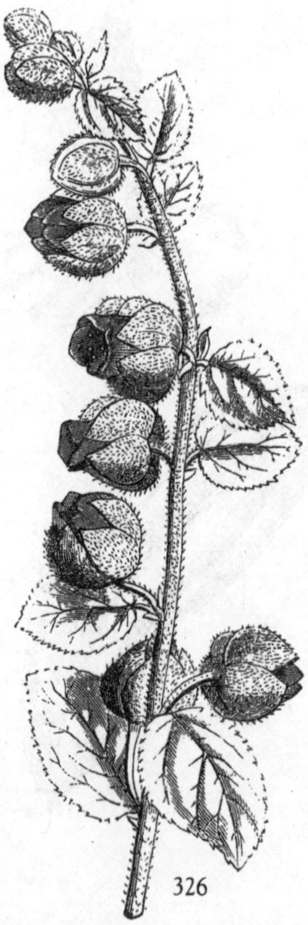
326

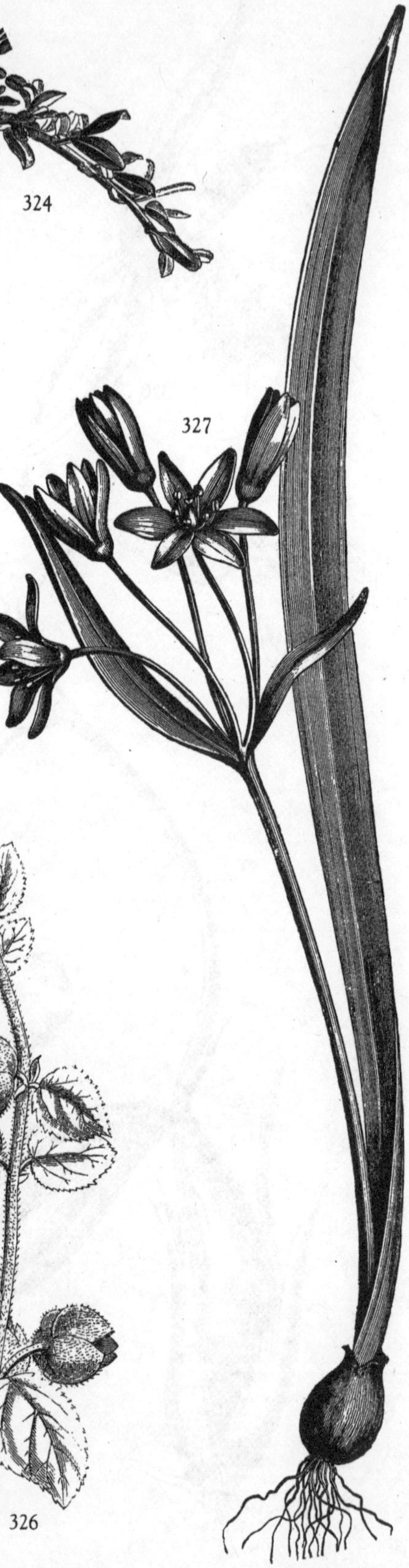
327

324. *Cotoneaster thymifolia.* A small prostrate evergreen hardy shrub with pink flowers; from the Himalayas. 325. *Dendrobium gibsoni.* An orchid with rich apricot flowers; from the Himalayas. 326. *Hermannia inflata.* A shrub with large inflated calyxes and short purple corollas; from Mexico. 327. *Gagea lutea.* See Fig. 289.

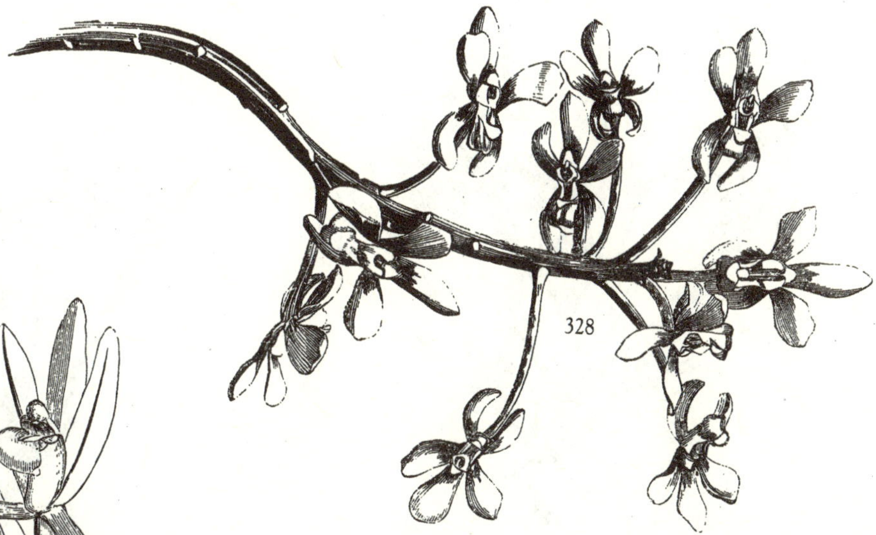

328

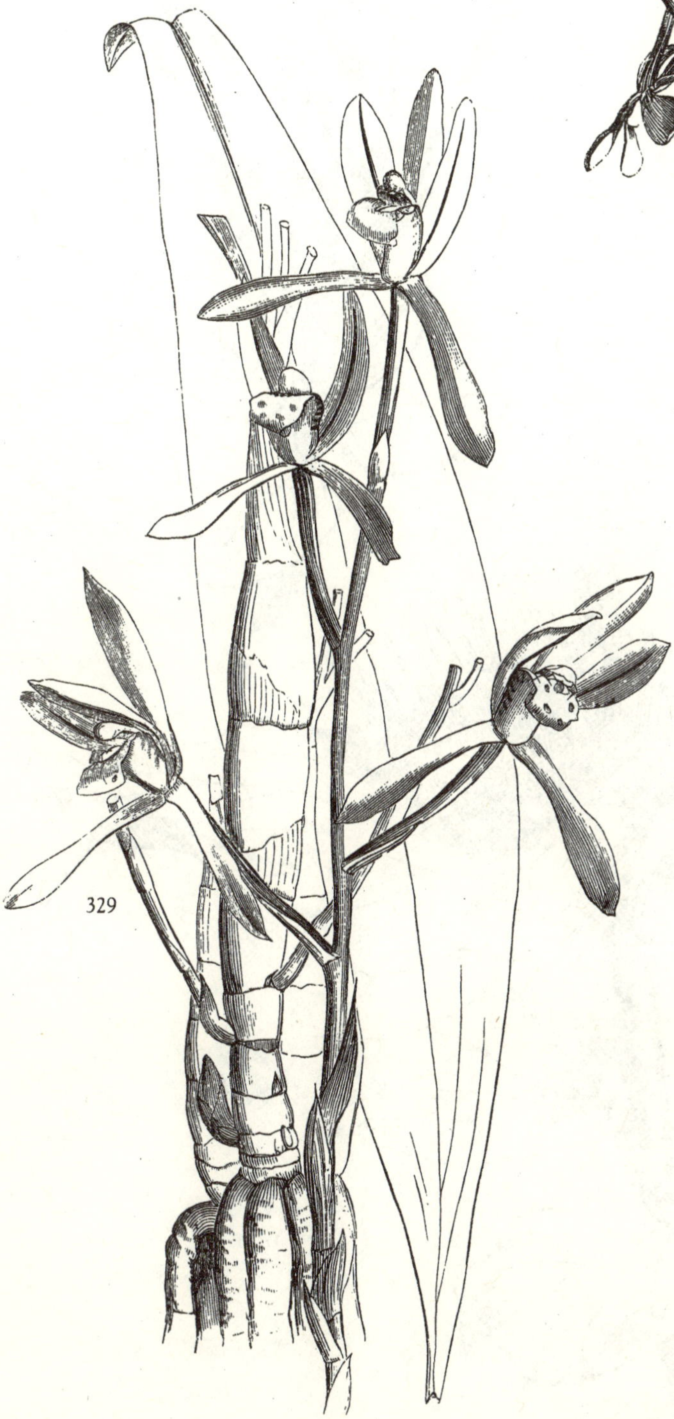

329

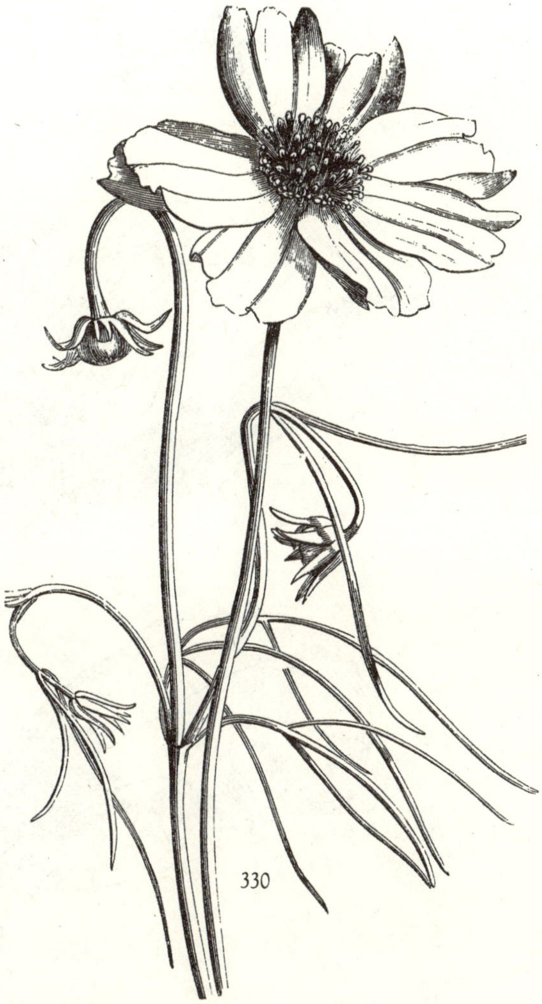

330

328. *Cleisostoma bicolor.* A struggling orchid with pink and purple flowers; from the Philippines. 329. *Cymbidium gibsoni.* A terrestrial orchid, flowers greenish with brown spots; from Asia and Australia. 330. *Coreopsis filifolia.* A hardy annual with bright yellow flowers; from Texas.

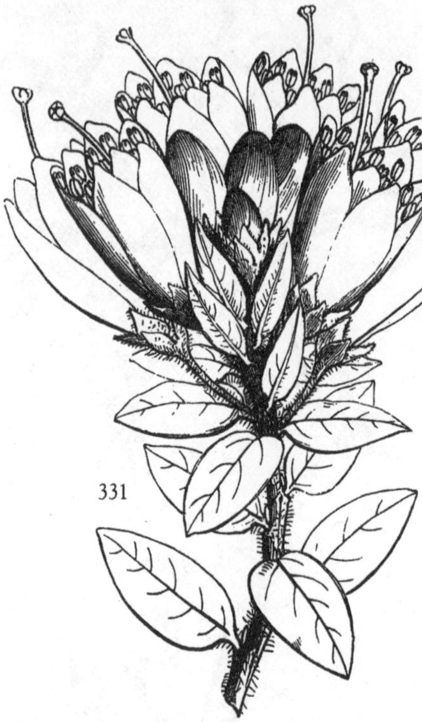

331

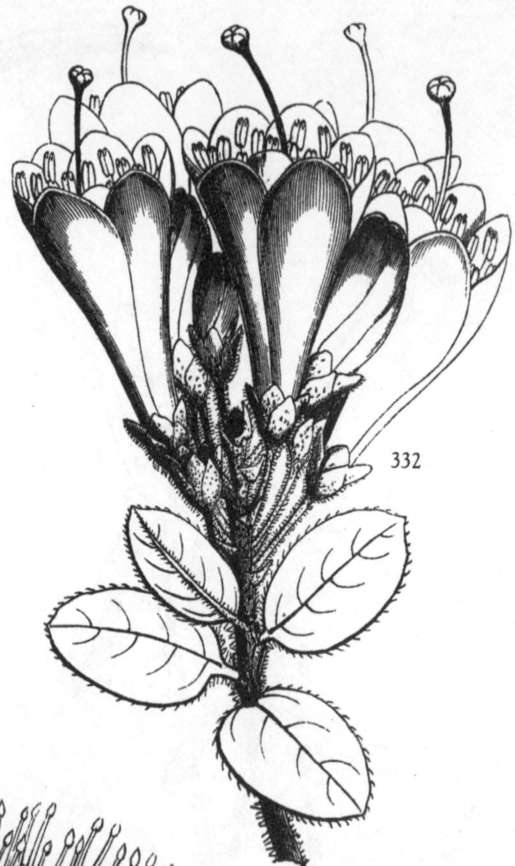

332

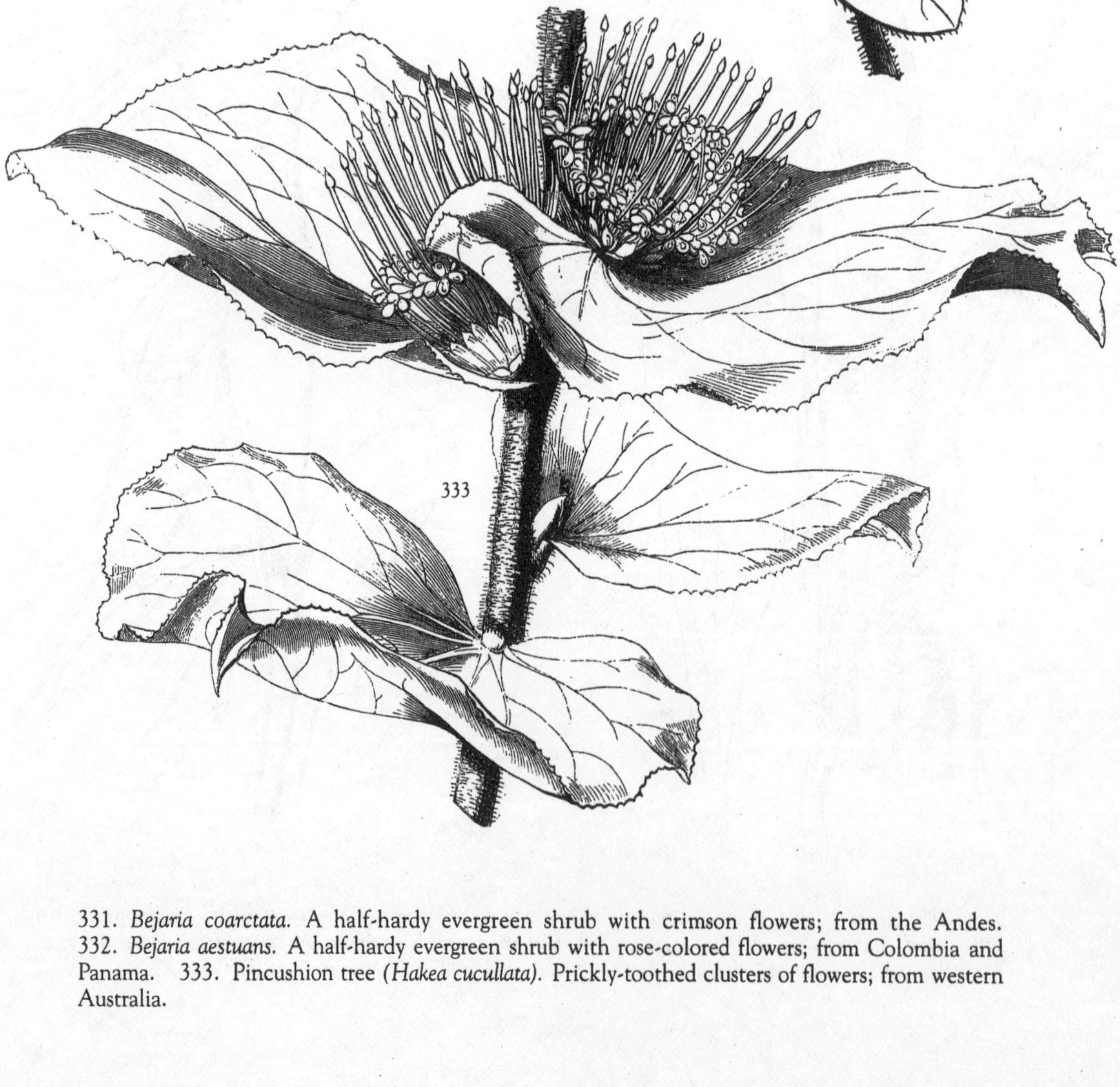

333

331. *Bejaria coarctata.* A half-hardy evergreen shrub with crimson flowers; from the Andes. 332. *Bejaria aestuans.* A half-hardy evergreen shrub with rose-colored flowers; from Colombia and Panama. 333. Pincushion tree *(Hakea cucullata).* Prickly-toothed clusters of flowers; from western Australia.

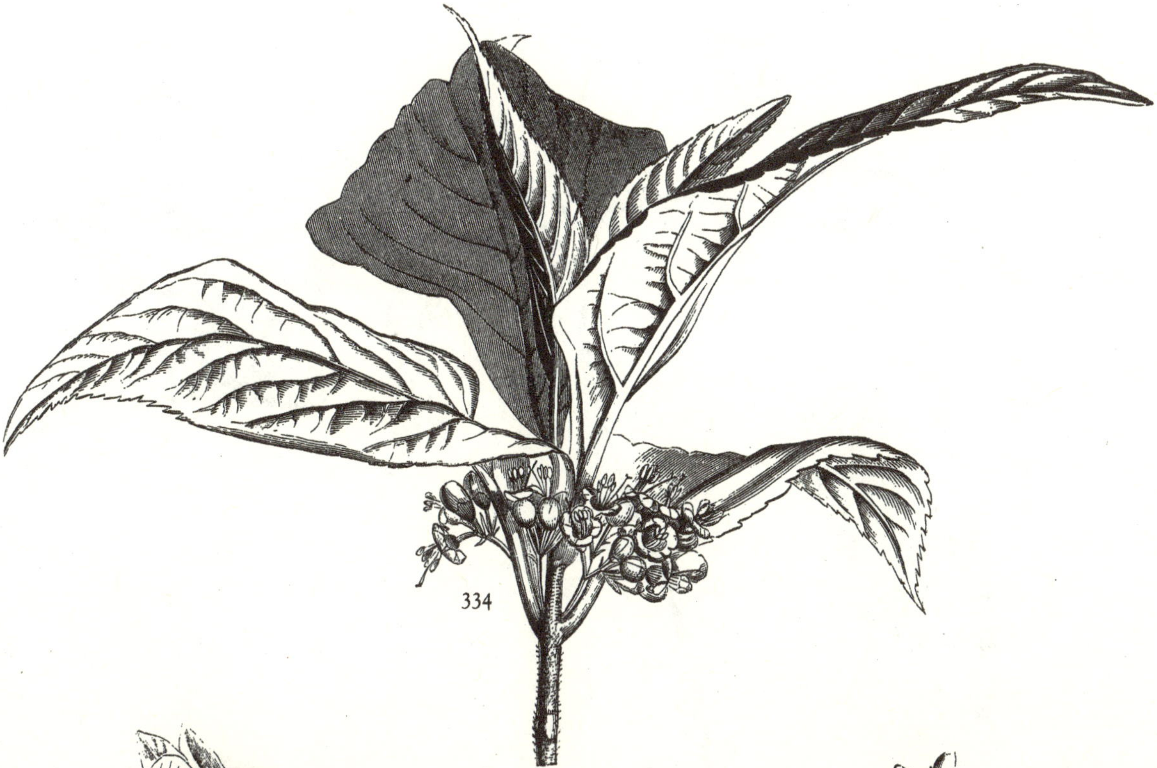

334

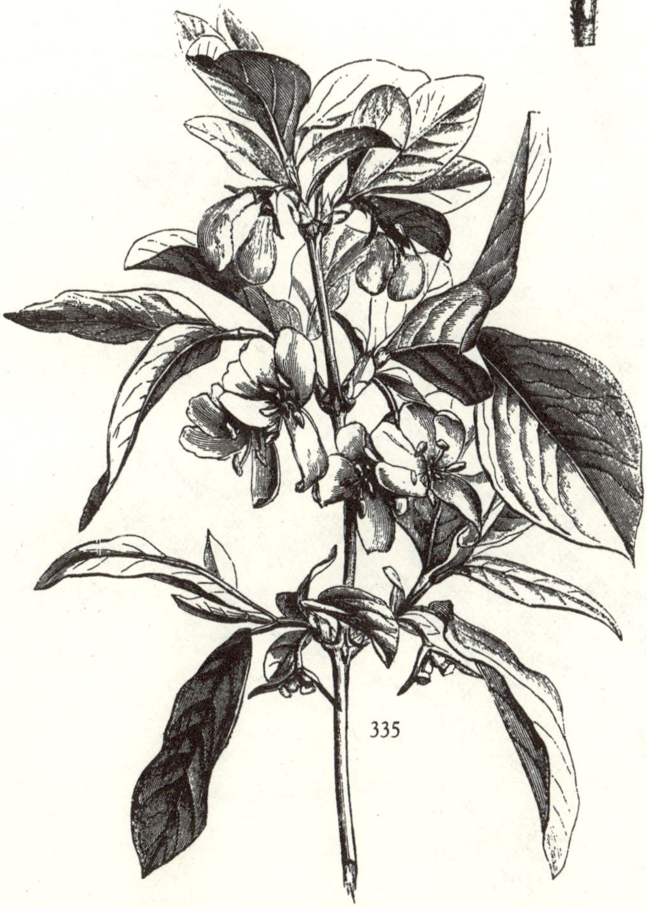

335

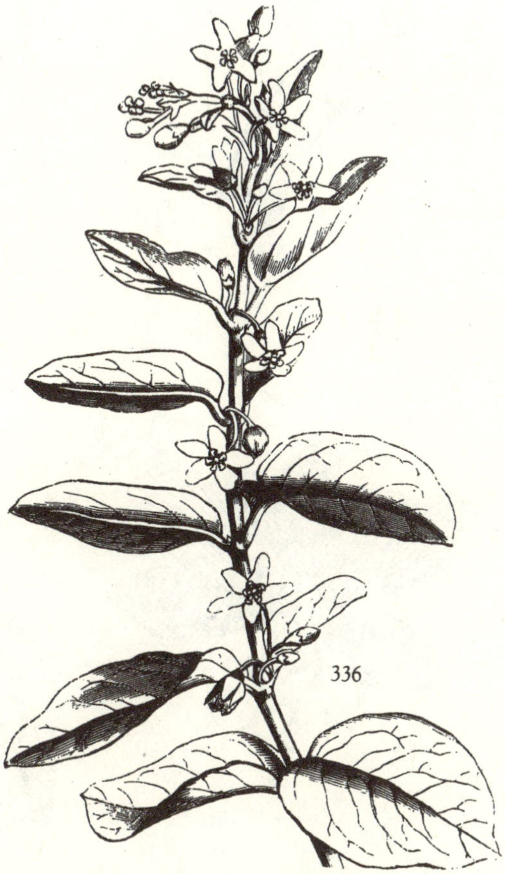

336

334. *Callicarpa japonica.* A half-hardy deciduous shrub with small pinkish flowers; from Japan.
335. *Lonicera fragrantissima.* A partly evergreen hardy shrub with whitish flowers; from China.
336. *Vincetoxicum japonicum.* A hardy herbaceous plant with pale yellow flowers; from Japan.

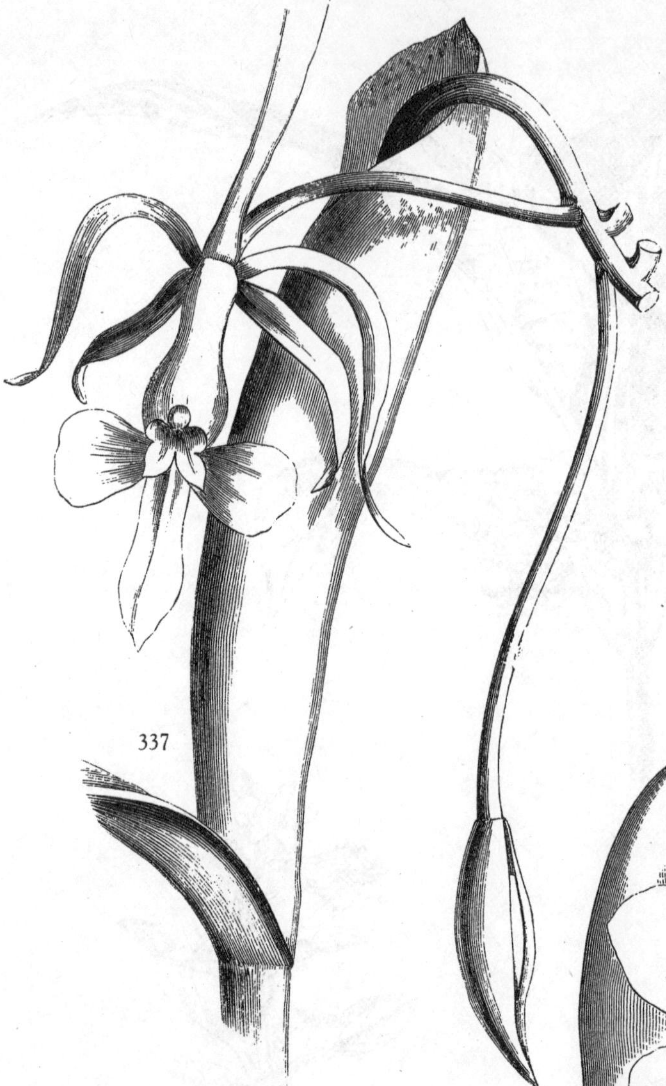

337

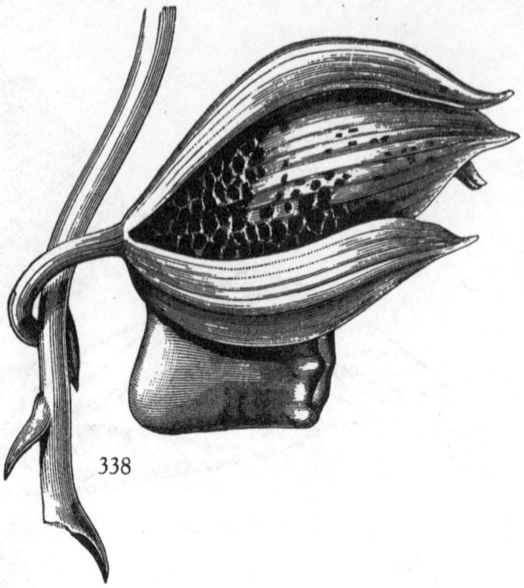

338

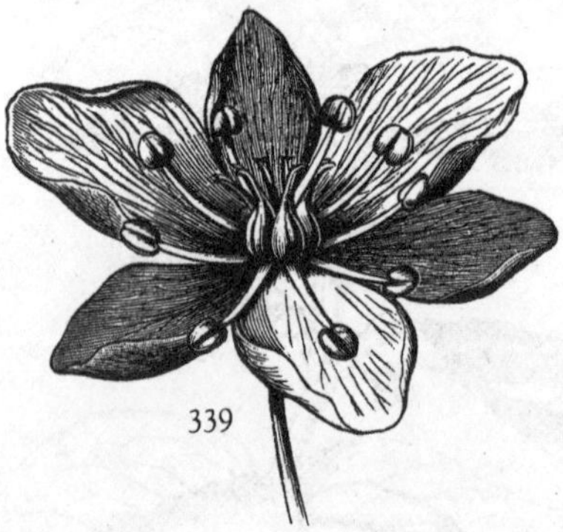

339

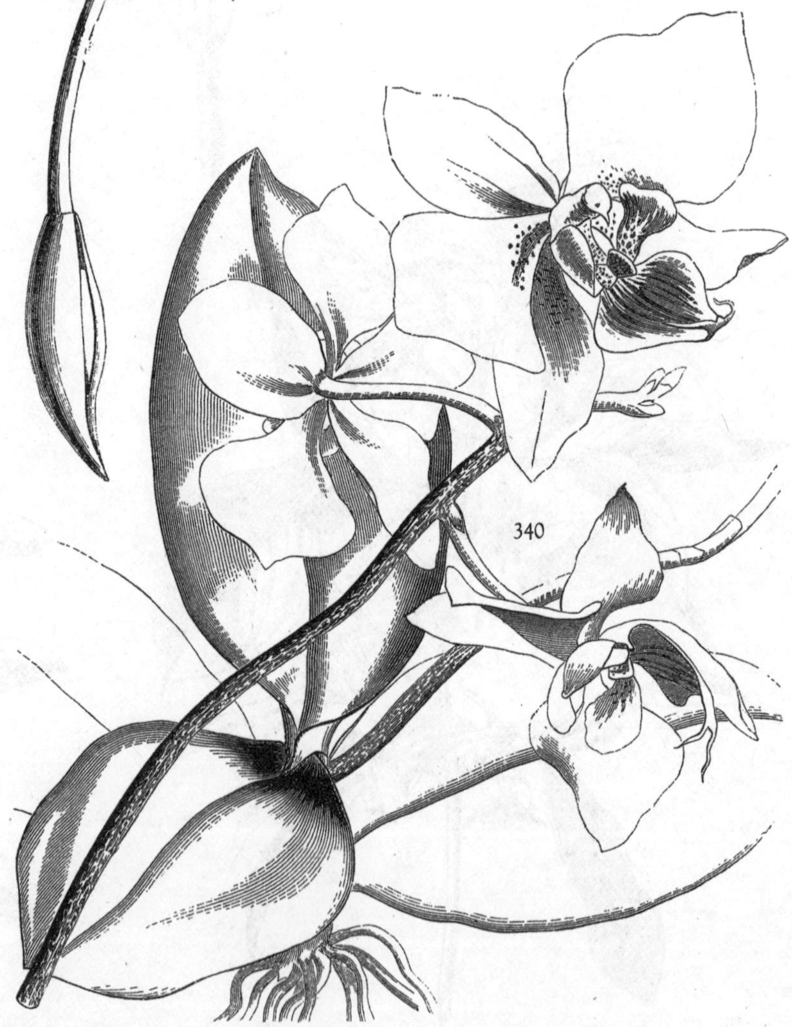

340

337. *Epidendrum leucochilum.* An orchid; flowers large, yellowish, with an ivory white lip; from Colombia and Nicaragua. 338. Jumping orchid (*Catasetum tridentatum*). Illustrating expulsive apparatus; from Trinidad and South America. 339. Flowering rush (*Butomus umbellatus*). Nine stamens in each flower; from northeastern North America. 340. *Phalaenopsis intermedia.* An orchid with white and deep rose flowers; from the Philippine Islands.

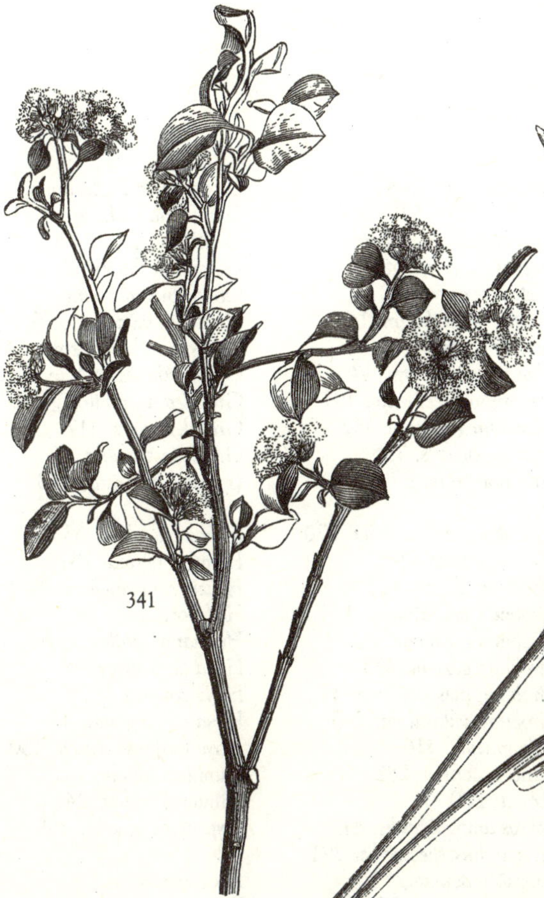

341

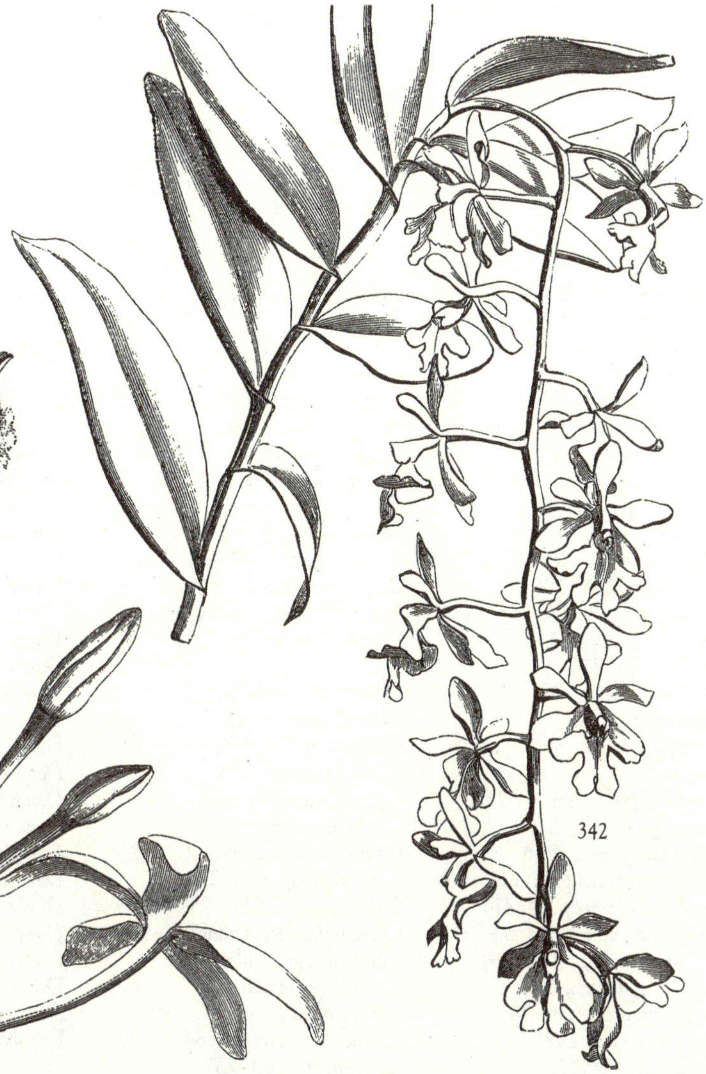

342

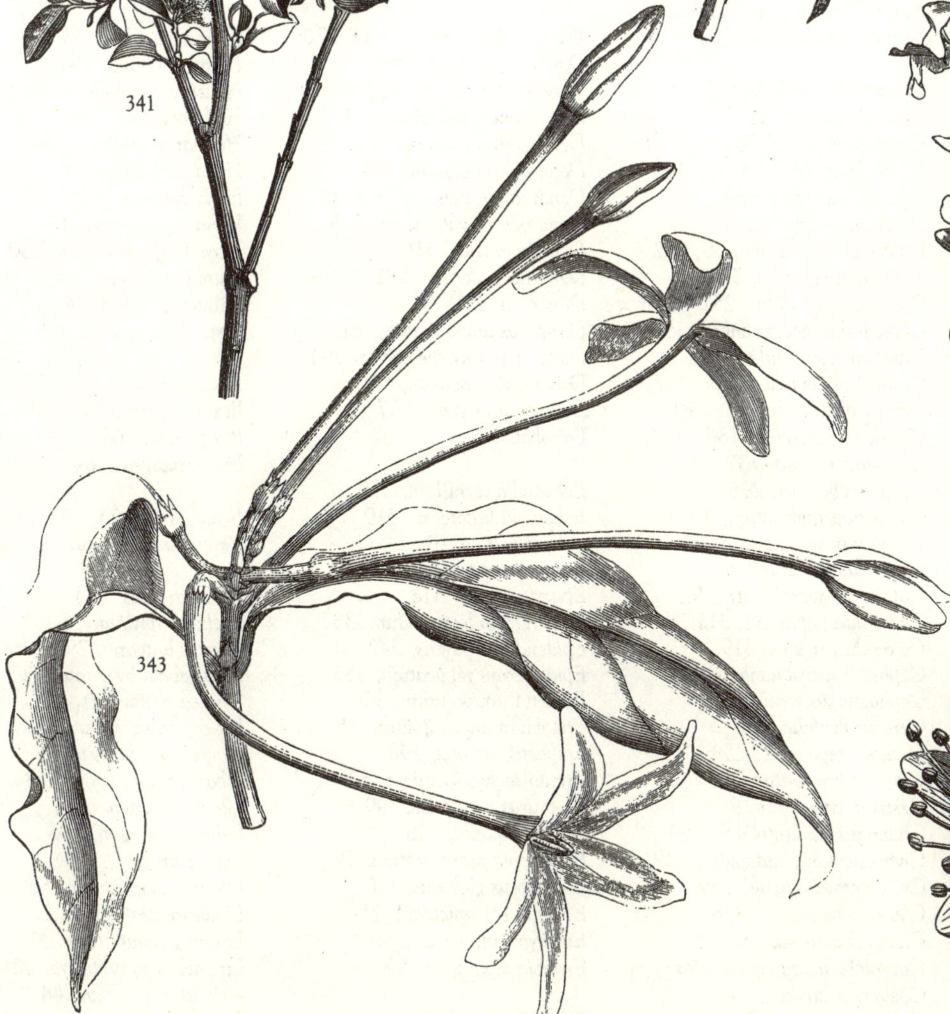

343

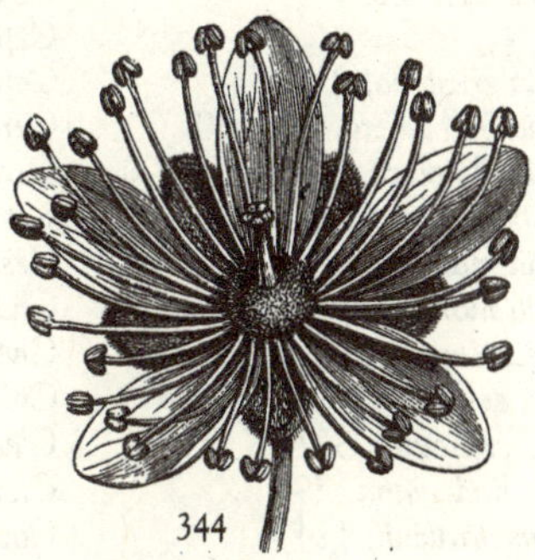

344

341. *Swammerdamia glomerata.* An evergreen half-hardy bush with small clusters of white flowers; from New Zealand. 342. *Epidendrum patens.* An orchid; flowers pale rust-colored or yellowish; from tropical and subtropical South America. 343. *Posoqueria revoluta.* A shrub with white flowers; from tropical South America. 344. Lime tree *(Tilia)*. See Fig. 278.

INDEX

Only scientific names are indexed.
The numbers are those of the illustrations.